HEROES OF SPIRIT

100 RABBINIC TALES OF THE HOLOCAUST

Stories of our Torah leaders who survived and
inspired during the terrible years of World War II
and the Reign of Communism

FOREWORD BY:
Rabbi Yosef Friedenson

INTRODUCTION BY:
Rabbi Avrohom Chaim Feuer

Rabbi Dovid Hoffman

ואנחנו בשם ה' אלקינו נזכיר

ISRAEL BOOKSHOP
PUBLICATIONS

HEROES

ואנחנו בשם ה' אלקינו נזכיר

אלה ברכב ואלה בסוסים

# of SPIRIT

100 RABBINIC TALES OF THE HOLOCAUST

Stories of our Torah leaders who survived and
inspired during the terrible years of World War II
and the Reign of Communism

Rabbi Dovid Hoffman

Book & Cover design by:

SRULY PERL • 845.694.7186
mechelp@gmail.com

Distributed by:

 Israel Bookshop Publications
501 Prospect Street
Lakewood, NJ 08701
Tel: (732) 901-3009
Fax: (732) 901-4012
www.israelbookshoppublications.com
info@israelbookshoppublications.com

Printed in the USA

DEDICATION

לעילוי נשמות

ר׳ אברהם יוסף שמואל אלטר בן ר׳ טוביה ז״ל,
ורעיתו האשה רישא רחל בת ר׳ אברהם שלמה ע״ה

ר׳ נפתלי טוביה בן ר׳ ישראל ז״ל,
ורעיתו האשה פעסל בת ר׳ יהודה ליב ע״ה

*As descendants of Holocaust survivors,
we are proud to bear your name. From four special
neshamos who lost a life of what was, you rebuilt
from nothing and achieved the ratzon haborei.
Complete families replete with yiddishe nachas,
are our tribute to these great individuals.*

*Zaidy & Bubby Kurz and Zaidy & Bubby Minzer -
you are our personal heroes. Heroes of spirit;
Heroes of ruchnius; Heroes that inspire us forever.*

*As young adults, you endured and triumphed over
unimaginable horrors and atrocities during the
war-torn years of the Holocaust. You were young,
but through it all you brought with you
the flavor of the "Alter Heim."*

*You buried your pain and loss deep in your hearts and
showed us the joys and purpose of living. You taught
us by example your deep love of Hashem. You bridged
generations and now you reap the fruits of your labor.*

*We draw our strength from your strength, because
that is how you survived - by being strong!*

Zaidys and Bubbys - you are our heroes!

Table Of Contents

Mid–War II: A Cry from the Depths

POST-WAR: REBUILDING AMONG THE ASHES

MUSEUM | A LIVING
OF JEWISH | MEMORIAL
HERITAGE | TO THE
| HOLOCAUST

April, 21, 2009

The Holocaust has played a major and devastating role in Jewish History and has shown the indomitable spirit of our great people through the many survivors and their remarkable tales of salvation.

It is my passion, as a child of the Holocaust, to educate our young people about the atrocity and reality of Churban Europa. Working with the Museum of Jewish Heritage on their Speakers Bureau, I have the opportunity to bring this important and extremely relevant message to many.

We must keep alive the memory of those who died and suffered *Al Kiddush Hashem*. It is crucial that we must never FORGET.

The wonderful stories my son Rabbi Dovid Hoffman has researched and compiled in this book will not only educate but also reinforce the incredible emunah and heroic efforts of those amazing men and women who lived during those horrific years (1933-1946).

It means a great deal to see that my son, who is not only a Talmid Chacham but also a historian, understands that we have an obligation to remember that European Jewry was nearly annihilated and we must keep their legacy alive. These heartwarming and inspirational stories will bring them to life.

With Much Yiddish Nachas,

Helen Hoffman

MUSEUM OF JEWISH HERITAGE

Speakers Bureau
hhremember@aol.com

Spiritual Leader
Cong. B'nai Abraham
75-03 Main Street
Flushing, NY 11367-
Tel. 718-261-4580

Rabbi Shlomo Dov. Shapiro
73-09 136th Street
Kew Gardens Hills, NY 11367-2826
Tel. 718-263-1574 Fax. 718-263-1575
בס"ד

שלמה דוב שפירא
באאמו"ר תור"הצ
מוהר"ר מרדכי שפירא זצוק"ל

"מ(ש)נכנס אדר מרבים בשמחה"

יום ג' שהוכפל בו כי טוב, א' דר"ח אדר, תשס"ט

Rabbi Dovid Hoffman Slit'a, is the son of our good friend, Rabbi Pinchos Hoffman Shlit'a, a pillar of tzedakah and chessed in our community. Reb Dovid Shlit'a grew up in our Synagogue in Kew Gardens Hills, a few years ago he started publishing a weekly Torah Sheet entitled "Torah Tavlin," distributed via e-mail to thousands of Jews both nationally and internationally. Many individuals have improved their life style as a result of this weekly news letter of Torah and Halacha Most recently the "Torah Tavlin," weekly sheet was published in book form.

Reb Dovid Shlit'a did not rest on his laurels, instead embarked on a new project, he collated a collection of inspirational writings of the great luminaries of the past and present generation. The new projected book called "100 Rabbinic Tales of the Holocaust and Other Stories," Their words of Chizuk under adverse and tragic conditions will serve and inspire the reader to better serve Hashem and Klal Yisroel.

I wish him Hatzlacha Rabba in his work.

With Blessings for success.

Shlomo Dov. Shapiro, Rabbi

THE SHTETL
THE LIVING HISTORY MUSEUM OF THE JEWISH WORLD
"A Shtetl Grows In Rishon LeZion"

Erev Rosh Chodsh Iyar, 5769

Rabbi David Hoffman's book: "Heroes of Spirit: 100 Rabbinic Tales of the Holocaust" is magnificent!

In my own work: "Hasidic Tales of the Holocaust" I attempted to portray the grandeur, fortitude and courage of Hasidic Jewry in the face of horrific death and destruction. It is an honor and pleasure to note that Rabbi Hoffman's: "Heroes of Spirit: 100 Rabbinic Tales of the Holocaust" seeks to carry on my ideal of "Becharta BeChaim" – "Choose Life" by showing the miracles of the success stories of those who persevered against all odds. Like we say at the Pesach Seder: Not an angel, Not a messenger, but G-d Himself, descended into Egypt to bring us out. So too, anyone who survived, it was because he at least had a Malach (angel) standing next to him!

Here, David uniquely presents a very Jewish view of Rabbis, Heads of Yeshivos, Hasidic Rebbes and little known stories of Sephardic Rabbanim, along with many other unsung heroes, and never-before-told stories of our people.

In so doing, David gives us a rare glimpse into a vanished world bringing alive a whole spectrum of Jewish life during the war. The stories tell the tales of a generation of Jewish leaders whose virtue, faith and personal greatness, were able to overcome adversity, providing inspiration for us to learn from.

Much is written about our Jewish heroes who physically resisted the Germans. Much greater and less advertised are those whose spiritual strength in the One Above was put to the ultimate test under the most

THE SHTETL
THE LIVING HISTORY MUSEUM OF THE JEWISH WORLD
"A Shtetl Grows In Rishon LeZion"

torturous conditions.

I am so happy to see Rabbi Hoffman's book with so many beautiful and inspiring stories of the Holocaust.

Our younger generation never saw this. It is so important to impress upon our youth such stories telling of the greatness of our fallen brothers and the victories that G-d wrought through the miraculous stories of those who survived.

Today it is rare to meet anyone who is a survivor and soon the generation of the war and the testimony that they bear will be gone forever. It is funny that after over 50 years and so many wars, this war has gone down in history as "The War …"

Unlike many histories of the Holocaust today, which captivate by the sheer terror and horror of the time, Rabbi Hoffman's book seeks to bring out the positive in short, captivating stories.

May we welcome the day when all those who were killed will return alive to greet us on the day that: "Uvla HaMaves LeNetzach" with the long awaited welcome of Moshiach Tzidkaynu! Please G-d. Ken Yehi Ratzon.

I am sure that they will give Rabbi Hoffman a big "Yasher Koach" as do I.

Dr. Yaffa Eliach

Dr. Yaffa Eliach
PRESIDENT AND FOUNDER - THE SHTETL FOUNDATION

"THE SHTETL- THE LIVING HISTORY MUSEUM OF THE JEWISH WORLD"
300 EAST 54TH STREET SUITE. 23K, NEW YORK CITY, NY, 10022, PHONE: 212-319-2927, FAX: 212-751-7932, EMAIL: YAFFA@SHTETLFOUNDATION.ORG
A PROJECT OF SHTETL FOUNDATION • WWW.SHTETLFOUNDATION.ORG

חולים רופא

RCCS
ROFEH CHOLIM CANCER SOCIETY
WE FUND MIRACLES

Rosh Chodesh Iyar, 5769

Dear Readers,

As the son of American-born parents, it would seem strange for me to comment on a book replete with stories of the European Holocaust. But as the son-in-law of Reb Yosef Friedenson, arguably the greatest living Holocaust historian in the Orthodox Jewish world, I gained a vantage point that just may be unique among American bred Jews.

The many stories of faith amid the flames that I heard over the years through my association with Agudath Israel of America and *The Jewish Observer*, as well as the subsequent miracles of ashes to renewal, make it obvious that the biggest tragedy to befall Klal Yisroel since the *Churban Beis Hamikdash* cannot be seen through the prism of secular thought. The intelligent mind knows that only a Torah-true outlook can relate any real meaning to that era.

Holocaust memorials are meaningless without proper Torah *haskafa*. And this *hashkafa* must be handed down to our children, to counter the constant barrage of "Shoah business" that we are bombarded with from without.

And that is why I am personally thrilled with this offering by the author of *Torah Tavlin*, my good friend, Rabbi Dovid Hoffman. What better way of transmitting this *emunah*, this faith in *HaShem*, this testament to spiritual greatness amid the greatest challenges of all time, than by preserving tales of *Kiddush Hashem*, tales of spiritual heroism -- tales of real strength -- the kind that will, and must, endure forever?

May this book add to the *Kiddush Hashem* of those who died *Al Kiddush Hashem*.

Rabbi Yosef C. Golding
Executive Director
Rofeh Cholim Cancer Society

762 BEDFORD AVENUE I BROOKLYN NY 11205 I TEL. 718.722.2002 I FAX. 718.722.4757 I WWW.ROFEHCHOLIM.ORG

Acknowledgments

We live in a unique, and somewhat paradoxical, time. It has been almost sixty-five years since the end of World War II, and as the years continue to roll by, fewer people remain alive who can personally recount the horrors of that time. Conversely, a never-before treasure-trove of information, documents, videos and audios of Holocaust material is out there for the taking. In this, the "Electronic Age", the tools needed to research documented material, historical facts, and relevant information about people, places and events during the years spanning the rise and fall of Nazi oppression, have become readily available and attainable. I have attempted to use every resource at my disposal and did my utmost to preserve and present as much factual information as I was possibly able to in this book. Most accounts that I have written, including the facts surrounding many of the personal recollections and anecdotes that were told to me verbally, have been carefully portrayed based upon the backdrop of documented history. I believe it is so important to not only tell a great story, but to tell it in as factual a way as possible. This adds to the greatness - as well as the integrity - of the story.

Much of the source material for this book was culled and adapted from interviews, personal recollections, various speeches and shiurim, *seforim* and publications. These include:

A Sacred Trust: Stories of Our Heritage and History,
Drs. Eugene Labovitz and Annette Labovitz; Torah

Lives, A Fire in his Soul, Amos Bunim, Ma'ayan Hashavua, R' Sholom Wallach, Nor the Moon by Night, Devorah Gliksman, Branded for Life, Raize Guttman, Operation Torah Rescue, Yecheskel Leitner, A Path Through the Ashes, collected from the pages of the Jewish Observer, Rav Breuer, His Life and his Legacy, The Rabbi Dr. Joseph Breuer Foundation, Hasidic Tales of the Holocaust, Professor Yaffa Eliach, Rescuing the Rebbe of Belz, Yosef Israel, Lulek: Child of Buchenwald, A Netanel, Aleinu L'Shabeach, R' Yitzchok Zilberstein, Insights; A Talmudic Treasury, R' Saul Weiss, Ma'aish Tam, From a Pure Fire, R' Moshe Aharon Stern zt"l, transcribed and translated by Yitzchok Meir Goldstein, The Brisker Rav, R' Yosef Shimon Meller, The Reichmanns; Family, Faith, Fortune and the Empire of Olympia and York, Anthony Bianco, The Klausenberger Rebbe, The War Years, Translated and Adapted by Judith Lifschitz from Lapid Aish by R' Aaron Sorasky, The Mashgiach, Rebbetzin Shulamit Ezrachi, Ish L'Rayahu, R' Y' Weinberger, To Save a World, D. Kranzler, E. Gevirtz, Visions of Greatness, Yosef Weiss, Making of a Godol, Nathan Kamenetzky, Stories of Spirit and Faith, D. Sutton, The Jewish Observer, R' Yerachmiel Tilles: www.ascentofsafed.com, The Holocaust and Jewish Destiny, R' Gershon Weiss, Lev Sholom, R' Sholom Schwadron, Chaim Sheyesh Bahem, Pirkei Avos, R' Yitzchok Shraga Gross, Modesty - An Adornment for Life, R' Pesach Eliyahu Falk, Silent Revolution, Miriam Stark Zakon, From the Summit, Simcha Leib Grossbard, Nes Hatzalah shel HaRebbi M'Gur, R' Moshe Prager, The Torah Profile, For Love of Torah, R' Shimon Finkelman, Yalkut Lekach Tov, R' Yaakov

Yisroel Beifus, Avoseinu Sipru Lanu, Haggadah Shel Pesach, R' Sholom Wallach, Rav Pam, The life and Ideals of Rabbi Avrohom Yaakov Hakohen Pam, R' Shimon Finkelman, Reb Elchonon, The life and ideals of Rabbi Elchonon Bunim Wasserman of Baranovich, R' Aaron Sorasky, Reb Elyah, The life and accomplishments of Rabbi Elyah Lopian, R' David J. Schlossberg, Rebbes of Ger, Sfas Emes and Imrei Emes, A.Y. Bromberg, Reb Moshe, The life and ideals of HaGaon R' Moshe Feinstein, R' Shimon Finkelman / R' Nosson Scherman.

A book of this magnitude requires a collective effort and consequently a great many people need to be acknowledged for their invaluable and unique contributions. My parents, Rabbi Pinchos and Helen Hoffman, were, are and continue to be my foremost "educators" - the ones from whom I learn the most. My father's gift to point out errors in print - and judgment - is critical for the success of any book, and the adjustments he made in this book's manuscript were invaluable. My mother's life-long commitment to educating today's youth through her speeches on behalf of the Holocaust Heritage Museum and retelling her mother - my grandmother's - personal account of survival, is absolutely my inspiration to write this book. May their efforts continue to bear fruit and may they see much *nachas* from this project.

My in-laws, Rabbi Yisroel and Leah Blonder, are a great help in so many ways. As children of European parents and second generation Holocaust and Siberia survivors, they have brought fascinating details to light, as well as a personal perspective on the war years. My mother-in-law's attention to detail has come in handy on more than one occasion, whether with my weekly Torah Tavlin or with this book. I thank them dearly for all their efforts and bless them with *nachas*, happiness and health from their entire family.

As an *"Ezer K'negdo"* my wife, Estee, is second to none. As a model of support, warmth and a deep understanding of the human psyche, she amazes me time and time again with her ability to say what needs to be said and do what needs to be done! The dedication that she wrote for this book displays a sensitivity that is unusual and unique, especially in this day and age. As the expression goes, "She's all heart!" It is no wonder that our children, Yitzy, Pepi, Tzvi, Alti, Naftoli, Daniel, Yehudah and (Shlomo) Yedidyah, *Kn"h*, surely follow in her impressive footsteps. Their assistance in every aspect of this book, including collecting material, copying, collating, proofreading and offering nuggets of suggestion literally took this concept from a whimsical idea to a final and concrete product. Each one is special and I pray that Hashem should continue to shower them with health, ability and *"koichos"* their entire lives.

In Yerushalayim lives a Rebbetzin, who in the family is known as the one with the "Red Phone" - her own private and direct line straight through to Heaven. (Believe me - it's true!) This Rebbetzin, none other than my sister, Raize, is also a gifted writer, speaker and - perhaps her greatest natural talent - a poet extraordinaire! The heartfelt poems that she composed for this book leave me breathless each time I read them. She was intimately involved in every stage of this book and her advice and suggestions clearly emanate from a *"Daas Torah"* perspective. Not to minimize in any way, the input and impact that my older sister, Elisa, added to this project. Her wise words and eye for perfection will b"H enable this book to become a classic. I cannot thank both of them enough, as well as my brother Alexander, for all their efforts and *chizuk*.

I would be remiss if I did not give proper thanks to Drs. Eugene and Annette Labovitz, Dr. Yaffa Eliach, Rabbi Gershon Weiss, and others who wish to remain nameless, for sharing their personal material, illustrations and stories and allowing me to use them in this book.

Of notable mention is Rabbi Shimshon Sherer, who has so many stories to tell, a number of which are printed here in this book; Rabbi Yitzchok Feldheim, of Feldheim Publishers, who is extremely supportive and a wonderfully gracious individual; the "Rabbi Dr. Joseph Breuer Foundation" for granting permission to reprint the story, Rav Josef Breuer:An Unlikely Savior, taken from the book (Chapter 7): "Rav Breuer—His Life and His Legacy."

A great measure of thanks to Reb Sruly Perl from Vividesign for his beautiful artistic work. The cover design, the layout and typesetting, are magnificent and eye-catching. His helpful approach and positive attitude never ceases to lift my spirits when I speak with him. Once more, Vividesign has done it again!

Mr. Moshe Kaufman and the staff of Israel Bookshop deserve no small amount of gratitude. After our first collaboration on Torah Tavlin, I fully believe in Reb Moshe's expertise and I trust his judgment. And he didn't disappoint. Of notable mention are Mrs. Malkie Gendelman, of the Israel Bookshop staff, and Mrs. Shayndy Abrahamson, who proofread the manuscript and perfected it. May Hashem bless Israel Bookhshop and all its members with continued success both in business and personal efforts.

There are so many people who deserve to be thanked for the production of this book, but none more so than my dear and close friend, a man of conviction, principles, good taste in sons-in-law and bad taste in Scotch, Rabbi Yosef Chaim

Golding. His scrutinizing eye and real desire to see this book through to its ultimate success was heartening and inspiring. He is a busy man, a man with many responsibilities and accomplishments under his belt, but the fact that he took so much of his valuable time to edit the entire manuscript from beginning to end, attests to his underlying integrity, decency and professionalism. He was also the one who put me in contact with his esteemed father-in-law, Reb Yosef Friedenson, and assisted in enabling the moving and powerful foreword to be written for this book. A special measure of thanks for Rabbi Friedenson, as well as Rabbi Avrohom Chaim Feuer, for graciously writing their beautiful words of introduction. R' Yosef Chaim, I cannot thank you enough for all the effort you put into making this book as good as it is and I know that your ctitique and criticism - although often regular and constant - is always offered and received in a spirit of good faith and humor. May you and your family see continued *simcha*, *nachas* and happiness from the whole gang and *hatzlachah* in all that you do.

Hakadosh Baruch Hu, to Whom the greatest amount of thanks and gratitude is always appropriate and never-ending, and Who is consistent in His kindness and benevolence, should bless each and every one of the people I've mentioned above, and the entire Jewish Nation as a whole, so that we merit the future liberation from darkness to light and from exile to redemption, speedily and in our time.

Dovid Hoffman
Rosh Chodesh Sivan 5769

Introduction

By **Rabbi Avrohom Chaim Feuer Shlit"a**
Shaarei Chessed, Yerushalayim

Another book on the Holocaust? Enough!

The truth is that there can never be enough written on this bitter and painful subject which must be indelibly etched on to the hearts and minds of Klal Yisrael for all time.

We believe that every crisis and calamity which Almighty G-d brings upon His Chosen Jewish People is designed to teach the Jews and all of mankind many very precious and pertinent lessons; crucial lessons essential for furthering the progress and development of the history of mankind at that juncture and point in time. Therefore, we, the victims of the Holocaust, must continuously apply our minds to learning more and more lessons from the Shoah. The sheer magnitude of this horrendous event demands a massive and never-ending literary response. When those who love G-d humbly accept and learn from His lessons, albeit harsh ones, it is an act of supreme devotion and tenacious faith in our Father in Heaven.

However, the horror and destruction of the Shoah is really not what this book is all about. Quite the opposite, this wonderful work focuses upon the positive, the indestructible spirit of the Jewish people who refused to abandon their faith in our Almighty G-d even in the most desperate wartime situations.

Rabbi Dovid Hoffman is blessed with all of the unique talents which a gifted story writer must have. First, he has a real knack for gathering a vast array of fascinating stories about Jews in times of danger, each tale a powerful lesson of how faith in Hashem is well rewarded. Indeed, it has been said that: "The real reward for a good deed is not what we get but what we become." These tales of trial and travail reflect this idea in so many ways as we see the heroes and heroines grow in stature and spirit right before our eyes.

The second talent with which R' Dovid is blessed is his ability to present his exciting accounts in a clear and concise manner which keeps the reader riveted to the page from beginning to end. This writer powerfully engages us and literally draws us into the drama as it unfolds before our eyes.

Fortunate is the nation which is blessed with such talented authors who are not mere entertainers but rather glorious educators who enlighten the Jewish nation with the light of their pen.

Rabbi Avrohom Chaim Feuer

Foreword

By **Rabbi Yosef Friedenson Shlit"a**

The True Heroes of World War II

I remember the day very clearly. It was September 5, 1939 and the Germans had initiated their invasion of Poland and were progressing at a fast pace. An order had come from the Polish military commander of Lodz for all able bodied men over the age of sixteen to immediately go to Warsaw, ostensibly to reunite all Polish forces, in order to resist the German intrusion and occupation.

So my father, Rabbi Eliezer Gershon Friedenson, and I set out on foot from Lodz to Warsaw. We encountered the dreaded Luftwaffe many times along the road as we dove for cover when they swooped down upon us, machine guns blazing. But, by the time we got to Warsaw, the war — as far as Poland was concerned — was almost over. The "mighty" Polish army had been defeated by the Germans in less than a week. A few Polish divisions were still battling in Warsaw, continuing to resist the occupation of their capital. After two weeks, they, too, surrendered and capitulated.

I begin the foreword with this story as an attempt to respond to the ridiculous bantering of many secularists who claim that the six million *Kedoshim* went to their deaths like sheep to the slaughter. Nothing could be further from the truth. Spiritually, the majority of them heroically resisted the German onslaught. They went like heroes of spirit. Anyone who thinks that the Jewish masses could have united to defeat the Germans should just acquaint themselves with the history of World War II. If the well equipped Polish army could not last a full week under the Nazi onslaught, how could anyone dare say that the civilian Jewish population could have successfully fought back?

In the five plus years I endured under Nazi torture and degradation, I can testify that the Germans never broke the collective spirit of *emunah* and *bitachon* of the Jews. They may have been physically stronger, and, indeed, they succeeded in killing six million of our people, but they never defeated us. We survived their plan to annihilate the Jewish people and we triumphantly go on living, remaining the *Am Hanivchar*, G-d's Chosen Nation. This is certainly partly due to the valiant spirit of the majority of the *Kedoshim*, whose heroism was not fully revealed to this day.

Much has been written about the heroism of those who physically dared to resist the Nazi barbarians and were ready to die to avenge innocent Jewish blood. But in our opinion, the real heroes were those who chose spiritual resistance in order to help Jews survive and prepare them to rebuild Jewish life anew.

The real heroes were men like my father, *Hy"d*, who, in the Warsaw Ghetto, opened his window to throw scraps of bread to the starving, crying children outside. And when we children asked him, "*Tatte*, what about us?" his answer rings in my ears today as clearly as the day he spoke them: "Tonight, we had enough bread. *Oif morgan, vet G-t zorgen* (Tomorrow, let G-d worry)." The Germans were happy to see the Jewish children dying of hunger. But my father was determined to help them stay alive with the hope that they would somehow survive.

Who would ever allow their children to marry in the ghetto, with a seeming death sentence hovering over the young couple's heads? Well, I got married in the Warsaw Ghetto due to the heroic spirit of men like my father, whose encouragement of my marriage was built in his unshaken belief of the words of the *Navi Yeshayah*. In speeches in the Jewish courtyard, he encouraged his fellow ghetto inhabitants not to lose their faith in the eternity of the Jewish people. On the day when Hitler made a fiery speech, boasting about his Luftwaffe that ruled the skies, my father quoted the prophecy of *Yeshayahu Hanavi* (*Isaiah 14:13*) who predicted that Nevuchadnetzar, who spoke about his ruling of the heavens, would fall to his ultimate defeat. This, too, was my father's prediction about Hitler. He encouraged his listeners and promised that the day will come when Hitler and his murderous cohorts will also be defeated.

In a slave labor camp in Poland, under German rule, I can testify how Jews baked matzos in the 2,000 degree smelting ovens, with the rare cooperation of our German overlord who was not a real Nazi. I remember his incredulous look when he asked us how we could be worrying about Hashem's commandments in the situation we were in. "Didn't your G-d forsake you?" he asked. One of the elders of our group, humbly, but with inner pride responded, "Sir, not totally, and not forever." The astonished German took a step back and said, "I'm afraid the Fuhrer will never be able to defeat such a people." This man who had the courage to proclaim our eternity; wasn't he a true hero?

In the slave labor camps, in the extermination camps, on the death marches, at the firing squads, Jews who went to the *Kisei Hakavod* with Shema on their lips, with *Ani Ma'amin* in their hearts, they were the true heroes of spirit. There were many, many heroes of spirit.

Rabbanim, Admorim, Roshei Yeshivah, and the plain, *poshiter Yidden*; stories abound of their heroism. Most of these stories, however, went to their deaths together with the witnesses.

But many stories survived. And these stories are vital to be passed on to the next generation ... and the next ... and the next. Our children must know that physical resistance is only a minor part of heroism. Spiritual resistance is much more difficult.

The secular world lauds the Jews who physically resisted the Germans. But as I said, much greater was the spiritual resistance of those whose faith in Hashem never wavered, even under the most torturous conditions.

Holocaust memorials are meaningless without proper Torah *hashkafah*. And this *hashkafah* must be handed down to our children, to counter the constant non-Torah *hashkafah* onslaught that we are bombarded with from outside our camp. What better way of transmitting this *emunah*, this faith in Hashem, this testament to spiritual heroism than by preserving tales of *kiddush* Hashem, tales of real strength, the kind that will, and must, endure forever.

That is why I am so happy to see Rabbi Hoffman's book, replete with stories of the Holocaust that will inspire the younger generation to greater levels of *emunah* and *bitachon*. We lost a generation of great Jews, but this book will allow their efforts not to be in vain and their memories not to fade.

Kol hakovod on this wonderful undertaking. May Hashem bless you with continued *kochos* to be *mekadeish shem Shamayim*.

Yosef Friedenson
Editor, *Dos Yiddishe Vort*

{PRE-WAR:}

PRELUDE TO
DISASTER

Heroes of Spirit

by Raize Guttman

In every corner there are eyes,
Angry, hateful, in disguise.

Danger lurking up ahead,
All around us signs of dread.

In every generation they rise to destroy,
To crush our faith, to mar our joy.

Has the Wandering Jew ever found peace?
Yet we still dare to hope, will the suffering cease?

Will the eyes stop to pierce, bring the end to our story?
Will the merciful G-d uncover His glory?

Yes, oh yes! We need to be patient,
To yearn for redemption and not feel complacent.

Chambers of gas, pogroms, Inquisition,
Yet we slip through their fingers and retain our position.

They can mock, they can jeer, never touching inside,
Our enemies are numbed by our faith and our pride.

We are HEROES OF SPIRIT they know this is true,
And will soon come to honor the Immortal Jew.

From Seldes to Duluth

In 1917, during the last years of World War I, a Jewish-American soldier from Duluth, Minnesota by the name of Alex Lurye, was stationed in a small German town called Seldes. War was raging all around and Alex found himself caught up in all the turmoil.

It was a warm Friday evening and Alex decided to go out for a walk through parts of the town. The lone soldier felt out of place since America was at war with Germany. Being Jewish, however, he sought out the local synagogue where he was met in the street and greeted by a kind German Jew by the name of Herr Rosennau. Surprised to learn that this American soldier, who spoke a broken German, was actually a practicing Jew, he graciously brought him inside the local synagogue for the Shabbos prayers.

After *davening*, Herr Rosennau invited the serviceman to his house for the Friday night meal, which Alex happily accepted. It had been a while since he'd been treated to such a delicious, kosher, home-cooked meal, complete with wine and traditional Shabbos songs. The Rosennau family treated their guest as graciously as their father did and Alex enjoyed himself immensely. The family doted on him and the children curled around him, playing with the soldier's uniform and tags. Alex wished the night would never end.

Eventually, though, after the meal, he was forced to return to his station barracks with a heavy heart, not knowing if he'd ever see these wonderful people again. Indeed, the soldier was unable to come back to see this kind family, but the impression that was made upon him, the experience of that Shabbos in Seldes in the warm and caring Rosennau home, did not leave him. In fact, it meant so much to this young soldier that when he finally returned to Duluth after the war, he took the time to sit down and write a letter to the German family who had touched his life with such kindness.

In 1938, as the situation became unbearable for the Jews of Germany and anti-Jewish decrees were being plotted and enforced on a regular basis, the Rosennau family in Seldes was not immune to the danger, nor were they naïve enough to believe that they were impervious to the impending disaster. They recognized that their only salvation lay in escaping Nazi Germany and they began searching for a way out.

One bright day, Herr Rosennau's grandson was rummaging through his grandfather's desk. Reaching into the bottom of a drawer, he pulled out an envelope with a foreign postage stamp on it. It was from America and there was a letter inside. He removed the letter and read it. It was the thank you letter from the American serviceman, Alex Lurye, from twenty-one years ago.

He brought the letter to his grandmother who, after reading it, suddenly remembered the young man. Then she had an idea.

"Let's write to him!" she announced to her husband. "Maybe he will remember us and be willing to sponsor our family. This will enable us to escape this awful place and immigrate to America."

There was a problem, though, and it was quite a serious one. They did not have a current address for Alex and had no way of getting a letter to him. They knew only one thing: The American serviceman's name was Alex Lurye and he was from a town called Duluth. With not much more to go on but faith, Herr Rosennau wrote the letter and addressed it simply to: Alex Lurye, Duluth, USA. Then, with a wish and a prayer, he sent off the letter.

Alex, meanwhile, had become a wealthy businessman in Duluth, which was not a small town but a large city of over one hundred thousand people. In a rare display of proficiency by the U.S. Postal Service, the nondescript letter from Seldes, Germany reached Duluth, Minnesota, and, with the ever-present guiding hand of Heaven, was directed to the correct home, the home of Alex Lurye.

When Alex received the letter, he remembered the Rosennau family - even after the lapse of twenty-one years - and the warm feelings came rushing back to him. Of course he would do whatever he could to help these wonderful people. He immediately sent a return letter acknowledging his receipt and pledging to help bring the family to America.

With tremendous and heroic efforts, Alex kept his promise. The entire Rosennau family was rescued from the jaws of the Nazi beast and arrived in the United States in 1938. Eventually, they managed to reach the city of Duluth. The reunion with Alex and his family was heartwarming.

In Duluth, Minnesota, as in Seldes, Germany, the Rosennau family made sure that Shabbos would be joyously honored. Unfortunately, most of German Jewry was destroyed. Yet, the kindness that Herr Rosennau had showed to a stranger twenty-one years earlier had come full circle. Through the kindness he had displayed back then, without any thought of personal gain, Herr Rosennau's whole family was spared from the horrible fate of their fellow German Jews.

| CHAFETZ CHAIM |

"Siz Gut Tzu Kenen Shusin"

For many years, the problem of Jewish soldiers serving in the Czar's army was a difficulty that went unaddressed. The "Cantonist" problem went on for many years and thousands of young Jewish children were mercilessly whisked away from their families, their lifestyle and their religion, and forced to serve in the "glorious" army of the Russian Czar. But even in later years, in countries like Poland, Hungary and the U.S.S.R., young men who received draft orders to report to the local army commander to begin serving their army service had little recourse but to run away, whereby they would be hunted by the authorities and punished horribly, if caught.

One young man heard that he was due to receive his draft order and was devastated. Immediately, he traveled to Radin, to the home of the great Chafetz Chaim, Rav Yisrael Meir Hakohen Kagan *zt"l* requesting a blessing to be exempt from the draft in Czarist Russia. He waited until he came before the great man and then, with tears in his eyes, begged him to intercede in Heaven on his behalf to receive a deferment.

The Chafetz Chaim sat quietly for some time. Then, he looked at the young man and with an unusual pitch in his voice, he intoned cryptically: *"Siz gut tzu kenen shusin* - It's good to know how to shoot."

The young man was aghast at this response. Basically, the Chafetz Chaim was telling him that when he gets drafted, he should report and serve in the army! Once again, he pleaded for a blessing, for any words of hope and encouragement that would set his mind at ease. But the Chafetz Chaim simply sat in his place and repeated his words, *"Siz gut tzu kenen shusin."* The young man left Radin crestfallen and was soon drafted into the Russian army where he was forced to serve for a number of years.

Thirty years later, the Second World War broke out and this man, together with his family and his entire hometown, were herded into the narrow confines of the Warsaw Ghetto. He was one of the lucky ones and managed to escape from the ghetto and hide in the woods. Fortunately, he was not caught by the Germans; unfortunately, he was captured by Polish partisans in the forest who took him for a spy and intended to shoot him on the spot. He pleaded for his life, shouting loudly that he was Jew and would never collaborate with the hideous Nazi beasts. He even told them that he could help them fight the Germans, here in the forest, as a partisan.

The partisans just laughed and said they were not interested in training some Jew how to shoot a gun. They were too busy with their nightly missions of sabotaging and terrorizing the Germans to be able to carry a lone, worthless Jew. At that point, he told them that he was already trained from the years he served in the Russian army and even demonstrated, to the amazement of the partisans and their leaders, that he not only knew how to use a rifle, but was actually quite proficient in its use as well.

With G-d's help he survived the war as an active member of the partisans, always remembering the prophetic words of the Chafetz Chaim, *"Siz gut tzu kenen shusin."* A Yid generally avoids violence; but there comes a time when even a Jew has to stand up and fight.

| KAPYCZNITZER REBBE |

What Could be Worse Than a Double Betrayal?

A woman came crying to the Kapycznitzer Rebbe, Rav Avraham Yehoshua Heschel *zt"l*. She was on the verge of despair. Having survived the Holocaust, she came to the United States and managed to raise her family as best as she could. She valued her Jewish roots, however she was not a deeply religious person and consequently, neither were her children. Now, though, her grown son had gone too far; he had met a non-Jewish girl, courted her for some time and just recently, announced their engagement. She was horrified - her son was planning on marrying out of the faith!

Day after day she pleaded with him to reconsider. What could be worse for a woman made to suffer through the hellish fire of the concentration camps because she was born a Jew, only to see her children turn their backs on the same faith for which she suffered? She begged, cajoled, and even took her son to speak with many important rabbis. He was a good son and wanted to make his mother happy so he went along, but he never allowed himself to be convinced to drop his wedding plans.

"Mama," he would say, "don't you want me to be happy? I have met the woman that I want to spend the rest of my life with. So what if she's not Jewish? It's not as if we keep any of the Jewish laws, anyway. Why is this so important to you?"

His mother tried to explain, but she was at a loss. Now, as she stood in front of the Kapycznitzer Rebbe, she broke down in a torrent of tears.

The Rebbe looked at her with tenderness in his eyes. "Bring him to me," he said, "I will talk to him."

"But Rebbe," she persisted, "My son specifically told me that he refuses to speak to any more rabbis. He claims that there is nothing they will say to convince him that he is making a mistake."

"I will not try to convince him," replied R' Avraham Yehoshua. "Please let him know that I will not try to convince him to change his mind. I simply want to tell him something which is important for him to hear."

The mother brightened and hurried home. She told her son what the Kapycznitzer Rebbe said and although he argued with her that he was through speaking to rabbis, when she gave over the Rebbe's cryptic message, he became intrigued. Not try to convince him? Just listen to an important message? Couldn't be too bad - and if it made his mother happy, why not?

Mother and son came to the Kapycznitzer Rebbe and while the mother waited outside in the anteroom, the Rebbe welcomed the young man into his private study. The warmth exuded by this old rabbi totally disarmed the strapping young man and he immediately felt drawn to the words of the Rebbe.

"Much like your mother," began the Rebbe, "I, too, suffered under the boot of the Nazis, although surely not as much as she did. I was able to leave Europe in 1938, before the war began. But in the short time that I lived in Vienna, I did get a personal taste of oppression, German style.

"I recall one incident which stands out in my mind until today. It's about a man, a Jew, who practically lost his mind from suffering. But it wasn't the Germans who put him through this torture. It was his wife."

The Rebbe spoke in soft tones and the young man eagerly waited for him to continue. "When the Germans annexed Austria in April of 1938, their first order of business was to enact decrees against the Jews. Day by day, life became unbearable and everyone prayed that this was only a temporary blip on the radar of normal society. The lucky ones got out at their first opportunity.

"One day, the Germans announced the first of many *selektions* which would decide the fate of the Jews of Vienna. Every Jew was ordered to gather in one of the main city squares and a huge line was formed. In typical German fashion, Jews were sent to the right or to the left. For some it meant slave labor camps and work details, for others it meant a temporary respite before the next *selektion*. We were all terrified - but there was nothing for us to do about it. We all lined up."

The Rebbe looked wistful for a moment. "I remember the line, how long it was and how far back it extended. We all stood for hours, hushed and scared until it was our turn. But then, out of the clear blue, we heard loud sobs. A man, not far behind me on line, began crying hysterically. People tried to console him but he shook them off. In the stillness, his cries reverberated and nobody could make him stop. It was strange and out of place. We all should have been crying but we weren't. Only he was. Finally, I left my place on line and walked over to him.

"'My son,' I said, 'please don't cry. We are all in this together and we will all get through this together. We are *'Acheinu kol Beis Yisrael'* - all Jewish brothers, and we will gladly share your burden.'"

The young man was still sitting impassively, but he was listening.

"The man began shaking his head violently. 'No, no, you don't understand! Go away! Leave me!' He was heaving uncontrollably now but I refused to walk away. I again tried to console him, to at least get him to stop crying. And finally he did. But only long enough to tell me his story.

"'Rabbi,' he began, 'I was born and raised in a religious home. But I was somewhat of a rebel and, in my teen years, I fell in with the wrong crowd. There was an Austrian girl, non-Jewish, who I became friendly with. We were young and having fun and it wasn't long before I was abandoning my religious practices. When we became old enough, we decided to get married. But how would that work? I was Jewish and she was Christian. Okay, she said, so you'll become a Christian. What did I need to be Jewish for, anyway? There was no future for us if I was a Jew, so I did the unthinkable. I converted to Christianity. We got married and lived happily together for over twenty years.'"

Now, the young man sat up in his chair. This, no doubt, was the part he was meant to hear. The Rebbe continued, "The man on line was sobbing softly, but he insisted on finishing his story. 'When the Nazis announced this *selektion* a few days ago, they made it very clear that not only must every Jew report to the city square, but if a gentile knows of a Jew who did not report and they do not come forward to expose the Jew, they, too, will be arrested and made to suffer the consequences. My wife got scared. She knew that I was once a Jew and in order to save herself from potential arrest, she went straight down to the Gestapo headquarters and reported that I am a Jew. The Nazis came for me a short while ago and pulled me out of my house, away from my wife and family, and threw me into this square.'

"Suddenly, the man looked up and pointed across the street. 'Rabbi, you want to know why I'm so hysterical? Because right over there, across the street, my wife of twenty years is standing and watching. In fact, she's talking with a few people around her and she doesn't even look upset. When I look at her there, I cannot control my emotions.' The man let out a loud cry. 'Rabbi, this woman betrayed me not once but twice! First, she convinced me to give up my religion and turn my back on my Jewish heritage. Then, when it suited her, she decided that I was a Jew and should be taken away with all the rest of the Jews! A double betrayal by one woman! That's why I cry so hysterically!'"

A somber quiet enveloped the Kapycznitzer Rebbe's study. The meeting was over. There were no more words to say. Silently, the young man stood up and let himself out of the room.

His mother jumped to her feet when she saw her son. Then, she noticed the ashen look on his face. "Mama," he said quietly, "the wedding is off. You were right. How can I trust a gentile with something as important as the rest of my life?"

Charity Saves One From Death

For over a century, American Jewry has been widely regarded throughout the world as a charitable and generous group, looked upon in so many situations to provide assistance to their needy brethren spread all across the world. Numerous *rabbanim*, *roshei yeshivah* and rebbes, not to mention countless *shluchim*, have made the arduous journey from Europe, Eretz Yisrael and the like, and their brethren in America are generally counted upon to come through in times of need. And generally, they do.

The famed *posek*, Rav Chaim Ozer Grodzenski *zt"l*, in particular, held American Jewry in the highest regard. A young American *bachur* by the name of Akiva Chill, traveled overseas to learn in the sanctified halls of the Mir Yeshivah. When World War II broke out, the entire Mir Yeshivah began its legendary trek through a vast stretch of Eastern Europe, including Russia, eventually reaching the city of Shanghai, where they waited out the war.

One of the first stops that the yeshivah made was in Vilna, where thousands of Jews and many *yeshivos* sought refuge. The overcrowded conditions were merciless and the hardships facing the many refugees became unbearable. Through it all, the *rav* of Vilna, R' Chaim Ozer, worked tirelessly to provide for any and all who needed assistance. During that time, his door remained open for much of the day and night to answer all the questions, and provide advice and solace for the needy masses. R' Chaim Ozer was no youngster and the strain on him was tremendous, but he carried on resolutely on behalf of his people.

While in Vilna, Akiva received a correspondence from his family in the United States, imploring him to leave Europe and return home to safety. Although he understood the need to accede to their urgent request, he nevertheless felt that he should remain with his yeshivah, the *roshei yeshivah* and the student body. He did not want to abandon his studies and the thought of leaving the Mir Yeshivah in its most desperate hour was unthinkable. He was torn and unsure of how to act. Finally, he decided to bring his dilemma to the *gadol hador,* R' Chaim Ozer, and allow him to make the decision.

R' Chaim Ozer's home was a non-stop hive of activity. *Rabbanim* from everywhere were constantly coming with questions that required immediate attention. Important members of the *kehillah* were likewise ever-present, in need of the great Gaon's attention and, as a result, Akiva had a difficult time getting in to see the *rav*. His perseverance eventually paid off and one day he managed somehow to get in for a private moment with the *rav*.

After detailing his dilemma in clear and concise words, he waited with anticipation for a response. R' Chaim Ozer's answer came swiftly.

"*Bachur,* you should go back to America immediately because I believe that the Germans will never reach the shores of America. The reason for this is because I have heard repeatedly that the American Jews are renowned in the area of giving *tzedakah* and *Chazal* have made it abundantly clear that, 'Charity saves one from death.' Go back to America and you will be safe."

R' Chaim Ozer's prophetic words rang true then, and still do today. Akiva Chill went home and remained safe.

| RAV JOSEF BREUER |

An Unlikely Savior

On October 28, 1938, seventeen thousand Polish Jews, whom Poland had earlier disenfranchised, were banished from Germany and wound up stranded in no-man's land between the borders of the two countries. Among them were the parents of seventeen-year old Herschel Grynszpan who was living in Paris. When he received a letter from his parents describing their anguish and fears, Herschel decided to act. He entered the German embassy in Paris on November 7th and shot Ernst Von Rath, the Third Secretary of the Embassy. Von Rath died on the morning of November 9th and Nazi retribution soon followed.

That entire night and throughout the next day, anti-Jewish riots erupted throughout Germany. While the government spokesmen claimed that the riots were a spontaneous reaction on the part of German citizens to the murder of von Rath, the riots were carefully orchestrated and planned by the Nazis. Every plea to the authorities for protection was ignored and the police turned upon the Jews as well. Widespread attacks were made on Jewish homes and businesses throughout Germany and Austria and some 20,000 Jews were arrested and detained in camps. According to Nazi records, 191 synagogues were set on fire and 76 others were totally destroyed. Thirty-six Jews were killed while hundreds of others were injured. Kristallnacht - Night of Broken Glass - as the riots became known, was the final blow to German Jewry.

Rav Yosef Breuer *zt"l*, the esteemed *rabbiner* of the Frankfurt *kehillah*, and his family were hiding in their home on the Theobaldstrasse, as the wild mobs roamed through the streets. On the intercom that connected his home with the

Frankfurt Yeshivah, R' Breuer could clearly hear the ranting hordes breaking into and destroying his office. A huge crowd had gathered around the *kehillah's* synagogue, mesmerized as flames climbed through its magnificent towers. Fire equipment surrounding the burning edifice had been dispatched to the site only to ensure that the conflagration not spread to other buildings in the area. Later, the shell of the building was dynamited and bulldozers leveled the area.

Yaakov, the *rav's* son, had been studying at the teacher's seminary in nearby Wuerzburg when the events of Kristallnacht began and decided to return home. He was concerned for the welfare of his family and he thought that perhaps he could assist in some way when he got there.

Getting there wasn't easy. Pretending to be a non-Jew, he managed to travel inconspicuously until he reached the block of his parents' apartment building. What he saw along the way made him cringe. Bands of roving Nazi youth were setting fires and vandalizing anything that resembled Jewish property. Prominent Jews were being dragged from their homes and beaten mercilessly in the street.

Yaakov knew that he must remain undetected so he approached the block of his parents' home cautiously. What he saw there made his heart stop. Standing directly in front of the entrance to the building was an S.S. man, not much older than himself.

Yaakov needed to get inside the building, but how? Finally, he made the decision to approach and bluff his way inside. He walked jauntily up to the entrance and the Nazi saw him. Yaakov broke out in a sweat but the man waved for him to come forward. Then he said to him conspiratorially, "Hurry, go inside before anyone sees you."

It was then that Yaakov recognized the German. He was the son of the building's superintendent and he had stationed himself directly in front of the entrance to the Breuer family's building in order to protect the *rabbiner*, his family and his Jewish friends inside! The reason why no Nazis had entered the building all evening was because this one S.S. member was standing guard and not allowing anyone inside! When the Breuer family saw Yaakov arrive, they were thrilled and relieved to see him safe, as well as amazed at how a Nazi was actually protecting them!

Around noon on November 10th, the doorbell rang. Through the frosted-glass front door, the family could make out the figures of two men wearing raincoats and fedoras - the unofficial uniform of the dreaded Gestapo. The agents demanded to meet with R' Breuer who was learning at his desk. The men told the *rav* to pack a few belongings into a bag and accompany them.

The Gestapo agents took R' Breuer to an armory called the Festhalle where he, along with thousands of other men from the Jewish community, was forced to stand and wait for hours on end. Eight hours after he arrived, a brown-shirted member of the S.A. came forward and ordered all men over the age of sixty to step forward. Although his frailty gave him the appearance of being past that age, R' Breuer was fifty-six at the time and therefore remained in line.

The S.A. officer screamed at the *rav* to move forward and join the older group. R' Breuer did so and it is quite likely that his life was spared by this inexplicable intervention, for the younger men remained behind and were sent off to Buchenwald and Dachau where many were beaten and killed. When the *rav* returned home, to the joyful relief of the members of his family, the decision was made to escape Germany as quickly as possible.

The Breuer family immigrated to Antwerp, Belgium in December 1938, where a former student persuaded R' Breuer that he was needed on the American Jewish scene. He eventually settled in the Washington Heights section of Manhattan, where he became the spiritual leader of the Khal Adas Jeshurun (KAJ) German-Jewish *kehillah* for the next 42 years.

| THE REICHMANN FAMILY |

Honor Your Father, Save Your Life

In early 1938, Shmaya and Renee Reichmann began planning a grand celebration for the bar mitzvah of their oldest son, Eli (Edward) Reichmann. The Reichmann family had already established themselves among the respected families of Vienna and the entire city was looking forward to quite a bash from the well-to-do Reichmann family. A prominent hall in one of the grandest hotels in Vienna was reserved for the big day. Residents of Vienna as well as many out-of-town guests were expected, and just two weeks before the bar mitzvah, preparations and travel arrangements were at a feverish pitch.

The Reichmanns were expecting a very special guest: the Pupa Rebbe, Rav Yaakov Grunwald *zt"l*. On his frequent visits to Vienna for medical care, the Rebbe usually stayed with the Reichmanns. He had established a close connection not only with Shmaya and his wife, but especially with Eli, who had precociously invited the Rebbe a year earlier when he had accompanied him to shul one morning. The Rebbe pledged that with Hashem's help, he would come to Vienna the following year for young Eli's bar mitzvah. The added honor of hosting the Pupa Rebbe increased the excitement to unprecedented levels.

In 1938, not very many families had their own private telephone line in their home, but the Reichmann's were one of the fortunate ones. Due to their successful business operations and the many communal functions that they were involved in, they were in constant need and use of their telephone.

Just a few days before the big *simchah*, the family received an urgent call. They were informed that the bar mitzvah boy's paternal grandfather, R' Dovid Reichmann, living in Beled, a small village in Hungary, had suffered a serious stroke and was unable to travel to Vienna.

The family was stunned and dismayed. All their preparations and the great joy and celebration would be very much lacking if they were unable to share it with the patriarch of the family. They were at a loss as to what to do. Should they cancel the event so close to its date? Or should they hold the bar mitzvah celebration in Vienna and after Shabbos, go to Hungary to take care of their grandfather?

Only days before the grand affair, Eli's father, Shmaya, made a decision: They could not possibly celebrate a family *simchah* without his father present.

Without another moment's hesitation, Mr. Reichmann called the hall and the caterer to cancel the event. He attempted to notify as many of his guests as possible that the event in Vienna was being called off. They even contacted the Pupa Rebbe and explained the situation to him. Of course, he was very understanding and considered even going to Beled, which was not too distant from Pupa. (He was unable to attend because the anti-semitic violence which had spilled over into

Hungary the day before the bar mitzvah made traveling too dangerous). Then Shmaya, his wife, the bar mitzvah boy and one of his brothers traveled to the little Hungarian village of Beled, where his father was convalescing comfortably, while the rest of the Reichmann children remained in Vienna with a nanny.

They arrived a few days early and, instead of a huge catered event in a beautiful Vienna ballroom, Eli Reichmann celebrated his bar mitzvah in the small *shtiebel* in Beled where his grandfather *davened,* and a modest feast was enjoyed in the grateful presence of his beloved grandfather.

This all took place on March 12, 1938, the same day that the Nazis *ym"s* entered Austria, unopposed, and initiated pogroms in the streets of Vienna. Sunday morning, Shmaya Reichmann decided to check in on his family and business interests back home, to see if there were any messages for him, and make sure everything was running smoothly in his absence. He managed to locate a telephone at a neighbor's house in Hungary and called his house back in Vienna.

The gentile nanny answered the phone and relayed to Mr. Reichmann all the relevant information that he needed to know. Everything was okay, she said, nothing new. "Oh, by the way," the secretary hastened to add before Mr. Reichmann could hang up the phone, "you did have a few visitors last night."

"Visitors?" he asked, thinking that perhaps some of the non-notified guests had mistakenly come to his house looking for the *baal simchah.* "Who were they?" he asked.

She paused for a moment. "Mr. Reichmann, it was the Gestapo, a group of German agents, looking for you and your family," she said. "When they couldn't locate you, they left quite upset."

The Gestapo had been to his house! Mr. Reichmann found out that the Nazis had begun rounding up wealthy and prominent members of the Vienna Jewish community that Saturday night, and had they caught up with him, he, too, would have been arrested! He made the decision right then and there that he would never return to Vienna and hastily made arrangements to bring the rest of his family over to Hungary. Shmaya Reichmann never went back to Vienna and was fortunate enough to be able to liquidate whatever assets he could from a distance.

If not for the mitzvah of *kibbud av*, not wanting to celebrate a *simchah* without his father, who knows if the Reichmann family - and their many accomplishments on behalf of Klal Yisrael - would have ever escaped the Nazi inferno?

A "Resourceful" Menorah

After the terrible events of Kristallnacht on November 9, 1938, many Jews expedited their plans to emigrate from a once beloved, but now cold and unforgiving, German Fatherland. Once their minds were made up, they wasted no time in applying for the necessary visas and documents needed. A bittersweet taste was felt by these German Jews who understood the need to escape as quickly as possible yet, could hardly believe that the homeland where they invested so much of their blood, sweat and tears, was now their own individual ticking time-bomb filled with hate, terror and death.

The Geier family of Berlin was proud of their Jewish German heritage. It saddened them deeply that they were forced to leave under such terrible circumstances. Shortly after the devastation of Kristallnacht, the Geiers had received their passports and visas to leave Germany for the United States. On December 25, 1938, the eighth day of Chanukah, the family was packed and making their way to the railroad station where they were to board the train that would take them away from the land of their birth as well as from the murderous clutches of the Nazis. It was a sunny, but rather cold day, as their train bound for Holland pulled out of the Berlin station. The Geiers shared their second-class compartment with two very stern-looking German citizens.

Arnold Geier, age 12, and his sister, 15, sat quietly with their parents. Their father was inwardly upset over the fact that he would be unable to light his Chanukah candles that evening. Mr. Geier was a devout Jew and had packed a small menorah and some candles in his briefcase, just in case. In a whisper, Arnold overheard his mother reassure his father that Hashem would forgive him for not lighting the menorah that night. They traveled on in tense silence for a few long hours.

Not long after darkness, the train slowed and puffed its way into a special railway station at the German-Dutch border. They braced themselves for their final encounter with the dreaded Gestapo. Just a few more kilometers and the terror of the previous years under the Nazi-led government would be behind them. The train sat in the station and the Geier family watched as the Border Police, together with the Gestapo, compared lists and prepared to check each person's passport and papers.

Finally, small groups of officers boarded the train for the inspection. Mr. Geier looked tense and broke out in a sweat. This was the moment of truth. His life and the future of his family's existence depended on making it through the next few minutes without attracting undue attention from the Gestapo agents. They were all very afraid.

Then, without any warning, the lights went out! A sudden blackout darkened every light on the train and in the station. This didn't help to ease their heightened apprehension. A number of people lit matches for light and the glow on their faces made an eerie sight. Most people simply stayed put, except for Mr. Geier, who suddenly stood up, terrified but still of sound mind, and pulled eight small candles out of his coat pocket. With the hint of a smile on his lips, he struck a match and lit one candle. Using that candle he warmed the bottoms of the other candles and lined up all eight candles on the window sill of their compartment. At that moment, Mrs. Geier and the children began to comprehend their father's action and they all stood up in unison. He quietly recited the Chanukah blessings, and lit the candles. For the first time in a long time, a smile appeared on Mr. Geier's face.

Then, someone shouted, "Look. There's light over there!" The Border Police and the Gestapo agents soon came to the Geier's compartment, attracted by the eight candles that gave off more light than anywhere else in the entire station. With German efficiency, they used the light of the candles to conduct their inspection of everyone's passports and papers. They were polite and even a bit thankful. One of the officers commended Mr. Geier on his resourcefulness for thinking ahead and packing "travel candles." When it was time to inspect the Geier family's papers, the agent took a quick, cursory look at their papers and was done.

About half an hour passed and then, as suddenly as they had gone off, the lights flickered back on again. The officers again thanked Mr. Geier and left the compartment to finish their work throughout the train.

The irony was not lost on the fleeing family. "Remember this moment," Arnold Geier's father said to him. "Just as we say each year about what took place in the times of the Maccabees: 'Nes gadol hayay po. - A great miracle happened here!'"

| *CHACHAM* MACHLOOF EIDAN |

A Handy Receipt

The Jewish community of Djerba, Tunis, was one that was poor in material wealth, but extravagantly rich in spiritual content. The revered and respected leader, *Chacham* Machloof Eidan *zt"l*, firmly controlled the strictly religious nature of the community. The people hung on to his every word and followed his directives without question.

One day, the *Chacham* was walking down a busy street filled with food vendors and children at play, when he overheard one child scream and curse at another. Quickly, he approached the boy and demanded to know his name and his father's name. The embarrassed child apologized profusely and it took quite a bit of stern coaxing before he told the *Chacham* his father's name.

Without another word, *Chacham* Machloof headed off to the synagogue where he sought out the man in question. He told him what he had witnessed and heard with his own ears and expressed his deepest consternation and regret that a father should allow his son to talk in this manner.

In response to the father's feeble protestations that it was not his fault that his son had uttered a curse, *Chacham*

Machloof said, "Not only is it your responsibility to watch what passes from your children's lips, it is also a clear indication of a lack of proper guidance and *chinuch* in your household. When vulgarities are uttered, even accidentally, from one's lips, it reveals the innermost workings of that person's tainted soul. This must be halted and corrected immediately."

The *Chacham* then imposed a fine on the father and ordered him to bring the money to the local yeshivah, Ohr HaTorah, in Djerba. The sum was a significant one and the man was forced to pay up. He sent his child with the money to the yeshivah where they issued him a receipt. From there, the young boy hastened to the home of the *Chacham* to show proof that the fine had been paid and to apologize, once again, in person.

Chacham Machloof treated the boy very differently this time. He embraced him in his arms and expounded on the great level of a *baal teshuvah* that he had attained. Then he said, "Hold on to this receipt. It may just come in handy later on."

A number of years passed, and the Second World War broke out, encompassing the whole of Europe and parts of North Africa. Djerba, too, was not impervious to the effects of the war, and when the Nazi oppressors occupied the small Tunisian island, their first course of action was to impose typical Nazi regulations upon the Jewish community. Any Jew caught without his yellow star or appropriate documentation was sent away, or worse.

During this time, a shortage of wheat was heavily felt and necessary food supplies were in great demand. *Chacham* Machloof dispatched a group of citizens to an outlying area where it was heard that wheat was available. Among those in the group were the man and his grown-up son, the one who had cursed the other child so many years earlier.

After successfully completing their purchase, the group headed back to Djerba. On the road, they came upon a German checkpoint and were ordered to stop. The soldiers demanded to see their documents and working papers, especially their permit for purchasing and transporting goods. None of the members of the group had such documentation and the soldiers were preparing to arrest the entire group. "Arrest" may be too benign of a word. When a Jew was caught in the Nazi clutches, even in the far-removed theater of North Africa, they were almost never heard from again.

The older members of the group began to despair. There was no escape and no way out of their predicament, at least none that they could come up with as they prepared to face their destiny.

Suddenly, the young man remembered that he had a valuable document on him. He pulled out his receipt from years before from Yeshivah Ohr HaTorah and decided that he would give it a try.

Walking up to the nearest soldier, he produced the paper, with its Hebrew writing on it, and announced that he "found" the permit. The German looked at the paper, then at the young man, then at his companions, before shrugging and allowing the group to pass.

The *Chacham* had said it would come in handy at a later date - and it most certainly did!

A Double Kindness

Before he came to America and established the great yeshivah in Lakewood, N.J., Rav Aharon Kotler *zt"l* was already an eminent *rosh yeshivah* in Kletzk, Lithuania, and considered one of the *gedolei hador*. *Bachurim* would flock to hear his dynamic *shiurim* and the yeshivah in Kletzk was a bastion of Torah in the pre-war days. But then, the Nazis came to power. Jews all over Eastern Europe tried to find means of refuge to escape the terrible Germans, *ym"s*.

R' Aharon, along with a group of leading *roshei yeshivah* and *rebbes*, managed to escape war-torn Europe through a series of incredible events, with a wide range of assistance from individuals, organizations and even the American government. Unfortunately for many Jews, salvation eluded them and they met their untimely demise together with the majority of European Jewry. No one, though, could fault them for a lack of trying.

Thousands upon thousands of Jews rushed to every available government office to try to procure visas - it didn't matter to where - for themselves and their families in order to get out of Europe. Some people traveled for weeks and then stood on line for days after that, before even coming face to face with an officer. Panic and confusion reigned supreme.

Yehoshua* was one of the many students who rushed to the city of Kovno to attain a visa. It was said that the Dutch consul was granting permits, as well as a senior officer in the Japanese consulate, a righteous gentile by the name of Shiune

*not his real name

Sugihara. People grabbed onto these "straws" of hope and flocked to the city.

When Yehoshua arrived in Kovno, he made his way directly to the visa office. He was hardly surprised to find a line of people waiting their turn, but the line was so huge, so much longer than he expected. What could he do? He had no choice but to wait.

Hours passed. Yehoshua began to panic. What if there would be no more visas by the time it was his turn? As the sun began to dip over the horizon, he became desperate. Without thinking, he began pushing his way to the front of the line. The people in front of him were annoyed and were arguing with him to get back in line. No one offered to let him move in front of them in line, until one young man standing near the front just looked at him questioningly, and then graciously gestured Yehoshua forward, directly in front of him. It was nice of him and Yehoshua was grateful.

He stepped forward, looking at the person now behind him. What if Yehoshua received the last visa and this *bachur* did not? He may have just given his life-line away to a total stranger! Such a great act of *mesiras nefesh,* and without an unkind word like from some of the other people.

Soon after, Yehoshua's turn came and, after him, the young man. They both received their precious visas to their great relief and both were able to escape Europe. Later, Yehoshua discovered that the young man was none other than R' Aharon's son, Rav Shneur Kotler *zt"l.*

Eventually, Yehoshua came to America and joined *Beth Medrash Govoha* in Lakewood. It was an honor to be considered among the *talmidim* of R' Aharon and he excelled in his studies.

In Kislev 5723 (1962), darkness again enveloped the Jewish world. R' Aharon Kotler passed away. Yehoshua was shattered. He had lost his *rebbi*, the one person who had helped him rebuild his life after the catastrophe in Europe.

Before the funeral procession began, the coffin of R' Aharon was placed in a room where people were able to go inside and recite Tehillim. Yehoshua made his way to the small room. If he would no longer be able to listen live to his *rebbi's* words of wisdom, at least he could spend a little more time with him by sitting near his *rebbi's aron*.

Yehoshua was not the only one who wanted to snatch a few final minutes with the *rosh yeshivah*. The tiny room was packed with students saying Tehillim. There didn't seem to be room for Yehoshua at all. But Yehoshua's mind was preoccupied. Once again, without thinking, Yehoshua began to push his way into the room. As he tried to find a small space near the *aron,* one man quietly moved aside and gave up his place.

Grateful, Yehoshua glanced at the man's face. Then he froze. It was R' Shneur! R' Shneur Kotler, son of the *niftar*! Once again R' Shneur had given up his rightful place for another.

| RAV YECHEZKEL ABRAMSKY |

A Torah Education Overrides Shabbos

Before the onset of World War II, a number of organizations were involved in saving as many Jewish lives as they could. Groups of youngsters were sent outside the borders, in what was known as "Kindertransport" and they crossed through countries until their arrival in England. Enemy aircraft and missiles had not yet brought widespread destruction to the British Isle but the German intrusion, it appeared, was imminent, and Prime Minister Winston Churchill guaranteed the people "blood, sweat and tears."

The young refugees were taken in by various Jewish organizations, both Torah observant groups as well as those lacking any connection to the Jewish religion and heritage. The religious organization organized a camp with counselors, teachers and educators, plus a kitchen and a "camp mother." Obviously, all this required a lot of funding.

At a time when inflation was sky-high and unemployment abounded, donations gradually subsided, as many donors went bankrupt and others simply could not part with their wealth out of fear for the unknown. The organizers gathered in the home of the Chief Rabbi of London, Rav Yechezkel Abramsky zt"l, to report on the grim situation.

"Rabbi, the money has been depleted, and we are compelled to cease operations. The youth will have to be given over to other groups where they will at least receive food and shelter, but without a Torah education. We have no choice."

They shook their heads. They had already turned to everyone; they had tried everything. There was, they said, one certain noble, a Jew by birth who had lost all ties to Judaism. He observed nothing other than the day of his parents' passing, when he would go to the synagogue to recite kaddish. Despite his immense wealth, they did not even bother approaching him. He was as far away from religion as east is from west.

Right then and there, the rabbi telephoned the wealthy man and scheduled a meeting.

"I come for a matter of life and death," the rabbi said as he sat opposite the man. He proceeded to tell him about the organization. The man sat and listened until the rabbi finished, and then replied, "I already support life-saving operations. I provide funding for the Red Cross and other similar organizations. Forgive me, rabbi, but this institute is not involved in saving lives. The youngsters were saved once they left their homelands. Here, in England, their lives are secure, and it makes no difference to me where they receive their education."

"Judaism maintains that Torah education is also considered saving lives," responded the rabbi. "Detachment from the fountains of Torah and observance of *mitzvos* is equivalent to the loss of life!"

"I'm sorry, but I don't exactly understand what you mean when you say you are 'saving lives.'" With that, he stood up, and the interview came to an end. R' Yechezkel left empty-handed.

That very same week, on Friday night, at 11:00 PM, the telephone rang in the wealthy man's residence. Shabbos for him was like a weekday, and so he picked up the phone. "Hello?"

The voice coming from the other end was familiar. "This is Rabbi Abramsky, the chief rabbi of London. I am calling you on Shabbos eve, because saving lives overrides Shabbos, and educating children towards Torah and *mitzvos* constitutes saving lives. Is this a clear enough indication that I am speaking here of saving lives?"

The man was startled. The chief rabbi of London was calling him on the phone on Friday night! "How much money does the rabbi need?"

R' Yechezkel told him the amount, an enormous fortune, and after Shabbos the nobleman came personally with the money. The operation continued, and lives were saved as the youngsters were given a Torah education.

| RAV AVRAHAM PAM |
A "Mistaken" Deferment

Mass immigration to the United States was a direct result of a wave of pogroms throughout Russia after the Bolshevik Revolution. The Pam family was among those refugees who were forced to escape and, in 1929, they ultimately settled in the Brownsville section of Brooklyn. Young Avraham Pam was sent to learn in Mesivta Torah Vodaath, the yeshivah he ended up heading in his later years.

At age nineteen, Avraham Pam embarked on a two-year *semichah* study program to master the four sections of *Shulchan Aruch*, with all the major commentaries. When he had completed the program, he and two friends were tested by three renowned *rabbonim*: Rav Moshe Binyamin Tomashov *zt"l*, the senior *rav* in Brownsville, Brooklyn; Rav Yehudah Leib Graubart *zt"l*, a distinguished *rav* in Toronto who was visiting New York at that time; and Rav Yaakov Kantrowitz *zt"l*, *Av Beis Din* of Trenton, New Jersey, who later succeeded Rav Dovid Leibowitz *zt"l* as *rosh yeshivah* of Torah Vodaath. (R' Yaakov was one of the greatest surviving *talmidim* of the Volozhiner Yeshivah in Lithuania and he was also the uncle of the great *posek*, Rabbi Moshe Feinstein *zt"l*; letters in halachah to him appear in *Igros Moshe*. Tragically, he was injured in a fall less than a year after coming to Torah Vodaath and was unable to continue as *rosh yeshivah*.)

For his *semichah* examination, young Avraham Pam was required to sit with R' Kantrowitz as *shochtim*, butchers and others came before the *rav* with all sorts of halachic questions. Before ruling on any matter, R' Kantrowitz first turned to his young charge and asked him to state his opinion. After a week of such "testing," R' Kantrowitz was duly impressed and presented him with a certificate of *semichah* in which he wrote: "I have found him to be fluent in matters of halachah; he has a clear mind and a deep comprehension to analyze a Talmudic topic in accordance with halachah. I have spoken with him in matters of practical halachah, and have found in him wide-ranging knowledge in major portions of *Yoreh De'ah*, as well as knowledge of *Even HaEzer* and *Choshen Mishpat*, like an experienced *rav*."

When Avraham Pam turned thirty, he became engaged to Sarah Balmuth. The young couple received a blessing from R' Kantrowitz, who wrote a beautiful letter expressing his warm wishes and fervent hope that the new couple will merit to build a beautiful Jewish home. R' Pam cherished this letter and kept it with him at all times.

On December 7, 1941, the Imperial Japanese army attacked Pearl Harbor and plunged the United States into the Second World War. The country began mobilizing for war and all able-bodied young men were required to report to their local army office for recruitment. Those men who were able to submit valid proof that they were either rabbis or full-time Talmudic students were deferred.

R' Pam entered the office where fifteen army officers were individually interviewing fifteen potential recruits. A long line stretched out of the waiting room as each young man waited his turn. For yeshivah students, a letter of approbation from their institution or a valid rabbinic ordination (*semichah*) paper was needed in order to secure the deferment. There was an officer in charge, a secular Jew who, it was said, could read Yiddish, who would peruse each document and validate its authenticity.

Finally, R' Pam's turn came to be interviewed. After a few short questions, R' Pam submitted his letter of *semichah* from R' Kantrowitz and the secular officer looked it over carefully. Then, without another word, he picked up his stamp and issued a deferment to the relieved young rabbi standing before him.

After R' Pam left the office, he discovered that he'd made a mistake. Instead of submitting the letter of *semichah* which vouched for his rabbinic status as a full-time Torah teacher, he had mistakenly submitted the letter from R' Kantrowitz wishing him mazel tov on his forthcoming marriage! The officer in charge had read through his letter of congratulations and through Divine Intervention, he had rubber stamped the coveted deferment!

When R' Pam would tell over this story, he would insist that his deferment was nothing short of a miracle.

| THE "LEICA FREEDOM TRAIN" |

Righteous Gentiles

The Leica is the pioneer 35mm camera. It is a German product - precise and utterly efficient. Behind its worldwide acceptance as a creative tool was a family-owned, socially oriented firm that, during the Nazi era, acted with uncommon grace, generosity and modesty.

E. Leitz Inc., designer and manufacturer of Germany's most famous photographic product, saved its Jews. Ernst Leitz II, the steely-eyed Protestant patriarch who headed the closely held firm as the Holocaust loomed across Europe, acted in such a way as to earn the title, "the photography industry's Oskar Schindler."

As soon as Adolf Hitler *ym"s* was named chancellor of Germany in 1933, Ernst Leitz II began receiving frantic calls from Jewish associates, asking for his help in getting them and their families out of the country. As Christians, Leitz and his family were immune to Nazi Germany's Nuremberg laws, which restricted the movement of Jews and limited their professional activities. To help his Jewish workers and colleagues, Leitz quietly established what has become known among historians of the Holocaust as the "Leica Freedom Train," a covert means of allowing Jews to leave Germany in the guise of Leitz employees being assigned overseas. Employees, retailers, family members, even friends of family members, were "assigned" to Leitz sales offices in France, Britain, Hong Kong and the United States.

Leitz's activities intensified after Kristallnacht on November 9-10, 1938, when synagogues and Jewish shops were burned across Germany. Before long, German "employees" were disembarking from the ocean liner Bremen at a New York pier and making their way to the Manhattan office of Leitz Inc., where executives quickly found them jobs in the photographic industry. Each new arrival had the symbol of freedom around his or her neck - a new Leica camera. The refugees were paid a stipend until they could find work. Out of this migration came designers, repair technicians, salespeople, marketers and writers for the photographic press.

The "Leica Freedom Train" was at its height in 1938 and early 1939, delivering groups of refugees to New York every few weeks. Then, with the invasion of Poland on September 1, 1939, Germany closed its borders. By that time, hundreds of endangered Jews had escaped to America, thanks to the Leitzes' efforts.

Leitz Inc. was an internationally recognized brand that reflected credit on the newly resurgent German Reich. The company produced range-finders and other optical systems for the German military. Also, the Nazi government desperately needed hard currency from abroad, and Leitz's single biggest market for optical goods was the United States.

Even so, members of the Leitz family and firm suffered for their good deeds. A top executive, Alfred Turk, was jailed for working to help Jews, and freed only after a large bribe was paid.

Ernst Leitz's daughter, Elsie Kuhn-Leitz, was imprisoned by the Gestapo after she was caught at the border, helping Jewish women cross into Switzerland. She eventually was freed but endured rough treatment in the course of questioning. She also fell under suspicion when she attempted to improve the living conditions of 700 to 800 Ukrainian slave laborers, all of them women, who had been assigned to work in the plant during the 1940s. (After the war, Kuhn-Leitz received numerous honors for her humanitarian efforts, among them the Officier D'Honneur des Palms Academic from France in 1965, and the Aristide Briand Medal from the European Academy, in the 1970s.)

Why has no one told this story until now? According to a prominent freelance writer and editor, the Leitz family wanted no publicity for its heroic efforts. Only after the last member of the Leitz family was dead did the "Leica Freedom Train" finally come to light.

{ MID-WAR I }

The Inferno Unleashed

Ashreinu - We are Fortunate

by Raize Guttman

The room stood ready, the doors opened wide,
Those standing in line shuddered and sighed.
Skeletal figures, beards and payos shorn,
Departing this world with no one to mourn.

In the shadow of evil awaiting their fate,
Their pounding hearts deafening their ears.
Then one man burst forth with a spirit so great,
Singing, dancing - dissolving their fears.

They clasped one another, each man to his brother,
Swept up with the joy of a Jew,
They sang with one voice - "We can truly rejoice,
We serve only Hashem - and not you!"

The onlooking guards with incredulous eyes,
Sparking with anger and unmasked surprise.
"Crazy Jews, don't you know this is the moment of
death?
What's that you dare sing with your very last
breath?"

"Ashreinu," *they answered,* "we are singing with joy,
For your Final Solution will never succeed.
We Jews are eternal - we can never be destroyed,
Our bodies can be killed but our souls will be freed!"

Dumbstruck, in awe, and against their own will,
The Germans screamed, "Get out, schnell, YOU we won't
kill!"
Still dancing and singing the Jews fled all together,
Singing, "Mah Tov Chelkainu - *ASHREINU FOREVER!*"

What a Jew Really Is!

On the day before Sukkos, 1939, after being thoroughly demolished by the fierce German onslaught - the "Blitzkrieg" - which began only four short weeks earlier, the hapless Polish army surrendered unconditionally and a ceasefire was established.

The people of Warsaw emerged from bomb shelters, grateful for the quiet, and the following wonderful scene took place: Thousands of Jews, who had just come out of cellars in every corner of the city, hurried to pull planks and doors out of the debris, and began building kosher *sukkos* for the coming Yom Tov.

Many *sukkos* went up, only to be torn down by furious German soldiers who would then chase the Jews away. The Jews of Warsaw, bursting with love for the mitzvah, would find another place and build a *sukkah* there. The Germans, joined by enthusiastic Poles, would knock down that *sukkah* as well.

But, in the end, the spirit of the Jews won out and by the time Yom Tov began, hundreds of *sukkos* were standing. Though perhaps not decorated, they were all kosher *l'mehadrin*, attesting to the tremendous love the Jews had for Hashem's *mitzvos* and their devotion to Him at all times and under all conditions.

On that very same day, Erev Sukkos, the Brisker Rav, Rav Yitzchak Zev Halevi Soloveitchik *zt"l*, was notified that an *esrog* was waiting for him by the Lubavitcher Rebbe, Rav Yosef Yitzchak Schneerson *zt"l*, who lived at the other end of town, well over an hour's walk from his house. A brave young Gerrer chassid volunteered to go, at great risk to his own life, and bring the *esrog* to the Brisker Rav. Through a series of miraculous events, he was successful in procuring the *esrog*, and word quickly spread that there was a kosher set of *arbaah minim* in the vicinity, in the possession of the Brisker Rav.

It was still dark, very early the next morning, when the Brisker Rav woke up to the sound of a great crowd outside his home. He opened his door a crack to see what was going on and discovered, to his amazement, a long line of people stretching from his doorway into the distance. It was truly inspiring to see just how precious the *mitzvos* of Yom Tov were to the downtrodden Jews of Warsaw.

Suddenly, just before dawn on the first day of the *chag*, from seemingly out of nowhere, the sound of trucks rolling in and horns honking broke the stillness. The trucks were full of German soldiers coming to break up the illegal gathering. They lashed out right and left, striking defenseless Jews dressed in holiday garb, viciously butting them with their rifles. The Jews scattered in all directions, and many suffered painful injuries, moaning and bleeding in the street. Having finished the job, the soldiers piled into the trucks and just as quickly sped off.

No more than a few minutes passed before the crowd of tenacious Jews had reassembled in their places, waiting in silence for the sunrise and their chance to fulfill the *mitzvos* of the *arbaah minim.*

The sun came up and the people began taking the *arbaah minim* one after the other. Each one made a *brachah,* shook the *lulav* and *esrog* and quickly handed it to the next person. The Germans returned, again and again, throughout the day to disperse the crowd, and some people at the end of the line did not even manage to perform the mitzvah before sunset. They did not despair, though, and came back the next day to try their luck again; perhaps they would merit the mitzvah on the second day of Yom Tov.

Among the many people who came to make a *brachah* over the *arbaah minim,* the Brisker Rav noticed one man who, when he took the *lulav* and *esrog* in his hands, made a heartfelt *brachah,* and his joy in performing the mitzvah was extraordinary. R' Yitzchak Zev asked for an explanation, and, in response, the man recounted that all his family had been killed in the bombings over the last month. His last child left alive had been killed by an exploding shell a few hours before the beginning of Yom Tov! He had nothing left but the *mitzvos* that he performed and his gratitude to Hashem for allowing him to do so!

The Brisker Rav would later describe the length of the line of people, comparing it to the distance from his Jerusalem home on Press Street to the Zichron Moshe shul. "It was then that you saw," he added emotionally, "what a Jew really is!"

Masquerading to Save a Life

The story of the daring escape of the holy Belzer Rebbe, Rav Aharon Rokeach *zt"l*, from Nazi Germany, is one replete with open miracles, unnatural occurrences, and full of inspiration which clearly portrayed the *Yad Hashem* (Hand of Hashem) at every turn. Just the idea of whisking the *tzaddik*, who was so weak from continuous fasting, praying and sleep deprivation, out of the jaws of the hideous Nazi beast, was a daunting task. But due to the heroic efforts of a host of righteous individuals, the *chassidic* dynasty of Belz survived to establish a glorious link to pre-war *Yiddishkeit*.

As late as May 1943, the Belzer Rebbe, along with his distinguished brother, Rav Mordechai *zt"l*, the Bilgoray Rav, was still hiding out in the Bochnia ghetto. "Hiding" is a relative term since there were very few people, including the Nazi commandant, his evil cohorts, the Jewish policemen, the Judenrat, and most of the ghetto residents, who did not know that the "*wunder rabbiner*" was in their midst. In fact, the chief Nazi, a sadistic tyrant by the name of Muller, went so far as to visit the Belzer Rebbe, receive a blessing from him and offer to double his rations and release him from forced labor! Such was the esteem that even the Nazis held for the saintly Rebbe and they believed that keeping him contained within their midst was a "good luck charm" of sorts. As a result, sneaking the Rebbe out from under their very noses was doubly difficult since they were specifically looking after him to make sure that he remained.

Eventually a plan was hatched which called for the Rebbe and his brother to sneak out of their home in the early morning hours, climb through a loose plank in the ghetto wall behind their building, and take sanctuary in an apartment until daybreak. Then, a horse-drawn wagon would transport them to the village of Baczkow where they would wait in seclusion until after nightfall when an official car driven by Captain Shtaier, a legitimate and heavily bribed officer of the Hungarian Army counterintelligence staff, was to collect them and smuggle them out of Poland and into Hungary.

It would have gone off without a hitch if not for the fact that as their wagon rolled through the village of Baczkow early on the morning of May 13, a group of Jewish laborers on their way to work in the factory noticed the wagon, and the Belzer Rebbe was recognized. Immediately a rumor circulated in the ghetto that the holy Rebbe was escaping!

The Rebbe's *gabba'im* refuted this rumor but many people wanted to see for themselves. The *gabba'im* had no choice but to devise an ingenious scheme.

A young Belzer chassid by the name of Reuven Walkin disguised himself as the Belzer Rebbe, donning his distinctive silk *kapote*, white socks, half shoes, woolen *tallis* and *tefillin*, all the while imitating the Rebbe's voice to perfection. Since the Rebbe spent most of his day in his inner chamber and only his *gabba'im* and closest chassidim were allowed to enter with *kvitlach*, by sitting in the Rebbe's customary chair facing the wall with his *tallis* over his head in prayer, Reuven Walkin was indistinguishable from the real Rebbe.

The *gabba'im* purposely left the door to the inner room open a bit so all those in the outer waiting area could see the "Rebbe" praying as usual by his *shtender* while they continued to run in and out of the room, bringing petitions, pitchers of water and tea at regular intervals to foster the deception. It worked, and throughout the day, many people were convinced that they saw the Belzer Rebbe in his room, when all the while, the real Belzer Rebbe was buying valuable time for his escape.

All that day and into the next, the deception continued. Some Judenrat officials recognized the deception but decided to keep their doubts strictly to themselves. Other less scrupulous members, however, passed on their suspicions to the Gestapo. The Commandant decided to see for himself.

Luckily, the *gabba'im* were tipped off. "Muller, Rosen and Weiss (the *Lagerfuehrer*, Jewish police chief and Judenrat head) are coming! They're already in the building, officially checking if everyone's at work!" Reuven Walkin hastily tore off the Rebbe's garments and they all ran out into an abandoned ruin in Ghetto Two, all, except for the Rebbe's loyal *shammes*, Yechiel Mendel Green. Despite the peril, he stayed put. Perhaps, because of his young age, he might not be held responsible for the Belzer Rav's disappearance.

Suddenly, a commotion arose: The *Lagerfuehrer* himself was charging up the stairs into the Rebbe's apartment. Imposingly, Muller strode directly into the Rebbe's room but the *wunder rabbiner* was gone. Grabbing the frightened *shammes,* Yechiel Mendel Green, he barked menacingly, "Where is the *rabbiner?*"

Green shook his head in puzzlement. "I don't know," he admitted truthfully.

"How is that possible? You are always together with the *rabbiner.*" Green nodded slowly in agreement, "That's true ... He must have gone missing overnight. When I got up this morning, he wasn't here!"

By now, Muller's fury was almost uncontrollable. He ordered the *shammes* to be imprisoned and interrogated mercilessly, but the loyal young man would not tell him anything. Neither beatings, torture, nor threats of death could make him talk. He claimed he knew nothing.

Fortunately, Mr. Eliezer Landau stepped into the picture. In preparation for the inevitable repercussions of the Belzer Rav's disappearance from the ghetto, Mr. Landau acquired a rare diamond of three carats weight. Hurrying to Muller's office, he quickly placed it on his desk. "Herr *Lagerfuehrer*, this would make an excellent present for your wife's birthday!"

"First tell me, where has your *wunder rabbiner* gone?" demanded the Ghetto Commandant, eyeing the glittering stone distractedly.

Mr. Landau shrugged. "He's a wonder Rabbi, capable of miracles! Who knows where he is!" After receiving some more "presents," the Nazi calmed down and eventually freed Yechiel Mendel Green.

| RAV MENACHEM ZIEMBA |

Sanctioning the Warsaw Ghetto Revolt

B y 1943, only three *rabbanim* were left in the Warsaw Ghetto. They were: Rav Menachem Ziemba *zt"l hy"d*, Rav Shimon Stockhammer *zt"l hy"d* and Rav Dovid Shapira *zt"l hy"d*. The latter two rabbis had been deliberately included on the list of appointees for the Judenrat, the ruling body that dictated Jewish life in the ghetto and was responsible to answer to the German authorities at their every beck and call. It was a difficult job and many individuals took advantage of their position at the expense of their fellow brethren, but not R' Shimon Stockhammer or R' Dovid Shapira. On the contrary, they fulfilled their duties in an exemplary fashion and even absorbed the physical abuse and beatings at the hands of the Nazis, in order to protect older men who would not have survived the blows.

R' Menachem Ziemba was undoubtedly the spiritual leader of the ghetto and people at the very point of despair turned to him for a warm word, encouragement and sage counsel. He even found time to study Torah with his students, deliver *shiurim* and write a number of *chiddushim* (novella) in the ghetto.

Just before the final uprising that saw the destruction of the ghetto and deportation of the few survivors, the Polish clergy extended an offer to save the three rabbis and spirit them out of the ghetto. After much discussion, they decided to forgo the offer rather than forsake their families and fellow townsmen, even as they prepared to face the bitter end that awaited them. There wasn't much they could do physically in the ghetto, but their mere presence and the fact that they chose to remain with their brothers in solidarity, mightily raised the spirits of the ghetto inhabitants.

When the revolt of the Warsaw Ghetto was in its final planning stages, R' Menachem was asked to speak to the leaders and deliver the Torah point of view on the imminent battle. R' Menachem addressed them in his distinctive manner, explaining that kiddush Hashem in their unfortunate circumstance could no longer be a matter of passive martyrdom.

"The kiddush Hashem of past generations is not the same as the kiddush Hashem of today. In the eyes of *halachah*, if a Jew was given the option of living as a gentile, yet he chose to remain a Jew at all cost, this choice alone sufficed to constitute kiddush Hashem. This is how the Rambam rules. Today, though, when nothing is to be gained by apostasy, the

Divine Name is to be sanctified not by the death of a Jew but by his striving to live."

R' Menachem looked at the men in the underground bunker, men who had seen death and destruction in close proximity and were not afraid to do battle against their ruthless foe, and concluded, "As I understand the halachah, therefore, it is now a mitzvah to raise a revolt - and with the best battle strategy we can muster!"

On the first night of Pesach, R' Menachem conducted the Seder together with his family, in his gloomy hideout on the fourth floor of their building. He recited the Haggadah with all the fire and fervor of previous years and even shared inspirational insights into the Festival of Liberation with the people who sat around his table and looked to him in these, their final days.

The next day, the Nazis broke through the meager defenses of the ghetto resistance and stormed the streets. In an effort to smoke out their prey, they burned down building after building, before eventually blowing up the entire enclosure.

R' Menachem and his family were forced to flee their apartment for the safety of a nearby cellar.

The fire and smoke were everywhere and the heat was overpowering. R' Menachem shepherded his family across the courtyard and into the adjoining street, but as he was crossing over in a desperate bid to reach the building on the next block, a sniper's bullet struck him down and he collapsed in a pool of his own blood. He died right there on the street in view of his horrified family.

Thus died a great *tzaddik*; a man who scorned an offer of life and freedom, preferring to share the certain fate of his fellow Jews.

The Modzhitzer Niggun

Dark clouds began to cover the skies of Europe - the clouds of Nazism. In spite of the terrible decrees, the yellow patches and the ghettos, most Jews could not fathom what was about to befall them. Only a few managed to escape the clutches of Nazi occupation to safe havens. One of them was the Modzhitzer Rebbe, Rav Shaul Yedidya Elazar Taub *zt"l*, whose chassidim made a tremendous effort to save him. He was smuggled out of Poland to Lithuania, and from there he made his way across Russia to Shanghai, China, eventually arriving in America in 1940.

Meanwhile, in Poland, tens of thousands of Jews were being shipped off to their deaths in cattle cars that took them to places where their existence would no longer trouble the Nazis - to Auschwitz, Treblinka, Majdanek, etc. Inside the crowded cars, over the clatter of the cattle cars' wheels, rose the sounds of people gasping, sighing, weeping and dying. But in one such car, headed toward the infamous death camp Treblinka, the sound of singing could be heard. An elderly Jew, wrapped up in his ragged clothing, his face white as snow, was in the process of recalling the Yom Kippur *tefillos* back home. In his mind, this Modzitzer chassid, Reb Azriel Dovid Fastag *zt"l hy"d*, was standing at the *amud* next to his Rebbe on Yom Kippur, and it is he who was leading the prayer before the Rebbe and all the chassidim.

Suddenly, there appeared before his eyes the words of the twelfth of the Thirteen Principles of Jewish Faith: אני מאמין באמונה שלמה בביאת המשיח ואף על פי שיתמהמה עם כל זה אחכה לו בכל יום שיבוא - *I believe with perfect faith in the coming of Mashiach; and even though he may tarry, nevertheless, I wait each day for his coming.* Closing his eyes, he meditated on these words and thought, "Just now, when everything seems lost, is a Jew's faith put to the test."

He began to hum a quiet tune. There, amidst the death and despair on the train to Treblinka, the chassid was transformed into a pillar of song, bringing forth the song of the eternity of the Jewish People. He was unaware of the silence in the cattle car, and of the hundreds of ears listening attentively. He also didn't hear the voices as they gradually joined his song, at first quietly, but soon growing louder and louder. The song spread from car to car. Every mouth that could still draw a breath joined in R' Azriel Dovid's *Ani Ma'amin.*

As if waking from a dream, R' Azriel Dovid opened his eyes to the sight of the singing train. His eyes were red from crying, his cheeks wet with tears. In a choked voice, he cried out, "I will give half of my portion in *Olam Haba* (the World to Come) to whoever can take my song to the Modzhitzer Rebbe!"

A hushed silence descended upon the train. Then, two young men appeared, promising to bring the song to the Rebbe at any cost. One of them climbed upon the other's shoulders, and finding a small crack on the train's roof, broke out a hole from which to escape.

Bidding farewell to their brothers and sisters on the train, the two proceeded to jump off, one after the other. One was killed instantly ה"יל from the fall. The other survived, taking the memory of the song with him. He eventually found his way to Eretz Yisrael and the notes were sent by mail to the Modzhitzer Rebbe in New York.

Upon receiving the notes and hearing R' Azriel Dovid's tune of *Ani Ma'amin* sung before him, the Modzitzer Rebbe exclaimed, "When they sang *Ani Ma'amin* on that death train, the pillars of the world were shaking. The Almighty Himself said, 'Whenever Jews will sing *Ani Ma'amin,* I will remember the six million victims and have mercy on the rest of My People.'"

It is told that on the first Yom Kippur that the Modzhitzer Rebbe sang the *Ani Ma'amin,* there were thousands of Jews in the shul. The entire congregation burst into tears, which fell like water into the pool of tears and blood of the Jewish people. The tune soon spread throughout world Jewry.

"With this *niggun,*" said R' Shaul Yedidya Elazar, "the Jewish people went to the gas chambers. And with this *niggun,* the Jews will march to greet Mashiach."

| BRISKER RAV |

"It's Out of our Control."

For the first two years of World War II, under the terms of the non-aggression pact between Germany and Russia, the Jews of Vilna lived in relative comfort. Indeed, thousands of refugees streamed into Vilna continuously, including many *yeshivos* and great *rabbanim.* Although incomparable to what the Jews of Poland were enduring already under the yoke of the evil Nazis *ym"s* the Jews of Vilna did not have an easy life under the tyrannical rule of the Russian Communists, who gave preferential treatment to any Russian soldier and his family by confiscating Jewish homes and supplanting their own soldiers there. Addresses of Jewish homes that were potentially "available" at the whim and desire of any Russian officer were posted publicly and even printed in the local papers. The Jews were then given 48 hours to relocate to other living quarters outside the city in the event their homes were chosen.

The Brisker Rav, Rav Yitzchak Zev Halevi Soloveitchik *zt"l*, had been living with the members of his family who had escaped from Brisk to Vilna in a large and centrally located apartment, one that would no doubt be quickly snapped up by some Communist official. When the family saw the notices and found their own address prominently displayed as "available," they frantically ran to their father imploring, "Tatte, will we also have to move from Vilna? What is to be with us?"

R' Yitzchak Zev was learning in his study and he immediately got up and took out a *chumash*. Turning to *Parshas Vayishlach*, he said, "Our forefather Yaakov was running away from his brother Eisav and his large army of four hundred soldiers. He split his camp in two and carefully transferred them over the river, hopefully away from the imminent danger. When he went back to retrieve some items, he struggled through the night in hand-to-hand combat with the angel of Eisav, and held his own.

"The angel told him: 'For you have become great before G-d and before men, and you have prevailed.' Rashi tells us that *'before men'* is referring to Lavan and Eisav. Now, Lavan we understand - Yaakov just left him, fully intact. But he hadn't yet dealt with Eisav. Why, then, does the angel assume that Yaakov Avinu had already prevailed over his mighty brother, Eisav?

"The answer," said the Brisker Rav, looking at his family members, "is that we do not control what happens in this world. If one is to be successful and strong here, it has already been decided up in Heaven that this is to be so. Thus, it was quite clear that just as Yaakov had bested the Heavenly protector of Eisav, so too, would he have no problem prevailing over the physical and earthly element of Eisav and his minions."

Looking ruefully at his family, he added, "So what can we do here? Nothing. Our only hope is to beseech Heaven with our spiritual weaponry, so that all is well here, physically."

Over the course of the entire length of time that the Brisker Rav and his family lived in Vilna, multitudes of Russian officers and their finicky wives came by to inspect their coveted apartment. Witnesses report that on many occasions, the officers would haughtily prance through the apartment, opening door after door, and then wordlessly leave! There was no logical explanation, but the home of the Brisker Rav was never confiscated by the Communists. Furthermore, within days after the entire family left Vilna, a senior U.S.S.R. general arrived and immediately settled in the spacious apartment!

| RAV AVRAHAM KALMANOWITZ |

Feeling the Pain of Another Jew

Rav Avraham Kalmanowitz felt the pain of every single Jew and his heart went out - literally - to each and every one. It is said that news of Nazi genocide might never have reached the public were it not for Yitzchak Sternbuch, the Va'ad representative in Switzerland. He received his data from a Jew who had escaped from Auschwitz to Switzerland and reported not only the deportation and murder of a hundred thousand Jews from Warsaw, but also the reduction of their bodies into soap and fertilizer. Sternbuch warned that the same fate would certainly befall every Jew in occupied Europe, through a cable that he sent to the Va'ad's office.

This information was of such enormous import, however, that Mr. Sternbuch did not trust the cable alone. He immediately called the Va'ad's New York office and asked for R' Avraham Kalmanowitz.

The call came in and as Mr. Sternbuch spoke hurriedly, R' Avraham stood up and leaned over a nearby desk.

"*Ah zoi?*" (Really?!) he said in a loud tone. "*Ah zoi?*" he said again and again, louder and louder, all the while his face turning from a healthy pink to a crimson red and finally to an ashen gray. And then, the terrible facts became too much for him. Suddenly, he fainted right then and there. The pain was too much for him to bear.

As a secretary quickly brought water to revive the unconscious man, another person picked up the receiver and listened, silent and horrified, as Yitzchak Sternbuch ended with a command: "Publicize these vital facts, mobilize the Jewish community behind you and get President Roosevelt to stop the genocide."

Once R' Kalmanowitz regained consciousness, he wasted no time fulfilling Sternbuch's request. The horrifying news mobilized the entire Va'ad. Everyone set about raising money and putting pressure on key individuals in Congress and the State Department to stop the genocide.

During their many trips to Washington D.C. throughout the war, Rav Aharon Kotler *zt"l*, Mike Tress, Irving Bunim and other leaders of the Va'ad Hatzalah organization, worked tirelessly to save as many Jewish lives as they were able to, forging alliances with important government officials. Using determination, devotion and unflagging respect for those they visited, they succeeded, despite their lack of political clout.

As the war raged on and the Va'ad was forced to attempt ever more daring missions, no one was a more valuable contact than U.S. Treasury Secretary, Henry Morgenthau Jr.

Direct action was required in the matter of Vittel, a detention camp in France that held 240 Jews who possessed invalid Salvadoran visas and passports. George Mandel-Mantello, a Hungarian Jew, had become the Swiss-based Secretary General of El Salvador. On the suggestion of the renowned Sternbuch family from Switzerland, he issued thousands of Salvadoran papers, sending them without charge to any Jew requesting them. It was a good idea, for between 1941 and 1944, many used these papers to flee Europe.

Suddenly, in April 1944, this Salvadoran escape route was closed. An informer had told the German authorities that the papers were false, and the Nazis were sending anyone holding them to Vittel. The Va'ad got word that unless El Salvador or some other Latin American government would recognize the papers, these inmates would be sent to Auschwitz.

The day after the news was confirmed, R' Aharon, R' Avraham Kalmanowitz zt"l, the Mirrer Rosh Yeshivah in America, and Irving Bunim quickly traveled down to Washington D.C. and, bright and early, were in Morgenthau's office. As Bunim began to speak, Morgenthau politely shook his head: He had a medical appointment and then a 5:00 flight to catch. There was little he could do, he said, and he really had no time.

"Please," Bunim begged, "you must intercede with the State Department, with the President! Someone must ensure South American acceptance of the papers."

Henry Morgenthau, distant and reserved as always, said he thought it was politically unwise to intervene at that time.

As Bunim countered and Morgenthau remained resistant, R' Avraham Kalmanowitz became agitated. He began to pace back and forth, muttering frantically about the lives being lost. Finally, lips quivering and skin ashen, he toppled over on Morgenthau's carpet in a dead faint.

Shocked and white-faced, his heart racing and eyes wide with fright, Morgenthau quickly knelt by the side of the Mirrer Rosh Yeshivah.

"Rabbi," he said, patting R' Avraham's hand, "Rabbi, don't die. Don't die! I'll do anything you want." A moment later, R' Avraham's eyes fluttered open and he tried to speak.

"No, don't talk," Morgenthau said quickly. "Let me get you some water."

Morgenthau was so moved by the reaction of this Jewish leader to his people's predicament, that he canceled his appointment, postponed his flight, and for four uninterrupted hours worked successfully with the State Department and other agencies to ensure South American acceptance of the papers.

A Personal Delivery by the Hand of the Enemy

The guiding Hand of Providence was never more felt than during the daring and incredible rescue of the Gerrer Rebbe, Rav Avraham Mordechai Alter *zt"l* (*Imrei Emes*). As soon as the war broke out, the Rebbe and his family left the confines of their hometown of Ger (Gora-Kalwaria) and made their way to the large metropolis of Warsaw in the hopes of remaining inconspicuous. The Nazis' first order of business was always to arrest Jewish leaders; a person of the stature of the Gerrer Rebbe, a towering presence of world Jewry, was high on their list of priorities. The capture of the *"wunder-rabbiner Alter"* as he was known to the Germans, would demoralize the Jews of Poland, and the Nazis spared no effort to find and arrest him.

A plan was formulated to whisk the Rebbe out of Warsaw. Stefan Puriesky, a Polish aristocrat and a nephew of the president of Poland, was an official of the Italian Consulate in Warsaw. Before the war, he had managed the Warsaw branch of the Italian shipping company, Lloyd Triestino, and he was highly regarded by the *Imrei Emes* from a previous incident.

When the Gerrer Rebbe traveled to Eretz Yisrael in 1935, Puriesky had arranged a double cabin for the Rebbe in the first-class section of the ship. As a token of his appreciation, the *Imrei Emes* sent Puriesky two cigars. Puriesky valued this gift very highly, so much so that he presented one of the cigars to his uncle, the president of Poland, and kept the other cigar in his home as a good luck charm. At the outset of the war, his house suffered a direct hit from a German shell and was completely demolished. Miraculously, his family escaped injury. Also untouched was the cigar, which was discovered when Puriesky was sifting through the rubble of his house. He believed his family was saved due to the mystical powers of the cigar.

Now, Puriesky was asked to use his connections in the Italian government to obtain visas for the Rebbe and his family to allow them to escape across the border into Italy. This was, in and of itself, not the biggest problem. Through his contacts, and with additional pressure from a Jewish American congressman by the name of Sol Bloom, Puriesky was able to obtain eleven visas for the *Imrei Emes* and the members of his family, with only minor difficulties.

The bigger concern, however, was obtaining Ausreisevisums. These were German exit visas certifying the Gestapo's permission to leave Poland. Any Polish citizen attempting to leave the country needed this document to be stamped into his Polish passport and then signed by the head of the department in the Gestapo office in Krakow. The head of the Ausreisevisum Department, a Nazi officer by the name of Wagner, had previously served as leader of the Hitler Youth in Berlin but was transferred to the Ausreisevisum Department in Krakow to take charge of the department involved in issuing exit visas. No Ausreisevisum could be issued without being signed personally by Wagner. How in the world, thought Puriesky, would he be able to obtain such a document for an old Jewish rabbi, who was on the top of the Gestapo's "most-wanted list"? He did not have an inkling of where to begin.

And then, the wheels of fate began turning and the unbelievable occurred!

There were two hardworking Polish employees in Wagner's office who had won his trust completely. Wagner was indeed very grateful to them, because the long hours they put in and their dedication to work allowed him to spend less time at the office and more time in his favorite pub.

In fact, these workers were Polish loyalists who used their position to forge Ausreisevisums for members of the Polish underground. Due to their efforts, many partisans escaped Poland and joined General Sikorsky in England, where the Polish army was regrouping.

With more and more wanted Polish partisans turning up outside Poland, the Nazi regime in Berlin realized that something was amiss in Krakow. The Polish underground discovered that Berlin was secretly investigating the Ausreisevisum Department, and they warned their two colleagues that it was time for them to disappear. The underground supplied them with money and forged Polish passports, but they did not succeed in obtaining the necessary Italian visas.

Because there was no time to waste, the two workers approached Wagner directly, and told him a fabricated story of their need to go to Italy for a few days. They asked him to do them a favor and use his influence to get them visas from the Italian Consulate in Warsaw. Unaware of the Gestapo's investigations, Wagner was completely taken in, and he traveled with his two "loyal" workers to the Italian Consulate in Warsaw to see what he could do for them.

Meanwhile, Stefan Puriesky was sitting in Warsaw, racking his brains in his office at the Italian Consulate, trying to come up with a way to get to Wagner in Krakow and have him issue Ausreisevisums to the Alter family.

Just then, a Gestapo officer walked into his office and announced, "I am Wagner of the Ausreisevisum Department in Krakow and I need your help!"

Puriesky was flabbergasted! As he listened to Wagner's request to secure two Italian visas for his workers, he realized that a golden opportunity to acquire eleven Ausreisevisums for the Gerrer Rebbe and his family, to go along with their eleven Italian entry visas, just fell into his lap.

Puriesky decided that it was now or never. With as much arrogance as he could muster in the face of this Gestapo agent, he announced that he would help Wagner get the two visas only if he returned the favor and issued Ausreisevisums for eleven members of a family here in Warsaw. Wagner took the bait.

"I have the sole authority to issue Ausreisevisums," Wagner declared haughtily. "And I'll have no problem issuing them for you as a return favor."

Wagner's Polish workers, knowing that their boss's days were numbered, hinted to Puriesky that he should come directly to Krakow himself for the Ausreisevisums. That way, they told him, they could make sure that the Polish passports were properly stamped with the Ausreisevisums, and then signed.

Puriesky took the Alter family passports to the Gestapo office in Krakow at the first opportunity, but when he entered Wagner's office, he found him drunk and in a foul mood. Angry at Puriesky's intrusion, Wagner glanced at the passports, said the pictures all looked alike, threw them on the floor on top of a heap of similarly discarded passports, and shouted at Puriesky to leave.

Puriesky was heartbroken, but the two Polish workers standing outside Wagner's office told him not to worry and to return early the next morning.

When Puriesky returned, they helped him find the passports and stamped them. Later that day they presented the stamped passports to Wagner, who signed them without even a second glance.

The Remedy (רפואה) Before the Calamity (מכה)

The staff of Aharon, which sprouted blossoms and developed nuts (almonds) proving once and for all that Aharon Hakohen and *shevet* Levi were indeed the chosen tribe to serve in the Mishkan, was a miraculous stick. Many *Rishonim* learn that in fact, the staff of Aharon was one of the marvels that Hashem created on the first Erev Shabbos of Creation, during בין השמשות (twilight), and it was later hidden away. Ultimately it will be found in the hand of Mashiach, as he arrives to liberate the Jewish People. Hashem purposely created this staff well in advance to be a source of kiddush Hashem at a later time.

Living in a ghetto under the threat of *aktions*, disease, deportations and starvation, was a constant way of life for millions of Jews during World War II. Finding enough food to feed mothers, fathers, brothers and sisters was essentially a race to see who could locate and provide food before others found them. One young boy lived together with his mother and sole surviving sister in the ghetto and his life revolved around seeing to it that they had enough to eat and were sustained during those bitter days. He would go out daily, foraging until he could bring home his prize. His devotion to his mother and sister knew no bounds and he was prepared to risk his life for them.

One day, as he was returning home, a strange silence hung on the streets - the silence that followed death and *aktions*. Running into his room, he discovered that it had been broken into, looted and his sister, his one and only most precious sister, was gone! She had been taken by the Gestapo, explained a neighbor quietly.

Without thinking, he tore out of the room and ran straight to the Gestapo headquarters! Bursting into the room, he was met at the desk by a young clerk who was amused by the wild-eyed look of the Jew. "What do you want here, Jew," he asked, "to be shot on the spot? No problem." He unhooked his revolver.

"You took my sister," spat out the boy in an accusing voice which surprised even the Nazi.

"Really? Who's your sister?" obliged the clerk who obviously felt used to responding to orders when they were made in a demanding voice. At this point, he motioned to another S.S. officer to come into the room.

"My sister is the beautiful girl you just brought in today," replied the brother impatiently. "I want her back!"

The second German burst into laughter. "You want her back? What strange ideas Jews have these days. You know, that Jews come in here - they don't usually go out!" The clerk now joined him in laughter as the boy stood there defiantly. Once again, he shouted, "Give me back my sister!"

This time, the second German, obviously a senior officer, stopped laughing and looked menacingly at the boy. "So, you want your sister back? Well, I'll tell you what," he said with a sneer. "When you grow hair on the palm of your hand - I'll let your sister go!" He continued to stare with an intimidating scowl.

Unthinking, the boy opened his hand. Together, they all looked at the boy's palm - which was covered with a tangle of black hair! The Nazi began screaming, "You Jewish devil! Satan! Take your sister and get out of here before I kill you both!" Hysterical, he ran into the next room and brought out the girl. Instantly, the boy grabbed her hand and together they ran out of the Gestapo building, out of the ghetto and deep into the forest where they hid from the Nazis for the duration of the war.

How did such a thing occur? Was it a miracle? Much later, this Holocaust survivor recounted the amazing circumstances. "When I was a small child, I used to help out in a factory in my hometown. One day, my hand got caught in a machine - it was a terrible accident. Somehow, the doctors managed to save my shattered hand, and today, I have full use and power of it. Apparently, though, the skin that was grafted onto my palm came from a hairy part of my body and, in my teens, hair actually began to grow on the palm of my hand. Doctors tell me today that this is impossible, but the palm of my hand did not go to medical school!"

Obviously, Hashem destined this young boy to protect and save his sister in a most miraculous fashion and he prepared the remedy even before the calamity.

| PONEVEZHER RAV |

The Master Builder

If the Chazon Ish was the architect of Torah life in Bnei Brak, the Ponevezher Rav, Rav Yosef Shlomo Kahaneman *zt"l*, was the master builder of Torah throughout the entire Holy Land.

The Ponevezher Rav escaped war-torn Europe and arrived in Eretz Yisrael in 1940. The inspiration to establish a yeshivah came to him at the height of the war, when General Rommel was leading the Nazi armies across North Africa to the boundaries of Eretz Yisrael. Nazi forces were raging across Europe, and appalling reports had begun filtering in about atrocities and the mass murder of Jews. It did not seem to be the right time to think about, let alone build, new *yeshivos*. Furthermore, although no one wished to actually articulate the thought, the Nazi army seemed to be invincible, and the Holy Land was clearly in the Nazis' path.

The feeling that prevailed in Eretz Yisrael at the time was that of sinking despair. All were absorbed with the catastrophic losses in Europe, and the Ponevezher Rav was no less consumed than anyone else. However, he was even more consumed with the necessity to rebuild.

The Rav lay in a hospital in Jerusalem, stricken with a serious throat ailment. Doctors had given him strict orders not to speak, but news of Nazi atrocities did not allow him to remain silent.

He forced himself into a sitting position, and in a faint voice, yet conveying spiritual strength, he said to those around him, "The Lithuanian peasant is lazy by nature, but when harvest time comes, he becomes invigorated. And when he sees clouds on the horizon, the thought of his crop being ruined by rain sends a sudden burst of energy through his bones. One can hardly recognize the lazy farmer of yesterday."

The people around him begged him to save his voice but he would not stop - could not stop. In a voice charged with emotion, the Ponevezher Rav continued, "Now is the time! I will immediately begin the task of reestablishing the Ponevezher Yeshivah in Bnei Brak. Storm clouds hang overhead. There is no time to waste. We must act now!"

Some in the room protested, "Rebbe are you making a yeshivah while Rommel is invading?"

He replied, "That's exactly when we have to build Torah!"

And so he started - with five *talmidim*. Today, the Ponevezher Yeshivah contains thousands of students and its stature among the elite of the yeshivah world has been firmly established.

On another occasion, when he was describing his ambitious plans for rebuilding all the *yeshivos* of Lithuania to the Chief Rabbi, Rav Isaac Herzog *zt"l*, the latter told him, "Rebbe, you're dreaming!"

He answered, "True, I am dreaming, but I'm not sleeping."

| RAV AHARON KOTLER |

A *Heter* in its Proper Time

As conditions in Europe deteriorated for the Jewish population during World War II, activism in relief and rescue efforts increased ten-fold. Many of the great American *shtadlanim* continued to press any and every influential government official on this side of the Atlantic Ocean to do what could be done to save the remaining Jews caught in the clutches of the German vise.

The renowned leader of the Lakewood Yeshivah, Rav Aharon Kotler *zt"l*, and spiritual leader of the Va'ad Hatzalah organization, traveled quite often between New York and Washington D.C., accompanied by various Hatzalah leaders, including Elimelech (Mike) Tress *z"l*, Irving Bunim *z"l*, and others. R' Aharon hoped that the many meetings with top officials in the Roosevelt administration would bear fruit and, ultimately, salvation for his suffering brethren in the form of easing American immigration quotas for Jewish refugees, as well as ordering military strikes on strategic German landmarks and railroad supply routes. Unfortunately, more times than not, the government officials turned a deaf ear to their heartfelt requests or didn't even give them the courtesy of a face to face meeting.

Despite these setbacks, R' Aharon never lost his drive to save as many Jews as possible. At the same time, though, he was always concerned for those around him. Once, for example, he and the well-connected activist, Irving Bunim, scheduled an appointment with a State Department official on an urgent matter.

It was December 26, 1944, corresponding that year to Asarah B'Teves, the fast day commemorating the original siege of Jerusalem by the Romans. They traveled by train to Washington D.C. the night before the scheduled meeting. Mr. Bunim stayed in a hotel, while R' Aharon went to the home of a close friend.

The next morning, they met at their pre-arranged spot and R' Aharon handed Mr. Bunim a small satchel containing rolls and hot coffee. Mr. Bunim looked at the food in confusion. "*Vos is dos* - what is this?"

R' Aharon explained that it would no doubt be a grueling day of meetings, requiring all of Mr. Bunim's skill and energy. Certainly, he said, the fast of Asarah B'Teves is rabbinically decreed. But by eating and maintaining his strength on this important day, it might help Mr. Bunim sway government officials and, in turn, save Jewish lives.

Irving Bunim was hesitant. After all, it was a fast day and he was feeling strong and well at that time of morning. "Irving," R' Aharon wagged a finger at him, sensing his hesitation, "I hold you should eat."

"Rebbe," Mr. Bunim responded pleading, "I feel all right. Really." He smiled encouragingly at R' Aharon, hoping to alleviate his concerns.

Finally, R' Aharon gave a curt nod of approval.

"Good," he said, turning to go, Mr. Bunim fast on his heels. "If you feel well enough, then fast."

Mr. Bunim held out during the long, exhausting day, enduring tedious meetings with obstinate government officials. But the meetings were long, and when they finally concluded late in the afternoon, Mr. Bunim was weak with hunger. Returning on the train to New York, Mr. Bunim sighed and, looking distractedly out the window, he said, "Rebbe, now I feel like I could really use something to eat."

R' Aharon barely looked up from the *sefer* he was learning. "Now," he retorted gently, "you could fast." The effort was over and the *heter* was not needed.

But in truth, it wasn't over. From the train, R' Aharon and Irving Bunim went directly to make an appeal for critically needed Va'ad Hatzalah funds. Standing before a sizable crowd in New York, his head still light from fasting, he gave an impassioned speech which touched the hearts of his listeners.

| RABBEINU YITZHAK ALFIA |

Unknown Hero of the Battle

For some time, the Jewish community of Palestine had been growing more and more fearful. Though the roar of shells and the sound of tank treads could not yet be heard, the threat of a Nazi invasion was becoming greater. No one had to tell the Jews here what a Nazi victory over the

Allies would mean. Many of them had arrived at these shores fleeing Hitler's brutal madness. Everyone shuddered to think of what would happen if the German forces would break through the British lines in Egypt and make their way up the coast, bringing their murderous Final Solution with them.

These were not idle fears. For the past three years, the Middle East had seen heavy fighting, first between the Italian Fascists and the British in Libya, then between the Allies and the German "Afrika Korps," under the brilliant German general, Erwin Rommel. Known as the Desert Fox, Rommel had kept the Allied troops on the run, chasing them with his merciless Panzer tanks until he almost reached Alexandria in Egypt. The invasion of Cairo seemed inevitable, and, after Rommel conquered Cairo, he would surely march across the Sinai Desert toward Jerusalem.

As the news from the front grew more and more threatening, the Arabs of Palestine, longtime allies of the Nazis, gleefully planned how they would divide the Jewish property among them. The Jewish community in Jerusalem was spurred into the traditional Torah response to threat. A Jew's strength is in his mouth, and the Jews of Palestine opened their lips, and their hearts, in heartfelt, fervent *tefillos* for the safety of the land and its people.

A military historian would summarize the resources of the two opposing armies on the eve of the crucial battle in El Alamein, a small railway town just 60 miles out of Cairo, as so: On the Allied side was the British Eighth Army, commanded by Lieutenant General Montgomery, a low-key officer whose calm in the face of battle was legendary, with 195,000 men and several thousand tanks and artillery. Facing him was Rommel's Afrika Korps, comprised of 100,000 battle-hardened soldiers, with their own tanks and artillery.

As the Nazi threat came closer and closer, the Jews began to pray even more, pleading with their Creator to save them. Rabbeinu Yitzchak Alfia, scion of a distinguished Aleppo family who had moved to Yerushalayim, called for special days of prayer. He visited the graves of *tzaddikim*, begging them to intercede on behalf of their children. Despite the rigors of the journey, he traveled from tomb to tomb, hardly missing any holy spot. Except for one.

One night, Rabbeinu Yitzchak had a dream. He saw a holy, glowing countenance looking at him, its eyes luminous with wisdom, pity and just a touch of sternness. The figure spoke, "Why have you not come to me? Why have you not prayed at my grave as well?"

Knowing, even in his sleep, that this dream was fraught with meaning, Rabbeinu Yitzchak asked timidly, "What is the Rav's name?"

The vision then revealed his identity. "I am the author of *Abir Yaakov*. I, too, care for my children and wish to intercede on their behalf!'

Still in the world of dreams, Rabbeinu Yitzchak asked the *tzaddik*, "And where is the *Chacham's* resting place?"

"In the city of Demanhour, in the land of Egypt." And Rabbeinu Yitzchak awoke.

The *Abir Yaakov*! The saintly *Chacham*, Rabbeinu Yaakov Abuchatzeira *zt"l*, buried in Demanhour, otherwise known as Cairo, Egypt! At the best of times, Cairo was a difficult journey from Jerusalem. Now, in these worst of times, through a country occupied by German troops and Allied forces, a country beset by war and bloodshed - to travel to Egypt in these mad times was to risk one's life.

But Rabbeinu Yitzchak did not hesitate, "I shall go and pray there, in Demanhour, in Egypt!'

Rabbeinu Yitzchak made his way to Gaza, where the British headquarters was buzzing with rumors of great battles to come. For a civilian, and a poor Jewish scholar at that, to see the commander of the area at this critical time was almost impossible. For a messenger of the Almighty, however, nothing is impossible, and Rabbeinu Yitzchak was allowed to speak his piece.

In those difficult days of war, all commercial train service between Palestine and Egypt had ceased, with the exception of military transports bringing British troops to the war zone. It would take a miracle for the *Chacham* to obtain permission to travel on a military transport, particularly when troops were pouring into Egypt. Yet, once again, a miracle happened. Rabbeinu Yitzchak patiently explained to the commanding officer that he wished to pray for the welfare of the Jewish people and for the victory of the British Army at the grave of a rabbi who was buried in Cairo. Inexplicably, he was given permission to go.

At dawn the next morning, Rabbeinu Yitzchak traveled to Cairo and was greeted with cries of wonder and astonishment as he walked into the renowned Beit Medrash Keter Torah in Cairo. How did the great Rabbeinu Yitzchak Alfia of Jerusalem get here? Why had he come to them in these difficult times when so many were fleeing Egypt?

Rabbeinu Yitzchak told them the tale of his dream, and then how he traveled on a British troop transport. Within minutes, the word was out and dozens of Jews laden with food for the journey had joined him. They would all travel to Demanhour. They would all pray at the grave of the *Abir Yaakov*. With a pure and untainted belief in the power of the *tzaddik*, they knew they would prevail!

Rabbeinu Yitzchak journeyed to Demanhour in the first days of November 1942, at that very same time that General Montgomery launched his offensive near El Alamein.

As the British troops, led by General Montgomery, broke through German lines on Kidney Ridge, taking vast numbers of prisoners, the Jews of Cairo, led by Rabbeinu Yitzchak Alfia, stormed the gates of Heaven. For three long days and nights, Rabbeinu Yitzchak and the Jews of Cairo prayed and fasted, refraining from all speech other than that of Torah and holy matters.

On the third day, the almost silent murmur of prayer was broken by a great shout and the sounds of trumpets and celebration. The news soon reached Demanhour: The Germans had been defeated! The triumph was complete! The threat of Nazi invasion was gone!

Britain's Prime Minister, Winston Churchill, was convinced that the battle of El Alamein marked the turning point of the war. He later said: "Before Alamein we never had a victory. After Alamein we never had a defeat!"

Apparently, though, he never heard of Rabbeinu Yitzchak Alfia who remained the unknown hero of the battle.

| RAV YECHEZKEL LEVENSTEIN |

Advanced Planning for a Unique Torah Center

The amazing story of the rescue of the Mir Yeshivah as they escaped from Mir to Vilna, Keidan, Kobe, Japan, and finally to Japanese controlled Shanghai, is a tale that defies the normal levels of human belief and endurance. Yet, perhaps the most incredible aspect of their long-winded tale is the fact that the entire body of the yeshivah, 250 students, married *kollel* members and their families, plus the faculty and *roshei yeshivah*, managed to remain intact throughout the entire war. This reason, more than any other, was why the Mir Yeshivah, unlike any of the other major Torah institutions in pre-war Europe, succeeded in staying alive, active and functioning during and immediately after the war.

It is told that when a student asked the spiritual leader of the Mir Yeshivah, Rav Yechezkel Levenstein *zt"l*, whether it would be advisable for him to flee to Shanghai, the *Mashgiach* was completely flabbergasted at the selection of China as a place of refuge. He explained that Shanghai would be unacceptable because of the host of difficulties in trying to maintain a Torah way of life there. Yet, barely one year later, the Torah community's house of study had arrived at that same foreign place: Shanghai!

Of course, there were countless worries: how and where to find acceptable housing, how to support organized religious life and studies on the level demanded by these students of Torah. How could the rabbis, with their families, and hundreds of students, find the bare necessities of life in this overcrowded Chinese seaport and commercial center? Where would they find a building adequate to house the students and provide study halls with all the necessary supporting facilities for so many people?

But, once again, the impossible became reality. All their problems were solved as soon as they landed in Shanghai. The entire Mir Yeshivah group was placed in a single synagogue, an extraordinary synagogue with unusual facilities in an odd location that had been built by an eccentric individual under the strangest of circumstances. It was the solution to all of the refugees' problems and needs, and it made five years of the most creative Torah learning for the yeshivah community in far away China possible.

This edifice, the Beth Aharon or Museum Road Synagogue, stood in a strange location for a synagogue in the very heart of Shanghai's port and business district near the famous Bund, the docking area for all ships. This synagogue had stood empty and almost unused for the first ten years after its erection, except for occasional prayer sessions and wedding ceremonies, or as a temporary emergency shelter, until the day of the yeshivah's arrival. The synagogue was a modern structure and contained a sanctuary built to meet all requirements of religious law. Strangely, the number of seats in the synagogue, 250, corresponded precisely to the number of yeshivah students who would study there.

In addition to the main sanctuary, the building contained large dining and kitchen facilities. It had been built to meet the needs of a residential community and contained all the facilities for catering services, including halls for wedding celebrations and other communal affairs. But no such nearby Jewish community existed in Shanghai until the arrival of the yeshivah. The building provided for their spiritual and physical needs to an amazing degree. In a building adjoining the synagogue there was even a *mikvah,* which complemented the synagogue facility to almost supreme perfection.

Who was the thoughtful sponsor of this veritable palace of Judaism in the Far East? An outstanding rabbi? A deeply religious businessman? A famous community worker or philanthropist?

Heavenly Providence revealed itself in an apparently miraculous manifestation by choosing a seemingly most unworthy and inappropriate person to build this place of refuge for Torah. In fact, this Jew was so estranged from his own religion that he had married a non-Jewish woman. Silas Hardoon, a Sephardic Jew of unknown origin, was motivated by a dream to build this edifice. He chose a non-residential section on the basis of plans for a future Jewish neighborhood in the area. Silas Hardoon had, of course, never earmarked these buildings for a school or for the teaching and practice of Jewish law. Nevertheless, he called out his "mission" with almost perfect planning to fit, perfectly, the specific purpose and needs of the group of Torah scholars who landed a decade later on the shores of China. These inexplicable facts transcend any calculations or fantasies of the human mind. Once again, unbelievable circumstances had led to the rescue and continuation of Torah study.

For almost five years, these buildings housed the centers of Jewish thinking and scholarship. These were some of the most fruitful years in Torah research and history, years that left deep and lasting effects on the spiritual growth of almost every participant. In fact, it may even be fair to say that many rabbis and communal leaders, who later became famous on the American continent, owe their spiritual achievements, in large measure, to those productive years of studies in Shanghai.

| PIACZECZNA REBBE |

To Save a Child Above All Else

The Warsaw Ghetto evokes memories of resistance; the rare instance where Jews attempted to fight back against the Nazi oppressors, where Jews behaved like "heroes" and the world took stock of their efforts.

Heroes? If one would want to talk of heroes, there are many more Jews who fit that description. Jews who never lifted a gun in their lives. Jews who did not have the wherewithal to do battle in physical terms against the Germans, yet fought with the courage of a lion to their fullest spiritual capacity. Are these people any less deserving of the title "heroes"?

The Chassidic Rebbe, Rav Klonimus Kalmish Szapira *zt"l hy"d* of Piaczeczna was one such hero, one of the powerful spiritual forces of the Warsaw Ghetto. He suffered no less than anyone else - if not more, in fact - but he never lost his faith and never lost his unique ability to transmit this faith onto others and give them hope. He exemplified the type of courage that is so often overlooked by those who are fond of describing the Jewish reaction to Hitler and the Nazis in terms of passivity and resignation.

An example of R' Klonimus Kalmish's courage and compassion came to light in one of the darkest moments of his life. In the first days of the war, in early September 1939, the German air force attacked the city of Warsaw with a ferocious "*blitzkrieg*" that decimated the historical city and brought it to its feet in shockingly swift fashion. Horribly, thirty-four thousand Jews were killed in the span of a few days. At the time, life seemed to become unbearable for the Jews of Warsaw; little did they suspect that the worst was yet to come.

Two days before Sukkos, R' Klonimus Kalmish's beloved and exceptional son was mortally wounded. A few hours later, his son's wife, Rebbetzin Gittel, was killed while standing outside the hospital where her husband lay wounded, and at almost the exact same time, the Rebbe's sister-in-law, Rebbetzin Chana, was also killed. Death and destruction lay everywhere.

A young Chassidic boy, an ardent follower of the Piaczeczna Rebbe (known to many as the "children's Rebbe" due to his active interest in the religious well-being of not only his adult chassidim, but especially the children) knew that it was usual for the two *rebbetzins* to carry their jewelry with them at all times (in case they needed it to save themselves). He found the dead bodies and removed their jewelry. He had recognized these women and wanted to give their possessions back to the Rebbe before the gentiles had a chance to rob them.

Unfortunately, the boy was caught in the act by a German patrol and taken to Gestapo headquarters, charged with the heinous crime of robbing the dead. The Germans had no compunctions about killing people, but woe unto the person who thought to steal from the dead! This was a crime which carried the most severe punishment, especially in those times of chaos as the conquering soldiers were taking control of the city.

R' Klonimus Kalmish was confronted with two very difficult tasks: he must transfer his wounded son to a regular hospital where there was a better chance for his survival, and he had to arrange for the burial of his daughter-in-law and sister-in-law. However, when he heard of the boy's arrest, he immediately dropped these other matters and risked his life to run to the Gestapo and vouch for the boy's honesty.

Everyone trembled with fear, because it was well known that whoever stepped into Gestapo headquarters did not usually come out alive. Undaunted, the Rebbe presented his case to the Gestapo and somehow managed to find favor in their murderous eyes. After a brief consultation, he was told to return the next day and they would see what could be done.

The next day, the first day of Sukkos, the Rebbe's son's condition worsened. R' Klonimus Kalmish was desperate to transfer his son to a better facility but he knew that the time it took to accomplish this would not allow him to plead on behalf of the young child in the Gestapo prison.

The Rebbe made his decision. He asked one of the young chassidim to go to the cemetery, to his wife's grave, and ask her to pray for her son's life, while he himself set out for Gestapo headquarters, once again, to plead for the release of the arrested boy.

With the Almighty's help, he accomplished his mission: his sincere pleading won the boy's release. Among the many tragedies that were taking place all around him, witnesses would testify that the happiness that shone on the Rebbe's face, because he'd merited saving a Jewish life, was indescribable. The Rebbe of Piaczeczna was undoubtedly a "hero" of the Jewish People.

| KLAUSENBURGER REBBE |

Who Has Chosen Us From All the Other Nations

The Zohar writes: "The Divine Presence never leaves a Jew on Shabbos or Yom Tov, even on a weekday Shabbos." The commentators explain that a "weekday Shabbos" refers to a person who is undergoing extreme circumstances, or traveling and loses track of time. Thus, whenever he is able to keep Shabbos, Hashem is always with him.

In a Warsaw slave battalion there was a Jew from Lithuania who was an expert in metalworking. This made him very important to the S.S. He was allowed to walk around freely and was given extra food.

One day this man sneaked into the cabin of the Klausenburger Rebbe, Rav Yekusiel Yehudah Halberstam *zt"l*, and said, "Rebbe, in my work, I have to violate Shabbos by transgressing Torah prohibitions. I think it is better to be transferred to a group that has to carry heavy logs and boulders, which is not a Torah prohibition but, rather, only a rabbinical decree."

The Rebbe asked him how he was going to do this, and he said, "I will burn my hands with scalding water so that I will be unable to continue my delicate work. Then the Germans will have to transfer me to the other work groups."

"Carrying the boulders meant certain death," reflected the Rebbe later. "Many were not able to hold out for more than a few days. I tried to convince him not to put himself into such danger, but he insisted that he wanted to keep Shabbos as best as he could. Only with great difficulty was I able to persuade him that, as a metalworker, he was able to help the lives of many other Jews, and he relented. Certainly seeing such a Jew strengthened us all in the truth and wisdom of the words that we say each day in *davening*: 'Who has chosen us from all the other nations.'"

| RAV ELYAH LOPIAN |

Faith in the Silence of a Leader

In 1925, Rav Elyah Lopian *zt"l* was offered the position of rosh yeshivah in the Etz Chaim Yeshivah in London, England. Although London was then a spiritual wasteland, R' Elyah accepted the position, believing that he could influence the Jewish community there. In fact, not only was he successful in reinforcing a dedicated community full of religious observance, his move from Lithuania to England saved his life and the lives of his family members who were spared the horrors of the Holocaust. Only one son, Hershel, refused to leave his beloved Telshe Yeshivah and perished along with the entire community of Telshe.

R' Elyah was extremely sensitive to the concerns and problems of others and lent a helping hand or a word of encouragement whenever he was able. With widows and orphans, he went out of his way to be there for them since the Torah instructs us to be especially careful where the feelings of widows and orphans are concerned.

Near his home in London lived a certain widow and her orphaned children. No matter how heavily involved R' Elyah was in his countless responsibilities, he always found time for her. He would always receive her politely, listen to her with great patience, and offer her his advice.

He had left standing instructions that whenever this woman or her children came to his house they were to be shown in immediately. Others could wait, but not this woman. He would always stop whatever he was doing or interrupt any meeting, conference or activity in which he was involved, in order to give her his full attention.

When the Nazi war machine began its *blitzkrieg* against London during World War II, civilian sectors of the city were being heavily bombed. Terror reigned throughout the city, for casualties were everywhere and no one knew who would be next. The Battle of Britain was long and drawn out and it took a heavy toll on the mental psyche of the population. Many moved out of the city to the countryside while others attempted to leave the country outright. R' Elyah's house was in no less danger than anyone else's but he never considered leaving the people who turned to him on a daily basis for advice and consolation.

Early one Sunday morning, the widow who lived nearby came to R' Elyah's home in great anguish. She had an urgent matter to discuss with the Rav and, as always, she was immediately escorted in.

Without preamble, she burst out, "Rabbi, there is a ship leaving this Wednesday morning for South Africa," she wailed. "I am afraid for my children and myself. Do you think I should arrange for passage on that ship in the hope of saving our lives? The bombs are falling everywhere. Who knows when we will all be killed?" The widow was extremely agitated, barely able to face the burden of responsibility for the safety of her household at so frightening a time as this.

An unusual silence settled on the room. Finally, R' Elyah looked up, and with a reply totally out of character, spoke with words she had never before heard from him. "I'm sorry," he told her curtly, "I cannot think clearly. I don't have time now! Please come back later."

Surprised, but with little recourse, the agitated woman left the house, her mind unsettled and fearful. A few hours later, she returned and was again ushered in to R' Elyah, but again he explained to her that she had come at a bad time, for he was in the midst of preparing his *shiur*. He could not focus on her inquiry at this moment and she needed to return at a later time when he could give her proposal serious thought.

She came twice more on that day, and five times on the following day, but amazingly, each time, R' Elyah just could not find the time to discuss the matter with her.

When she was turned away several times again on the next day, Tuesday, she stopped coming. Without a clear response from R' Elyah, she gave up the idea of leaving for South Africa, for she would never have made a decision without R' Elyah's sanction.

The ship set sail for South Africa on schedule Wednesday morning, filled with people who hoped to be saved from the Nazi bombs. On Thursday, the news reported the terrible tragedy: the ship had been sunk by a German u-boat that had been lurking in unsecured water. There were no survivors.

The widow who, along with her children, was saved from tragedy because of her absolute faith in R' Elyah, was Rebbetzin Sternbuch, the mother of the Av Beis Din in Jerusalem today, Rav Moshe Sternbuch *shlit"a*. Interestingly, R' Moshe Sternbuch eventually did relocate to South Africa, where he led a prominent community before moving to Israel.

| BABA SALI |

A Blessing From the Heart

When the German Army's notorious *"Afrika Korps"* invaded and conquered North Africa in 1941, many of the large Sephardic communities of Tunisia, Libya and Morocco came under Nazi control and were made to suffer as their brethren in Europe did. However, the first order of the Germans, even before the round-up and persecution of the Jews, was the arrest of all important government officials. Governors, city leaders and men of civic distinction were seized and herded off to a massive holding facility in the city of Bodniv, Morroco, which happened to be the city where the great Baba Sali, Rav Yisrael Abuchatzeira *zt"l* served as Rabbi. One of the prisoners, the revered Arab ruler, Al-Haj Tahami El

Jilavi, a benevolent leader who treated Jew and Arab equally well, was also incarcerated in Bodniv.

On the day that the Arab leader was taken out to face his German captors, he was paraded through the streets in an effort to shame and embarrass him. As they were walking, El Jilavi looked out and noticed the holy rabbi of Bodniv walking on his way. Immediately he stopped and called out to the Baba Sali.

R' Yisrael also stopped. An interesting spectacle was unfolding between the Arab governor and the Jewish rabbi, and the Germans' interest was piqued. El Jilavi shouted, "Holy rabbi, do you have a son?"

Unsure if this was some sort of ploy, R' Yisrael hesitated, but remembering the benevolence of the Arab governor, he finally responded, "Yes, honorable governor. I have a son. His name is Meir."

"Splendid," called out El Jilavi. "Rabbi, I want you to bless him."

A strange request, but the Baba Sali complied and murmured a blessing to his son Meir.

"No, rabbi," said the Arab. "That's not the way one gives a blessing, murmuring under one's breath. From the depths of your heart, concentrate on your son and deliver a heart-felt blessing." This time, R' Yisrael closed his eyes and began to slowly intone a special prayer on behalf of his son. Suddenly, the governor interrupted him and called out, "Now, rabbi, include me in your blessing!" The Baba Sali paused, surprised, but then did as he was asked and included the name of the Arab governor in his prayer. Finally satisfied, El Jilavi allowed himself to be led away.

Very soon, thereafter, word got around that Al Haj Tahami El Jilavi, the Arab ruler, was set free and allowed to return to his provincial palace in Marrakesh. But before he left Bodniv, he made a special stop at the home of the rabbi of Bodniv to thank him as he attributed his fortuitous release to the blessing of the holy man.

When the Baba Sali asked him why he insisted on including himself in a blessing for his son, rather than request a blessing for himself, the governor smiled and said, "Rabbi, I'm sure you know that the Almighty in Heaven will listen to a prayer or blessing if it is delivered from the depths of one's heart. For me personally, I could not be sure that the rabbi's blessing would be perfectly sincere and genuine. But I knew that for the rabbi's son, he would surely muster up the emotion needed to evoke a Heavenly response. It was this blessing that I wanted bestowed upon me, and, obviously, the Almighty heeded to this heartfelt request!" The governor remained kind and a friend to the Jews all his life.

| RAV YECHEZKEL ABRAMSKY |

Torah in a Vault

During the Battle of Britain in World War II, London was victim to nightly bombing raids by the German Luftwaffe. Like all the city's residents, Rav Yechezkel Abramsky *zt"l*, then head of the London *Beis Din*, was forced to take refuge in the nearest bomb shelter. This meant going to the bank, one flight down from his apartment and entering a steel, walk-in vault. The bank's gentile director was a close acquaintance of R' Abramsky and he had built a special staircase descending directly from the rabbi's apartment into the bank to facilitate his family's flight to safety.

When the bombings would begin, at all hours of the day or night, everyone would rush into the vault, where they waited out the deadly raids. The bank workers who also found shelter in the huge vault noticed that each time R' Yechezkel entered the vault he would begin whispering something to himself, continuing to do so for the length of time they remained in the vault. People just assumed that he was praying for the safety of the refugees huddled inside and one finally mustered up the courage to ask the rabbi's son what prayer he was actually saying.

R' Yechezkel's son explained that his father was always praying for their safety, however, inside the vault, it was a prayer of a different sort that he was reciting.

"Throughout the course of my father's life, he has recited the verse from Tehillim, *"Tov li toras picha m'alfei zahav v'chessef* - I prefer the Torah of your mouth than thousands of pieces of gold and silver" countless times. But now, each time he enters this vault and is surrounded by millions of pounds sterling, my father immediately is filled with joy, because now he truly understands how he feels about the wisdom of Hashem. Indeed, he really feels deep down that he would not trade one drop of Torah for all the money in the world. It is this verse that you see my father whispering each time he walks into the vault!"

The Warmth of a *Niggun*

A bitter cold winter descended upon Mauthausen, a bastion of misery in the Austrian Alps. Many of the inmates died of exposure, disease, and starvation, but not Moshe, a young fourteen-year-old bundle of skin and bones. Moshe was the son of the head of the Bobover Yeshivah and a fervent chassid of the saintly Bobover Rebbe, Rav Benzion Halberstam *zt"l hy"d*, author of the Chassidic classic, *Kedushas Tzion*. Unbeknownst to Moshe, his Rebbe was already not among the living. On "Black Friday," July 25, 1941, Aktion Petliura was unleashed in Lvov, Poland. The Bobover Rebbe and his family were among the 2,000 Jews who were arrested. Four days later, on Monday, the fourth day of the month of Av, R' Benzion, dressed in his silk Shabbos *kapote* and *shtreimel*, marched to his death. He was urged to escape but he refused to leave his family. "One does not run away from the sound of Mashiach's footsteps," he announced as he continued to walk with his dignified stride in the direction of the open pits in the forest. He was murdered by the Nazis and their Ukrainian collaborators, *hy"d*.

In the misery of Mauthausen, however, young Moshe never lost faith in his Rebbe. He constantly felt the Bobover Rebbe guiding his steps, almost as if he were pulling him and pushing him, often in directions opposite those he would have normally chosen to follow. When Moshe's strength failed, he would try to concentrate and remember the beautiful melody the Rebbe used to chant the holy *Zohar* each Friday night. The memory of that melody would fill him with courage and determination to go on.

At times Moshe wanted to cry, weep, and express his pain and anguish, but his tears would not respond; all the wells of tears had dried up together with all other signs of humanity. Moshe would then concentrate on the Rebbe's *Zohar* melody and tears, warm, human tears, would fill his eyes and stream down his hollow cheeks, momentarily dispelling the harsh realities of Mauthausen.

It was a cold December day in 1944. It was "delousing day" and the prisoners' tattered striped uniforms were exchanged for clean ones, as they were all chased to the showers across the camp's huge square.

Suddenly, they heard the, familiar order: "*Zeil appell!*" Roll call! Kapos with truncheons and clubs began to chase the wet prisoners out of the showers and into the camp's square, into the howling winds of the subzero December winter.

Wet living human skeletons lined the square. The ritual of the head count began. There was a discrepancy between the list in the Kapo's hand and the number of prisoners in the square; one was missing. The head count began again but the inconsistency persisted. An hour passed. The bodies of the prisoners began to develop a thin layer of white frost; breathing became more and more difficult and people began to fall on the snow. The search for the missing man continued. The lines of standing prisoners thinned out, while the rows of bodies on the snow grew longer and longer.

Young Moshe tried to move his feet and his hands, but his body no longer responded to his will. He felt that he, too, was slowly freezing into a pillar of ice, being drawn and pulled to the white snow on the ground beneath him.

Suddenly he felt the presence of the Rebbe supporting him. R' Benzion's reassuring voice rang in his ears: "Don't fall, don't stumble! You must survive! A chassid must sing, a chassid must dance; it is the secret of our survival!"

The Bobover melody was burning in his head, ringing in his ears, but his frozen lips could not utter a single sound. His mind worked feverishly as if willing his lips to produce the sound in his head. Then, slowly, his lips began to move. A note forced its way through the colorless lips. It was followed by another and another, individual notes strung together into the Rebbe's *niggun*. Like burning coals, the tune scorched his lips and set his body aflame. One foot began to move, to free itself from its chains of frost. Soon, the other foot tore itself away from the clinging ice. The snow became red as skin from the sole of Moshe's foot remained grafted to the ice. Moshe began to sway and then to stamp his feet in the snow, to dance to the Bobover Rebbe's *niggun*. Moshe's heart warmed up, burning tears streamed down his face as his body and soul sang the Bobov melody.

Finally, the *Zeil appell* was over. The Mauthausen camp square was strewn with scores of bodies. But Moshe's red footprints burned the white snow with the glow of a Bobov melody.

A Country of Kindness

On April 9, 1940, Germany attacked and invaded Denmark. Soon after, a Danish resistance movement began and German military targets and businesses were hit by a wave of sabotage actions. There was also labor unrest with massive strikes in many Danish cities. But more notably, the Danes stood in solidarity with their Jewish compatriots and even undertook heroic efforts to shelter Jews from the insidious decrees of the Nazis.

One popular legend says that when the Germans ordered the Jews in occupied Denmark to identify themselves by wearing armbands with yellow stars, King Christian X of Denmark and non-Jewish Danes impeded the decree by donning the armbands themselves. It was said that King Christian sported an armband as he rode through the streets of Copenhagen on his daily morning horseback ride, explaining to citizens that he wears the star of David as a demonstration of the principal that all Danes are equal. Non-Jewish Danes responded to their king's example by wearing the armband as well, thus preventing the Germans from identifying Jewish citizens and rendering the order ineffective.

In September, 1943, it was decided by the German high command that the deportation of the Danish Jews to death camps was to begin. The Nazis were prepared to begin deportation of the 7,500 Danish Jews on October 1, 1943, but somehow the news leaked out and the Jewish community was forewarned.

On September 29th, two days before the projected round up, the chief Rabbi of the Krystalgaade Synagogue implored his congregants and the whole Jewish community to immediately go into hiding. The word was passed and many Danes offered their support, conveyed warnings, finding places for the Jews to hide. From all corners of Danish society and in all parts of the country, clergymen, civil servants, doctors, store owners, farmers, fishermen and teachers protected the Jews. Many Torah scrolls were hidden away in the crypt of a local church. Hundreds of Jews were hidden in the large Bispebjerg Hospital. Virtually the entire medical staff at the hospital helped save Jewish lives. Once it became known among Danes what the hospital was doing, money was donated from all over the country. Even the Danish police and coast guard helped the Jews by refusing to join in the Nazis' manhunt.

However, it was clear that Denmark was no longer safe for the Jews and in order to escape, many refugees were driven to the coast in ambulances belonging to the hospital. About one fifth of the Danish Jews escaped to Sweden via Gilleleje, one of the larger fishing villages. Local fishermen agreed to transport them to Sweden, but successfully completing the two-mile boat trip without being intercepted by German patrol boats was not easy. A committee of local people quickly initiated rescue aid and helped find hiding places and food.

One of the survivors, Leif Wassermann, recalls the boat trip in the middle of the night, the hushed voices, the people crowded inside and the rotten smell of fish.

"We stayed very low on the floor. There were German patrols everywhere. We saw flashlights through the windows."

Although the fishing boat was boarded regularly by German soldiers, the refugees were never discovered. The boat made more than a dozen trips with groups of five to twenty people crammed inside the hull, thus saving many Jewish families from annihilation.

Over the course of a few days, more than 7,000 Danish Jews reached safety in Sweden. Only 481 were captured and sent to a Nazi concentration camp at Theresienstadt.

The Danes, though, continued to protect the unfortunate Jews whom the Germans were able to capture. Through political intervention, Danish officials managed to keep the Jews of Denmark out of the extermination camps. Almost all of the Danish Jews in the camp survived through the solicitude and support of the Danish civil service and church organizations. Month after month, the blessed Danes sent over 700 packages of clothing, food and vitamins to the Jews in the camp.

Thousands of years after the original exodus of the Jewish people from Egypt, a different sort of "exodus" occurred for the Jews of Denmark who survived - almost in their entirety - the horrors of World War II.

To Save a Soul Amongst the Jewish People

This is the story of an incredible woman and her amazing gift to mankind: Irena Sendler. An unfamiliar name to most people, this remarkable person defied the Nazis and saved 2,500 Jewish children by smuggling them out of the Warsaw Ghetto. Her courage enabled not only their survival but also generations of their descendants.

In 1942, the Nazis herded hundreds of thousands of Jews into a sixteen block area that came to be known as the Warsaw Ghetto. The ghetto was sealed and the Jewish families ended up behind its walls, only to await certain death. Irena Sendler, a non-Jewish health worker, was so appalled by the conditions in the Ghetto that she joined *Zegota,* the council established to provide aid for Jews, organized by the Polish underground resistance movement, and directed the efforts to rescue Jewish children.

To be able to legally enter the ghetto, Irena managed to get a pass from Warsaw's Epidemic Control Department (WECD) and she visited the ghetto daily, reestablished contacts and brought food, medicine and clothing. About 5,000 people were dying a month from starvation and disease in the ghetto, and she decided to focus her efforts on helping the Jewish children get out. For a young mother like herself, persuading parents to part with their children was in itself a horrendous task. Finding families willing to shelter the children, and thereby willing to risk their life if the Nazis ever found out, was also not easy.

"Can you guarantee they will live?" Irena later recalled the distraught parents asking. But she could only guarantee that they would die if they stayed. "In my dreams, I still hear the cries when they left their parents."

Irena began smuggling children out in ambulances. She recruited at least one person from each of the ten centers of the Social Welfare Department. She issued hundreds of false documents with forged signatures and successfully smuggled almost 2,500 Jewish children to safety, giving them temporary new identities. Some children were taken out in gunnysacks or body bags. Some were buried inside loads of goods. A mechanic took a baby out in his toolbox. Some kids were carried out in potato sacks, others placed in coffins.

Irena had a remarkable record of cooperation when placing the youngsters. "No one ever refused to take a child from me," she said. The children were given false identities and placed in homes and orphanages. Irena Sendler carefully noted, in coded form, the children's original names and their new identities. She kept the only record of their true identities in jars buried beneath an apple tree in a neighbor's backyard, across the street from the German barracks. She hoped that someday she could dig up the jars, locate the children, and inform them of their past. In all, the jars contained the names of 2,500 children.

The Nazis became aware of Irena's activities, and on October 20, 1943, she was arrested, imprisoned and tortured by the Gestapo, who broke both her legs, but no one could break her spirit. Though she was the only one who knew the names and addresses of the families sheltering the Jewish children, she withstood the torture that crippled her for life, refusing to betray either her associates or any of the Jewish children in hiding. Sentenced to death, Irena was saved at the last minute when *Zegota* members bribed one of the Gestapo agents to stop the execution. She escaped from prison but for the rest of the war she was pursued by the Nazis.

After the war, she dug up the jars and used the notes to track down as many of the children as she could in order to reunite them with relatives scattered across Europe. Unfortunately, most had lost their families during the Holocaust in Nazi death camps. The children had known her only by her code name Jolanta. Years later, after she was honored for her wartime work, her picture appeared in a newspaper.

"A man, a painter, telephoned me," said Irena, "'I remember your face,' he said. 'It was you who took me out of the ghetto!'"

Irena Sendler did not think of herself as remarkable. She claimed no credit for her actions. "I could have done more," she said. "This regret will follow me to my death."

She has been honored by Yad Vashem in Jerusalem, with the Order of the White Eagle, Poland's highest distinction, and she was announced as the 2003 winner of the Jan Karski award for Valor and Courage. In 2007, she was nominated to receive the Nobel Peace Prize. She died on May 18, 2008.

Selfless to a Fault

During World War II, shortages in every area of everyday life were the norm, both for Jews and non-Jews. People had to make do with what they had. Children went hungry for long stretches of time and complaining about it wouldn't make any difference.

One year before Pesach, the Skulener Rebbe, Rav Eliezer Zusha Portugal *zt"l*, made tremendous efforts, investing time and money, to locate extra supplies of flour and other necessities. Amazingly, under the terrible conditions of the time, he was successful in obtaining several hundred kilograms of wheat for the upcoming Pesach holiday. Although, the Rebbe had been forced out of his home and was now living in the city of Chernowitz, he still managed to set up a small matzah bakery to supply the townspeople with matzos. The residents of Chernowitz were thankful for his efforts and a mere two weeks before Pesach, began distributing them, limiting the allocation to three matzos per family, thereby allowing for the maximum number of people to benefit.

Jews from all around the city gathered daily while the Rebbe and the members of his family distributed no more than three matzos per family. Each person gratefully accepted the Rebbe's matzos, happy to be able to perform the mitzvos of the upcoming Yom Tov.

When the son of the Seret-Vizhnitzer Rebbe, Rav Baruch Hager *zt"l* reached his turn on the distribution line, he made a strange request. "My father, the Rebbe, asks to receive six matzos for Yom Tov."

The Skulener Rebbe knew who this young man was and gently informed him that a system had been set up whereby each family received just enough for Yom Tov so that the limited quantity could supply the maximum number of people. It would not be feasible, explained R' Eliezer Zusha, to give more than the allotted amount - to anyone.

The young man, however, insisted that he had received specific instructions from his father, the Seret-Vizhnitzer Rebbe, not to settle for anything less than six matzos. The distributors, including the Skulener Rebbe, were surprised at the tenaciousness and assertiveness of the young man and his refusal to accept what everyone else was getting. His insistence bordered on chutzpah and the family members believed that this young man should not be allowed to talk to their father this way. They had it in their minds to ask him to leave but the Skulener Rebbe stopped them. He was, after all, only a messenger. Finally, the Skulener Rebbe decided not to continue the argument and gave the man six matzos.

Erev Pesach, late in the afternoon, the Rebbe finally finished handing out the last matzah - literally - he had given out every last matzah, leaving himself and his son with nothing to fulfill the mitzvah on the night of Pesach. Their activities had taken up all their time and energy that they simply hadn't thought about saving a few matzos for themselves. Now, they would be forced to celebrate the Yom Tov without performing this precious mitzvah.

In the waning minutes of the afternoon, a messenger suddenly arrived at the home of the Skulener Rebbe to deliver a package. Upon opening it, the Rebbe found three whole matzos. The messenger explained to the puzzled family members that the Seret-Vizhnitzer Rebbe had purposely requested three additional matzos so that on Erev Pesach, he could return these matzos to the Skulener Rebbe.

R' Baruch, the Seret-Vizhnitzer Rebbe, was indeed very intuitive. Understanding human nature and the incredible *ahavas yisrael* (love for his fellow Jew) of the Skulener Rebbe, he had realized that R' Eliezer Zusha would very likely hand out his entire stock of precious matzos until the very last one. He wanted to make sure that both the Rebbe's and his son's families were provided with matzah for Yom Tov. If not for his foresight and his son's persistence in carrying out his father's request, both the Skulener Rebbe's family and his son's family would have been deprived of even the barest minimum of matzah for Pesach.

A Spark of Humanity

The holy Torah discusses many issues pertaining to war. In fact, the Jewish people are instructed exactly what the requirements of being a soldier in the army of Klal Yisrael were. A Jew must always fight with a spark of humanity, for the honor and glory of the Almighty, not for the sake of killing other human beings. If war can be avoided, that is obviously the best case scenario. But where it cannot, one must fight with honor, integrity and above all else, humanity.

It was September 1939, and it had just been announced that Germany invaded Poland. There was a mad scramble to get out of Warsaw as it became a victim of relentless German bombing. It was a time when every Polish citizen, Jew and non-Jew, tried to run, hide and contact family.

A young Jewish woman who had been working in Warsaw at the time decided to get out of Warsaw and make it to her hometown of Chelm to see her family and take them with her safely to Russia. She had some connections and needed certain permits before she left. She went about procuring them from various agencies in Warsaw.

On one of her dashes around the city, the air-raid sirens began to wail, which foretold of a coming bombing raid. When the sirens went off, terror gripped the city and people jumped into the first available shelter. It was a fairly civil minded Warsaw at that time and people actually tried to help others. There was usually someone willing to provide shelter in their basement for those who became stranded when the sirens sounded. The woman found herself huddling in the basement of a small house, as the bombs fell all around her. In those days, this was known as the "bomb-lottery."

It is said that if you hear the sound of a bomb exploding, you can breathe a sigh of relief. It has already exploded and you have lived to hear it. It was this feeling of terror and impending doom which blanketed the city of Warsaw and every home and shelter where people huddled in masses. So many houses, buildings and hiding places all over the city were being demolished every single day, along with their huddled and terrified occupants.

As the woman huddled, a sudden terrible crash and shake enveloped the house. They had obviously been hit. There was a perceivable moment between the initial impact and the time the bomb ripped through the floors of the house. But then - no explosion. This was the real moment of terror. They had definitely been hit, but the bomb had yet to go off. Surely it would be just a matter of moments until the massive trauma of the shrapnel and heat would rip through the house and themselves.

But more moments passed. Nothing happened. There was the faint sound of whimpering and crying; the sound that only people can make when they are too frightened to make noise. Slowly, the crouching strangers got up and gingerly moved about. It took about two minutes to locate the unexploded shell. Everyone had a sense of where it had fallen. It was big and shiny, and had broken into several pieces on impact. Perhaps this was what it was supposed to do.

The more fearless of the bunch touched the metal pieces, and found that there was no material, powder or explosive inside. Indeed, it was an empty shell. However, there was something there. A piece of card or paper had survived the impact, and lay in between two of the broken pieces. A brazen man picked it up and found that it contained some scrawled German. One of the people read it, and translated it into Polish: "War benefits no one. This is the best we can do."

No one knew who wrote it, but they all knew why. Some decent person was doing his bit to stop the waste of human life about to occur with the dropping of the bomb. Even in the heat of battle - humanity must overcome all else!

{ MID-WAR II }

A Cry from the Depths

A Mother's Sacrifice

by Raize Guttman

Amidst the helpless, broken crowd,
Of shattered hearts and spirits worn,
A piercing wail is heard aloud,
The time has come - a child is born.

The SS guards point guns and bombs,
While a Jewish mother caresses and cries,
Her heart filled with love, her lips citing Psalms,
She turns to the Heavens with tears in her eyes.

This day - the birth of her newborn son,
Should be the happiest time of her life,
But she knew - yes she knew - there was nowhere to run,
As the Nazi approached, clutching a knife.

Without hesitation, she grabbed for the blade,
Instinctively, she knew what she needed to do,
"Who has commanded us to do Milah," she called out
unafraid,
At least she was comforted, he will die as a Jew.

| REB YOSEF FRIEDENSON |

It's More Important to Warm the Soul

As a Holocaust survivor and one who lived through the horrors of the war first-hand, Reb Yosef Friedenson received, in his own words, "seven diplomas from seven German universities of murder and atrocity." One incident that stood out in his mind involved a fifteen year-old girl from the town of Chust.

During his time in Birkenau, Reb Yosef and his friend Aviezer, from the Lubliner Yeshivah, had been assigned the unsavory task of transporting the garbage refuse from the various depositories - outside the kitchens, the latrine, and so on. They filled the wagon they lugged around the camp and emptied it into the dump. No one would call the job a pleasant one, but it was considered one of the best in the camp. Quite often, extra morsels of food could be found in the kitchen scraps, and it gave them a certain sense of freedom to roam the camp at will.

One day, as they were pushing the malodorous cart past the ditch that separated the men and women compounds in Birkenau, they caught sight of a young girl, waving frantically and calling to them. A strong wind was blowing toward her, and her voice did not carry well. She held her arms together and, shivering, called out numerous times, until they could hear her voice: *"Kent yir mir kriggen a ... vetter?"*

Aviezer looked at Yosef for an explanation. "It's cold. I think she wants a sweater," he offered.

His first reaction was a shrug of the shoulders. "Where does one get a sweater in Birkenau?" he asked incredulously.

Several days later, they happened to pass a warehouse that stored clothing and the personal effects of the victims of the gas chambers. Wordlessly, Aviezer slipped through the door and emerged a few minutes later as if nothing had happened. As he returned to his place pushing the refuse cart, he said to Yosef under his breath, "I put on a warm, woolen sweater under my prison shirt." In his emaciated condition one could not even detect the difference.

The next day, as they passed the women's compound again, the same girl was standing at the same spot, as if waiting for them. Aviezer took off his jacket, removed the sweater and hurled it over the barrier. She picked it up, shook it out and looked at it quizzically. "What's this?" she shouted.

"A sweater," Aviezer replied. "You said you needed one."

"A sweater? No!" she cried out. "I said a 'siddur' - I want a siddur! Next week is Rosh Hashanah and I was hoping you could get me a siddur to *daven* from!"

Yosef and Aviezer looked at each other sheepishly. They were so occupied with mere physical survival, food to eat and a way to warm their bodies, it never dawned on them that this young girl required a siddur to warm her soul. The next time they passed the storage area, Aviezer smuggled out a siddur, which eventually found its way into the girl's hands.

Reb Yosef recalls that they, too, wished to *daven*, however, the main impediment was the load that wafted its offensive smell right into their faces, as they pushed the refuse cart from station to station. Finally, they hit upon a solution: They would pull the cart rather than push it, putting their putrid load out of sight and, when facing a head wind, out of mind.

"Aviezer and I would start from the beginning of *davening* - *Mah Tovu*, *brachos*, and so on - helping each other when memory didn't work, picking up a cue from the young girl from Chust, who was cold without a siddur."

| BLUZHEVER REBBE |

Clinging To Life:
The Merit Of Our Ancestors

It was a cold, dark, wintery night in the Janowska death camp. Suddenly, a shout pierced the air: "You are all to evacuate the barracks immediately and report to the vacant lot. Anyone remaining inside will be shot on the spot!"

Pandemonium broke out in the barracks. People pushed their way to the doors while screaming the names of friends and relatives. In a panic-stricken stampede, the prisoners ran in the direction of a big, open field. In the middle were two huge pits. Suddenly, the inmates realized where they were rushing that dark night deep in the Polish countryside, in a nightmare known as Janowska.

Once more, the cold, healthy, German voice roared into the night: "Each of you who values his life and wants to cling to it must jump over one of the pits and land on the other side. Those who miss will get what they rightfully deserve." Imitating the sound of a machine gun, the voice trailed off into the night followed by wild, coarse laughter.

It was clear to the inmates that they would all end up in the pits. Even during the best of times it would have been nearly impossible to jump over them, all the more so on that cold night. The prisoners standing at the edge of the pits were skeletons, feverish from disease and starvation, exhausted from slave labor and sleepless nights. Though the challenge that had been given them was a matter of life and death, they knew that for the S.S. and the Ukrainian guards it was merely another devilish game.

Among the thousands of Jews on that field in Janowska was the Bluzhover Rebbe, Rav Yisrael Spira *zt"l*. He was standing with a friend, a non-religious, freethinking Jew from a large Polish town whom the rabbi had met in the camp. A deep friendship had developed between the two and they looked out for each other.

"Rabbi, all our efforts to jump over the pits are in vain," said the friend to the rabbi. "We only entertain the Germans. Let's sit down in the pits and wait for the bullets to end our wretched existence."

"My friend," said the Bluzhover Rebbe, as they walked in the direction of the pits, "man must obey the Will of G-d. If it was decreed from Heaven that we be commanded to jump, then jump we must. If we fail and fall into the pits, we will reach the World of Truth one second later. So, my friend, we must jump."

The Rebbe and his friend were nearing the edge of the pits; the pits were rapidly filling up with bodies.

As they reached the pit, R' Yisrael closed his eyes and commanded in a powerful whisper, "We are jumping!" With a mighty effort, the Rebbe and his friend left their feet and jumped. When they opened their eyes, they found themselves standing on the other side of the pit.

"We are here, we made it, we are alive!" the friend repeated over and over again, "Rabbi, for your sake, I am alive; indeed, there must be a G-d in Heaven. Tell me, how did you do it?"

The Bluzhover paused. "I was holding on to my ancestral merit, clinging to the coattails of my father, my grandfather, and my great-grandfather, of blessed memory," said the Rebbe as his eyes searched the black skies above. "But tell me, my friend, how is it that you reached the other side of the pit?"

"I was holding on to you!" replied the Rebbe's newly religious friend.

| BOBOVER REBBE |

Flying in the Lion's Den

The Bobover Rebbe was faced with a dilemma. For more than four years, Rav Shloime Halberstam *zt"l*, his young son Naftulche (R' Naftali Halberstam *zt"l*), and a large number of family members had been continuously on the run from the dreaded Gestapo who were looking for them since their escape from Poland. In mid-1944, R' Shloime and his son managed to reach Romania and found themselves hiding out in the city of Arad.

R' Shloime urgently needed to reach the capital, Bucharest, in order to obtain legal residency papers and focus on helping his family trapped in Romania and Hungary. The problem was getting there.

Late one night, the Rebbe sat with his host, Mottel Farkash, to discuss the limited options. "There are two ways to get there," Mottel said. "One is impractical and the other one is impossible!"

The Rebbe looked at him puzzled. "You mean by train or by ... air?" asked the Rebbe. Mottel nodded. It was well known that the Romanian police were avid Nazi sympathizers who patrolled every train headed to the capital. At every station, they would board to check each passenger's papers and examine every person's face. Papers can lie but a Jewish face tells it all, and they were experts in this sort of determination.

Traveling by train was truly impractical, but the other alternative - flying on an airplane - was even more dangerous and virtually impossible. Every air field was controlled by the Nazis. To board an airplane, one would need a special government permit, which was impossible for a Jew to obtain. Only military officials, Gestapo agents and wealthy German businessmen were allowed to fly the decidedly "unfriendly" skies.

But the Rebbe was pacing again, his mind working furiously. "There has to be a way," he thought. "There just has to be ..." And then, the roots of a plan began to take shape.

A few days later, a "gentleman" arrived at the government airfield with a recently purchased plane ticket in hand. While the technicians checked the military airplane, the controller announced in guttural German, and then in his native Romanian: "Flight from Arad to Bucharest, leaving Airstrip 14 at 17:20 hours."

All the passengers prepared to board their flight. A number of Army officials in full dress and some others dressed in civilian clothes, milled about. Yet, they were all most obviously Nazis. Who could fail to notice their arrogant strut or their steely blue eyes? After the customs official checked their permits he left.

The "gentleman" - clean-shaven and dressed in a crisp civilian suit, found a seat on the small aircraft and breathed a sigh of relief. Obtaining the gentile papers and permits had been difficult, but that was nothing compared to what would come next. Here, literally inside the lion's den, sitting among the very officials he had been hiding from, the Bobover Rebbe felt an urge to *daven* to Hashem, but he was afraid to draw attention to himself. Putting a cigar between his lips, he began to murmur silent prayers with all his heart and soul.

The turbulence of the flight did little to calm the Rebbe's nerves. "Could anyone see through my disguise?" he thought. "Do I look like a Nazi? And how was Naftulche?" Since the Rebbe could not possibly procure a military pass for the child, Naftulche had to travel by train, escorted by a gentile woman.

He sat tensely for the duration of the flight and it took all his composure to maintain a calm and even casual exterior.

Stealing a furtive glance at the other passengers, R' Shloime noticed that one was staring at him. Slowly, he turned back toward the window, his heart pounding furiously. He left his seat, ostensibly to stretch his legs, and wandered down the narrow aisle. Sure enough, the man's gaze remained focused on him. R' Shloime tried to stay calm as he returned to his seat.

Along the way, the plane made a short stop and the watchful Gestapo officer disembarked. A few minutes later, out of the corner of his eye, the Bobover Rebbe noticed a crew of policemen boarding the plane. Were they coming to arrest him? With all his willpower, he stopped his hands and feet from trembling, praying that the Gestapo officer had not informed on him.

The policemen boarded the plane, chatting congenially among themselves. They found seats, settled down, and thankfully paid the gentleman with the cigar no heed. R' Shloime relaxed somewhat, but he longed for the ordeal to end.

Finally, the plane touched down in Bucharest. R' Shloime followed the other passengers off the plane, being sure to steer clear of any watchful German eyes.

Just as planned, and right on schedule, Hatzalah activist Sammy Baraf was waiting with his car to whisk the Rebbe away to safety. Not until they arrived at his pre-arranged lodgings did the Rebbe thankfully discard his disguise and relax. It was a truly terrifying ordeal, but one that only a man with the courage and audacity of the Bobover Rebbe would be able to pull off.

It wasn't until 1947, after much self-sacrifice and tremendous effort to rescue thousands of his brethren, did R' Shloime finally leave the blood-soaked shores of Europe for America, where he was reunited with his son, Naftulche, and other members of his family.

| RABBEINU YITZCHAK HAI TAYEB |

"Ribi Hai Tayeb is Not Dead, He Lives On"

E very traditional Sephardic community has its favorite *chachamim*, *poskim* and/or kabbalists who become legendary figures of towering stature, with the passing of every generation. They are an inseparable part of the Mediterranean and Middle Eastern Jewish heritage, who never knew an irreligious, "enlightened" culture, as did many of their European counterparts. These Sephardic *chachamim* are perceived as heroes among their people. They are not only part of the community; they have always been part of the individual Jew who identifies with them and takes strength and example from them.

The great *chacham* of Tunis, Rabbeinu Yitzchak Hai Tayeb *zt"l* was one of these beloved rabbis. He was born in Tunis in 1743 into a family of *chachamim* and served the Tunis community for many long years, until his death in 1837 at the age of 94. His community adored him and hung onto his every word and many miracles were attributed to their holy *chacham*.

The Sages tell us: "Yaakov Avinu never did die." His presence was, and is, continuously evident within the greater population of Jews all throughout the world, and our nation's very identity - Children of Israel - is viewed through our holy patriarch Yaakov, in name and action.

Rabbeinu Hai Tayeb was similarly held in very high regard. In fact, after he passed away, a poem was composed and chiseled on his tombstone, ending with the words: "Ribi Hai Tayeb is not dead, he lives on." As far as the hearts of Tunisian Jewry were concerned, this statement was not an exaggeration; these words actually proved to be prophetic, as well.

The graves of *tzaddikim* have always been popular pilgrimage sites in the Old Country, and stories of the many Sephardic righteous men are likewise handed down from parents to children. Today, these stories, transmitted in book form, are the equivalent of religious "best-sellers" in every Sephardic community.

One of the best-known stories about the great *Chacham* Yitzchak Hai Tayeb, took place in 1942, after the Germans invaded Tunisia to confront the Allied armies stationed in Morocco, Algeria and western Tunisia. The occupation lasted less than a year, but that was ample time for the S.S. war machine to set up an efficient, true-to-form Nazi operation, which included confiscation of Jewish property, creation of local labor camps, and regular shipments of Jews to the European gas chambers.

Towards the end of the occupation in 1943, the Allies began bombing Tunis every day, hoping to force the Germans to surrender. The city took a massive pounding and the Jews, who had lived through confiscations, hunger, roundups and deportations, were at least fortunate to still have roofs over their heads. But now this, too, threatened to disappear. They had only one option, which had sustained them through centuries of occupations and invasions: heartfelt prayer by the gravesites of the *chachamim*.

The Jews of the *hara* (ghetto) gathered and went in a group to the cemetery to the grave of their *tzaddik, Chacham* Yitzchak Hai Tayeb. The bombers droned toward the city even as they walked and the terrified masses straggled along. Upon arrival at their destination, they started reciting Tehillim and tearful petitions.

The explosions, distant at first, became louder as the air force hit new targets. The prayers continued and so did the bombing, closer and closer to the cemetery. Finally a lone plane flew over the cemetery, with the earsplitting sound of weapon deployment.

The huddled Jews froze. The sound was unmistakable. They threw themselves face down on the ground as a huge bomb began its whistling descent right down on top of their heads. With a tremendous thud, the bomb landed beside the gravesite, directly in front of the horrified Jews, and then ... nothing happened! The Jews waited, hearts still. After a hair-raising moment, they looked up and saw half a bomb protruding from the earth. It was a dud!

When they grasped what had happened, they jumped up and shouted praises to Hashem. Their *tzaddik*, Rabi Hai Tayeb was indeed not dead; he was watching over them at that very moment, protecting them and keeping them alive!

| KLAUSENBERGER REBBE |

"I Defeated the Resha'im!"

The seven days of Chag haSukkos were terribly difficult for the saintly Klausenberger Rebbe, Rav Yekusiel Yehudah Halberstam *zt"l*, during the years that he spent under inhuman conditions at the Muldorf Labor Camp. Aside from the rigors of daily life as a slave laborer for the Nazi war machine, the Rebbe had no sukkah, no *arbaah minim*, and no *ushpizin*. This lack of holiday *mitzvos* caused him added pain and distress, for the Rebbe lived his entire life for the performance of *mitzvos*.

When Shemini Atzeres was but a day away, the Klausenberger Rebbe decided that it did not matter that he was a prisoner. No one - not even the ruthless Germans - would take away his special Yom Tov; this special day when Hashem communes exclusively with the Jewish people. There was no way, he reckoned emphatically, that he was willing to forgo his celebration.

The camp doctor, Dr. Greenbaum, a Jew by birth, had agreed to issue the Rebbe an exemption from work because he required extra rest and the Rebbe was fortunate to be able to spend the whole Yom Tov of Sukkos in the infirmary. He planned to do the same for Shemini Atzeres as well.

On Hoshana Rabbah, a young man and acquaintance of the Rebbe, Moshe Eliezer Einhorn, who had obtained the Rebbe's medical exemption for him, was informed that on the following day the *Oberfuehrer*, the senior commander of the camp, was coming to conduct a special inspection and selection. Together with him would be a certain Dr. Plukan, a very evil woman who was known for her practice of quickly weeding out the weak and sick inmates and sending them to the crematoria in Dachau. It was imperative for anyone who wanted to remain alive to show up for work and prove that he was strong and capable of working. Woe to anyone who was missing at roll call!

Moshe Eliezer hurried to Dr. Greenbaum and asked him to add the Rebbe to the list of those assigned to work for the next day. The doctor was surprised by the sudden request, since he was prepared to do the opposite, but Moshe Eliezer insisted. Although he could not explain why, the Rebbe could not be excused from work the following day.

The Rebbe, however, was understandably upset. Since he did not know why he had been reassigned to a work detail, he could not imagine forfeiting his Yom Tov solitude and decided not to report to work on Shemini Atzeres. He remained in the barracks and experienced the Yom Tov as only he was capable. He *davened* with tremendous emotion and his heartfelt prayers truly captured the spirit of the day.

When the prisoners were inspected and counted, it became clear that a prisoner was missing. Immediately, guards were sent to look for the missing prisoner. They found the Rebbe standing in his barracks, deep in prayer, and dragged him to the prisoner lineup. There, they proceeded to beat him mercilessly in front of all the rest of the prisoners. When they finished, the Rebbe was so badly hurt that he was barely breathing. He was taken to the infirmary for immediate medical attention.

The poor Jews who witnessed this scene went to work, certain that the Rebbe had not survived. They had witnessed with their own eyes the horrific beating and they helplessly cringed with every blow. It was as if each blow that connected to the Klausenberger Rebbe's body was felt by the many onlookers who considered him their mentor and leader.

When the work was finished for the day and the inmates returned to their barracks at night, they were astonished to find the Rebbe not only alive, but back in his own barracks. He was limping around a small stool, holding a few pages from a small torn mishnayos in his hand. This was the Klausenberger Rebbe's *hakafos* in honor of Simchas Torah!

In his later years, R' Yekusiel Yehudah would often mention his experiences on that Shemini Atzeres. With satisfaction evident in his voice, he would say, "True, I was terribly beaten and barely survived, but in the end I defeated the *resha'im* because I did not work on Shemini Atzeres."

Escape to Romania

During the years of the *Churban*, a large number of refugees from Poland converged on the Hungarian city of Grossvardein, an important center of Torah and *chassidus*, residence of the renowned Viznitzer Rebbe, Rav Chaim Meir Hager *zt"l* (1888-1972). The city also boasted a local Jewish committee which distributed funds to refugees on a regular basis. Reb Avraham Yitzchak Friedman *z"l* was one of the chief organizers of that committee. Also, Grossvardein was close to the Romanian border, and everyone hoped to sneak across that border to relative safety.

Although the deportation and demise of Hungarian Jewry did not commence until the German takeover of Hungary in the spring of 1944, life was far from easy and serene. The Hungarian Arrow Cross comprised of violent youths and anti-Semites believed themselves to be Nazi "wanna-bes," beating, torturing and maiming any Jew they could get their hands on. In addition, most adult Jewish males were shipped off to Hungarian slave labor camps.

R' Avraham Yitzchak, a highly proficient printer by trade, used his skills to forge exemption papers for himself and many others, to avoid being sent to labor camps. His print shop was soon besieged with hundreds of Polish and Hungarian Jews begging for counterfeit documents. R' Avraham Yitzchak remained holed up in his shop, which was adjacent to his house, creating documents until late into the night, tricking the Hungarian gendarmes into thinking he was away in a labor camp. He built a bunker behind a dummy wall in the shop to hide in case of a police search.

Then the Germans invaded Hungary, and in the early morning of May 5, 1944, the ghetto walls of Grossvardein were erected. R' Avraham Yitzchak immediately created counterfeit passes for his family to enter and leave the ghetto at will. Soon after, he met a Romanian peasant who, for a steep price, smuggled people into Romania. He engaged the man's services to move his entire family, in stages, to Romania. The peasant was found to be relatively reliable and R' Avraham Yitzchak promised him more money for more services rendered.

Having found a route to freedom, he selflessly aimed to save the Viznitzer Rebbe, R' Chaim Meir Hager, the *Imrei Chaim*, and his family. R' Avraham Yitzchak sent his oldest daughter, Chaya Sarah dressed like a Hungarian peasant girl to the ghetto to convey a message to the Rebbe: "Tonight there is a transport leaving for Romania. The Rebbe and his family are urged to join in the transport."

The Viznitzer Rebbe refused. His conspicuous beard might endanger the entire operation. Besides, he felt relatively safe going to work in the forest on the estate of a Hungarian count. He insisted, however, that his *rebbetzin*, their son, the present Viznitzer Rebbe of Monsey, Rav Mordechai Hager *shlit"a,* and his *rebbetzin,* be included in the transport. The girl left the Rebbe the name and address of the Romanian smuggler for future use. Soon afterwards, when the Germans rounded up the Jews of the forest for shipment to Auschwitz, the Rebbe and several others did get in touch with the smuggler who brought them safely into Romania.

On Friday night, May 7, 1944, part of the Friedman family escaped to Romania through a dense and damp forest. *Baruch Hashem,* they arrived on Monday morning by train in Arad, Romania, to be greeted by a group of smiling Jews who identified themselves by calling out, "*Amcha! Amcha!*" With unforgettable *hachnosas orchim,* they provided meals and lodging for everyone in the group. A few days later, the rest of the family - mother, four children, and several cousins - joined them. All those who chose to remain in the ghetto perished.

Like a faithful captain, R' Avraham Yitzchak was the last to leave Hungary. He wanted to make sure that everyone had made it safely across. He literally led the aged Viznitzer Rebbetzin by the hand, while R' Mordechai, his *rebbetzin*, two children of the Ziditchover Rebbe, as well as several Polish refugees crossed the treacherous border. Once across, all of them boarded a train for Arad; only R' Avraham Yitzchak remained behind to make certain that everyone was safe. It was then that the Viznitzer Rebbe, using the same Romanian smuggler, arrived safely on the Romanian side of the border.

Twenty years later, when the Rebbe had settled in Eretz Yisrael, he remarked to R' Avraham Yitzchak's son, Mordechai, "Never have I been as happy to see a Yid as when I saw your father at that small attic in Romania. It was your father who told me that my *rebbetzin* and my son were safe in Arad."

No sooner did R' Avraham Yitzchak arrive in Bucharest, though, than he set out to rebuild *Yiddishkeit*: He installed a kosher public kitchen, organized a Bais Yaakov, a Bnos Agudas Yisrael and a branch of Zeirei Agudas Yisrael. He also founded a *cheder* and a yeshivah headed by the Bobover Rav, Rav Shloime Halberstam.

"The Emissary of a *Mitzvah* is Not Harmed"

In England, during World War II, many children were evacuated from the larger cities and sent to the countryside to escape the almost constant bombardment by the German Luftwaffe. The blitz of London was in full swing and much of the capital city was destroyed or burning. Any child that could be evacuated was hastily removed from London and the other larger cities and spirited away to safety.

A group of Jewish children had been transported outside the city to the countryside. They were housed in a rural synagogue complex that had only recently been built. Next door to the main building, housing the *beis haknesses*, was a smaller, older, two-story building.

On Chanukah, the boys of the *cheder* held a party in the synagogue. A much needed burst of encouragement was offered and the children needed to take their minds off the drudgery of the war. They were just about to light the menorah when, suddenly, the air raid siren went off. Automatically, they formed a line and filed across the courtyard into the study hall, where another flight of steps led down into the bomb shelter. They were used to this already and some of the younger children grumbled about missing out on their Chanukah party. This time, however, the explosions sounded very close. They could hear bombs falling all around them.

After taking attendance and a proper head-count, the group leader announced, "Children, it is Chanukah. We must light the menorah and continue our party, even down here, in the shelter." This got the children excited once again, but when they looked about, they realized that in all the commotion, the menorah had been left behind in the main shul. They were very upset, but what could they do? The leader spoke again and said that Hashem would accept their good intentions, and consider it as if they had fulfilled the mitzvah, anyway.

One boy could not accept this. He really wanted to light that menorah! He decided to sneak across the courtyard and retrieve the menorah and candles. He couldn't ask for permission, because it would surely not be forthcoming; the leader would no doubt forbid him to risk his life. But he reminded himself of the words of the Sages, "The emissary of a mitzvah is not harmed," and slipped outside when no one was looking.

The whole sky was lit up by searchlights. It was terrifying. Running as fast as he could, the boy made it safely to the shul and grabbed the menorah and candles. But as soon as he opened the door to head back to the shelter as the conquering hero, a bomb hit the building next door! His earlier burst of courage had disappeared. Trembling, he forced his legs to run across the courtyard like a bolt of lightning - only to see a firebomb land on the roof of the synagogue!

Now, he stood frozen in place. Should he wait for a civil defense guard to notice the fire, or should he try to do something himself? Maybe they were too busy putting out fires, elsewhere. What about his friends and the leader in the shelter? Were they looking for him at that very moment? Perhaps they were, he reasoned, but in the meantime, the synagogue could burn down!

The courageous boy knew what to do. Bracing himself, he hurriedly ran forward and followed the fire protocol, as they had all been taught during repeated fire drills. There was no time to lose. He placed the menorah and candles on the ground and grabbed a ladder that had been prepared for just such an emergency. Within seconds, he was on the roof of the synagogue. On every roof was a huge bucket of water with a foot pump and rubber hose. He put the hose in the bucket and started to pump with all his might, spraying water on and around the fire. He kept on spraying until the flames had died down.

Baruch Hashem, the danger was averted. The courageous boy felt proud of his accomplishments even though no one else had seen him or would know what he did. Not wanting to risk getting into further trouble, though, and noticing a civil defense guard battling a fire on a nearby roof, he hastily climbed down the ladder and sprinted away.

Bursting into the bomb shelter, triumphantly carrying the menorah, the young boy lit the candles that night in a manner reminiscent of the *kohen gadol* in the Beis Hamikdash. It was truly a night to remember!

| SATMAR REBBE |

Finding the Right Person
at the Right Time

In one of the last transports to arrive in Bergen-Belsen towards the end of World War II was a Jew by the name of Reb Shmelke Schnitzler *z"l*. He was a chassid and Torah scholar, with warm, penetrating eyes. Most amazingly, he maintained a mood of genuine cheerfulness, a rare disposition to find in the inhuman environment of the camp. He worked hard to encourage his fellow inmates at every turn and make their lives a bit brighter.

At the end of 1944, though, as winter approached, R' Shmelke was nagged by a compelling problem, one that was increasing in urgency with each day: how could he possibly obtain oil with which to kindle the lights of Chanukah? The holiday was only a few short days away.

He consulted everyone with whom he came into contact, but no one had any oil or even anything that could be substituted for oil. Still, R' Shmelke did not give in to despair. The mitzvah of kindling Chanukah lights was much too important to him and besides, it would allow him to provide a surge of much-needed encouragement to the desperate Jews in the camp.

On the day before Chanukah, R' Shmelke had to hurry to one of the barracks near the far end of the camp, where someone, just that day, had died. He was assigned the job of removing the dead bodies of the many that died from starvation. Not far from the fence at the edge of the camp, he stumbled when his foot sunk into a patch of red earth covering a small hole. It was clear that someone had dug this hole on purpose.

He gazed at the shallow depression and saw there was a solid object buried there, now slightly revealed. He knelt down and scooped out some dirt with his hands. It was a small jar, half-filled with congealed liquid! He removed its cover and dipped his finger in carefully. It was oil! His thoughts immediately flashed to the original Chanukah miracle of finding a single flask of oil. How could this be happening? Was he dreaming? Then he noticed that the jar had been concealing other objects beneath it. He dug some more with his hands and uncovered a small package wrapped in a swatch of cloth. In it were eight small cups and eight thin strands of cotton! This was almost too impossible to believe!

Someone had intentionally buried this Chanukah stash, thought R' Shmelke, as he quickly replaced everything back in the hole, filling it with dirt and carefully smoothing the surface. It would be too dangerous to keep the materials in his possession until Chanukah began the next evening. Besides, perhaps someone would come back for it.

During the next day and a half, R' Shmelke circulated among as many of the inmates as he could, casually asking if anyone had concealed a quantity of oil in a hiding place. Everyone stared at him as if he were out of his senses.

The next night, R' Shmelke stealthily recovered the buried items and set up his menorah. All the Jews in his barracks crowded around as he lit the first candle. He struck the match, and recited the blessings with great emotion before touching the tiny flame to the thin strands of wick protruding out of the little cup. It was a scene from a storybook, in stark contrast to the harsh environment of the concentration camp, a ray of hope that repeated itself for a total of eight nights.

The elderly R' Shmelke managed to survive the next few months until the conquering Allied forces liberated the camp. His faith and hope had proven victorious. In time, he was able to make the journey to the United States of America, where he began the arduous task of picking up the pieces of his shattered life.

Not long after arriving on the shores of the U.S., R' Shmelke made it a point of visiting various rebbes, receiving blessings from them. On one of these visits, he found himself in the home of the holy Satmar Rebbe, Rav Yoel Teitelbaum *zt"l*, who lived then in Brooklyn.

The Rebbe welcomed him with great warmth. R' Shmelke spoke to the Rebbe and poured out his heart to him. The Satmar Rebbe held his hand and delivered words of *chizuk* that inspired and revived the elderly chassid. After conversing for a short while, the Rebbe suddenly said, "R' Shmelke, I hear that you had the honor of lighting Chanukah candles in Bergen-Belsen." R' Shmelke was surprised! How had the Rebbe known? He nodded his head as he recalled that incredible miracle.

R' Yoel bent over and quietly whispered into his astonished visitor's ear, "Did you ever wonder who left all those materials for your Chanukah lighting? I am the one who hid the oil, the cups and the wicks in that hole next to the fence when I was imprisoned in Bergen Belsen, the year before you arrived, before my miraculous escape!"

R' Shmelke was speechless. The Rebbe smiled. "I knew that Hashem would allow the right person to find it at the right time to do the right thing!"

| BOBOVER REBBE |

"You Will Not Die!"

A cup of flour; that was all it was. How hard the Bobover Rebbetzin had worked to procure a simple cup of pure flour in order to bake special challos, in honor of Shabbos. In the Bochnia Ghetto, during the height of World War II, even something as small and simple as a cup of flour was illegal for Jews to own, let alone use to bake challos for their holy day. Yet, the Bobover Rebbetzin persevered. A large amount of money to a black marketer was the only way she was able to go about acquiring such a precious commodity. L'kavod Shabbos, the *rebbetzin* succeeded in her quest, to her sublime joy and happiness.

The *rebbetzin* prepared the challos with lighthearted excitement. Golden brown challos baked in the tiny oven, their other-worldly aroma wafting all throughout the apartment. This Shabbos will be just like it used to be back in Bobov, she thought, as the bittersweet memories of a time forgotten came flooding back. And then, in an instant, that happiness quickly turned to horror. An angry Polish officer burst into the tiny apartment and caught her red-handed. Thrilled to snare a prized catch, he demanded, "Where is Halberstam? I want to see the rabbi, Halberstam!"

The Bobover Rebbe, Rav Shloime Halberstam *zt"l*, was a wanted man by the accursed Germans, and no amount of bribery or promise of further compensation, would dissuade the Polish officer from handcuffing the *rav* and roughly hauling him away to the dreaded Gestapo jail. It was said, almost always correctly, that no one reemerged from the Gestapo jail alive.

At the jail, the gleeful officer triumphantly showed off his catch to his superiors, charging him with possession of food reserved for the *Wehrmacht*. The Gestapo officers were pleased. As part of their responsibilities, they were involved in overseeing the day-to-day activities of the Jews of Bochnia and nothing gave them more pleasure than seeing a Jew suffer, no less a Jew of this caliber.

They beat the prisoner mercilessly, demanding a confession for his "crimes." When none was forthcoming, they pushed R' Shloime into a cell with a number of lowly Polish criminals who recognized the importance of their new guest and went out of their way to humiliate and bother him.

Meanwhile, the dreadful news spread quickly and, soon, everyone in the ghetto was talking about the Bobover Rebbe's arrest. Many *Yidden* gathered together, *davening* for his safe release. The Belzer Rebbe, Rav Aharon Rokeach *zt"l*, a resident of the Bochnia Ghetto, immediately asked for the Bobover Rebbe's mother's name and began saying Tehillim. Every hour he would briefly stop his prayers to ask if there were any new developments.

The *rebbetzin* contacted the Ordnungsdienst, the Jewish ghetto police. In most ghettos, the Jewish police were not religious and only wanted to find favor with the Germans. They would often collaborate with the Nazis against their fellow Jews. The Ordnungsdienst in the Bochnia ghetto, however, consisted mostly of well-meaning Jews, two of whom were religious. One of them, a man named Naftali Rapps, who used his influential position to save many lives, undertook to procure the Bobover Rebbe's release.

R' Shloime had endured a terrible beating and his wounds were quite severe, but this did not deter him. After resting for a short while, R' Shloime beckoned to one of the guards, and after a few whispered negotiations and a handsome bribe, the guard agreed to deliver a letter to the Rebbe's family.

It was late Friday afternoon when the guard returned. He came back empty-handed.

"No response?" the Rebbe asked, disappointed.

"None at all. When I got to your house, they were all just sitting around weeping, and no one had anything to say."

R' Shloime sank back onto his hard bench. He understood that his family had exhausted all of their options to have him released. With courage and fortitude that was his trademark throughout the war, the Bobover Rebbe began to prepare himself for the special mitzvah of kiddush Hashem.

He recited Tehillim with intense concentration, in order to bring himself to a state of *simchah*. Then, he decided to compose his will. Writing the date and name of the weekly *parshah, Tetzaveh,* at the top of the page, he reflected for a moment, trying to choose an appropriate *passuk* from the *parshah.* Finally, he wrote, *"Venishma kolo b'vo'o el hakodesh -* His voice will be heard as he enters the Holy." Through this will, thought the Rebbe, my family will hear my voice one last time before I enter into the holy sphere of Heaven - before I give my life in sanctification of His Holy Name.

He began writing his heartfelt words, imploring his family to remain true to Torah and *yiras Shamayim.* Mid-sentence, he suddenly stopped. The end of the *passuk -* how does it end? With the words, *"Velo yamus -* And he will not die." The Rebbe's face lit up and he tore the paper into shreds, believing now that true Providence had guided his thoughts to this specific *passuk*, for indeed, he will not die.

A short while later the jail door opened and an officer strode over to the Rebbe. "Halberstam," he demanded, "Follow me!"

This was the end, he thought, as most executions were known to take place in the evening. But the officer led him out of the building and through the dark streets of Bochnia. He then caught sight of a familiar figure.

"Naftali," called the Bobover Rebbe. There stood Naftali Rapps who assured him that he was to be released shortly, that he was only being taken to the protocol office for questioning.

Encouraged by his words, R' Shloime followed the officer. At the protocol office, he was again questioned, and again he maintained his innocence.

"Well, Halberstam," said the presiding officer, "we have no more business with you. Go home."

Hardly believing his ears, the Bobover Rebbe quickly left the office and hurried home. It was a forty-five minute walk to his house, and he walked in just as his *rebbetzin* was lighting the Shabbos candles. Overjoyed, his family told him about Naftali Rapps' extraordinary efforts. The man had collected a huge sum of money to bribe the right people and orchestrate the Rebbe's release.

| RAV SHULEM LEIZER'L HALBERSTAM |

Death With Dignity

The mere mention of the name of the *tzaddik*, Rav Shulem Eliezer Halberstam *zt"l Hy"d*, the second youngest son of the holy Sanzer Rebbe, still evokes awe and reverence in those who remember him. He was a saintly figure who lived for the Jewish people and his many followers from the town of Raczfert and beyond loved him dearly.

When the Nazis came to power, R' Shulem Leizer'l, as he was affectionately referred to, did his utmost to save his people from the destruction that had been decreed in Heaven. Many witnesses who spent the last Rosh Hashanah with R' Shulem Leizer'l in Raczfert in 1943 recall that right before the blowing of the shofar, he cried out in obvious anguish, "I see harsh judgments and a terrible Divine decree. Let us recite together the psalm 'My G-d, my G-d, why have You forsaken me?'"

Soon after the Nazi occupation of Hungary, in March 1944, the Germans began herding the Jews into detention centers and ghettos. On the last day of Pesach, they rounded up the Jews of Raczfert and transported them to nearby Nirdhaus. R' Shulem Leizer'l, then over 80 years old, was taken together with his immediate family and a number of his grandchildren. Many desperate attempts were made to try to save R' Shulem Leizer'l, but he refused to leave his community, saying, "I dwell among my people."

R' Shulem Leizer'l and his *rebbetzin* were eventually deported to the Auschwitz death camp. They were packed into cattle cars with no room to stand and little air to breathe. The *rebbetzin*, already in a weakened state, succumbed to her fate on the train; R' Shulem Leizer'l was taken from the platform and sent directly to the gas chambers.

All the Jews were ordered to undress and leave their clothing in the outside waiting room. The Nazis attempted to trick the unknowing newcomers into believing that they would get back their clothing and possessions once they had been sanitized and deloused in the showers. But few Jews fell for their misinformation.

As R' Shulem Leizer'l watched the other prisoners undress, his thoughts centered on what he must do before leaving this world and how he could do so with the utmost purity. He motioned to one of the Jewish kapos on duty.

"Please," he asked "let me go in with my shirt, my *tzitzis*, and my *kappel* (yarmulke). I cannot possibly offer myself up as a sacrifice in an unholy state of impurity."

The guard hesitated. Before the war, he had revered R' Shulem Leizer'l, as most Hungarian Jews did, and recognized him as the *tzaddik* that he was. But his request was impossible. It was unprecedented. No one had ever disobeyed the Nazi order of total undress. He would be risking his life to allow anyone to enter the gas chamber wearing even the slightest shred of clothing.

R' Shulem Leizer'l saw his hesitation and leaned forward. "I promise you," he whispered urgently, "if you do this act of kindness for me, you will survive the war."

The guard was visibly moved by these words and he acquiesced. R' Shulem Leizer'l was not forced to remove his shirt, *tzitzis* and head covering - perhaps the only Jew in the entire war who went into the gas chambers with clothes on. R' Shulem Leizer'l even asked for, and received, a bit of water to wash his hands.

On Wednesday, June 17, 1944 (17 Sivan, 5704), R' Shulem Leizer'l was murdered *al kiddush Hashem*. The *tzaddik* went to his death with dignity. This Jewish kapo was the only one of his group to survive the war.

| BLUZHEVER REBBE |

Even the Transgressors in Yisrael Are Full of Good Deeds

The soul of a Jew is pure. No matter how sullied the building, the foundation is never spoiled. We are assured that no amount of sin can totally sever the connection of a Jew from his Maker. Thus, Hashem gives us an opportunity each and every year to remove the stench of sin that we have brought upon ourselves through the *teshuvah* process on Yom Kippur. No matter what one's station is in life, Hashem is willing and eager to accept every last one of His children back into the fold. As we say: "With Hashem's consent and the consent of the congregation ... we pray even with the sinners."

The Jewish High Holidays were drawing near, and fear in the Janowska Concentration Camp mounted. It was widely known that the Germans, and their trusted helpers both Jew and Gentile alike, especially enjoyed inflicting added terror and death during the Jewish holidays. The prisoners huddled in fear, anticipating terrible suffering and sadistic persecution in the coming weeks.

A number of religious prisoners, however, were unconcerned and felt that they needed to celebrate the old holiday rituals under these trying circumstances, as best as they could.

In Janowska, there was a Jewish kapo (barrack foreman) by the name of Schneeweiss, one of those people one stays away from if he values his life. He was as sadistic as any Nazi toward his fellow Jews, but he was in charge and needed to be dealt with.

The day before Yom Kippur, a few prisoners approached a fellow inmate, the Bluzhever Rebbe, Rav Yisrael Spira *zt"l*, and asked him to be their representative to speak with this Jewish kapo to request that they be excused from work on the holy day of Yom Kippur. The Rebbe was hesitant, as the request alone could bring about his untimely demise, but he was exceedingly moved by the earnest desire of these prisoners, and decided to go ahead and ask.

With a heavy heart and tearful prayer to Heaven, R' Yisrael approached the kapo. "Tonight is *Kol Nidrei*. You are a Jew like me. There is a small group of Jews who want to observe and pray on this holy day. Can you do something about it? Can you help?"

To his great surprise, the Rebbe noticed a small tremor course through the kapo's body. Solemnly, the guard replied, "Rabbi, I cannot do anything for you tonight, as I have no jurisdiction over the night brigade. But during the day tomorrow, I will put you and your friends to work cleaning the officers' quarters without polish or water, so that it will not be against *halachah*. I, myself, will supervise."

True to his word, the next day, R' Yisrael and the others were brought to the S.S. officers' quarters and put to work. The Rebbe used a dry rag as he cleaned the huge windows and his companions polished the wood floor. Together, they chanted the Yom Kippur *tefillos* with tears of sincerity pouring forth.

At about noon, two Nazis suddenly burst into the room with heaping trays of aromatic food and set them down before the starving inmates with a simple demand: eat or be shot.

Nobody moved. The lead Nazi commanded: "You must eat this minute or you will be shot on the spot!"

Still, nobody moved and the Nazis' patience began wearing thin. They called in Schneeweiss from an adjoining room and demanded, "Make them eat now, or you will be killed along with them."

This same kapo stood up defiantly and said, "Today is Yom Kippur, a day holy to the Jews and we may not eat." Incredulous at the insolence of this Jewish *kapo*, they asked him to repeat that statement, which he did proudly and defiantly. The German unholstered his revolver and pointed it at Schneeweiss who did not even blink. A single shot rang out and Schneeweiss fell dead.

Much later, the Bluzhever Rebbe would recount this story to his chassidim. "It was only then, on that Yom Kippur day in Janowska, did I understand the meaning of *Chazal's* words: 'Even the transgressors in Yisrael are full of good deeds as a pomegranate is filled with seeds.'"

| RAV YISRAEL MEIR LAU |

A Child Among Men

In November of 1944, the Germans loaded all the residents of the Piotrokow ghetto onto the train platform in preparation for deportation. Naftali Lau, who was eighteen, had been placed with a group of men, while his seven-year-old brother, Yisrael Meir, was ordered to stay with their mother. Women and children were being shoved into one freight car, men into another.

The usual pandemonium ensued as people were trying to cling to their loved ones while Nazi soldiers were busy tearing them apart. At the last second, before boarding one of the trains, young Yisrael Meir's mother suddenly gave him a hard shove over to the side of the men, whom she hoped would not be killed but rather used for labor.

"Tulek!" she called out to Naftali, "Take Lulek (Yisrael Meir)! Take care of Lulek! Goodbye, Tulek! Goodbye, Lulek!" That was the last time the brothers ever saw their mother.

There had been no time to consider whether his mother's move was the right one but Yisrael Meir began yelling and fighting with his older brother to let him go back to the other side. He took out all his rage on Tulek, hammering on his chest with his small fists. Naftali tried to hold onto his younger brother, to soothe him and reassure him, but he refused to calm down. The men tried to help out by offering warm drinks on the cold train but nothing seemed to help. Eventually Yisrael Meir cried himself to sleep. It took quite a few years until Yisrael Meir was able to fully understand that the push from his mother had indeed saved his life.

The train transported them to the Czenstochova labor camp, near Krakow, where they remained for a short time. In January of 1945, they were again marched to a train station and this time, deported to a larger camp. As the train rolled into the station, the first thing they saw was a group of men in striped uniforms, shoveling snow. They called out to the prisoners and asked them where they were. In reply, the inmates drew their forefingers across their throats. This was Buchenwald.

Yisrael Meir was a child and it was known that children did not survive in the camp. Naftali smuggled his seven-year-old-brother Yisrael Meir into the camp, hidden in a knapsack. They got as far as the initial lineup but when the Nazis ordered everyone to throw their belongings into an oven as a precaution against spreading disease, the boy was forced to jump out and join the line waiting to be inoculated by a doctor. This doctor, a Czech gentile imprisoned because of his Communist affiliation, stood there like a robot, injecting arms without even looking at the faces.

Suddenly he saw no arm before him and looked down to see a little boy. "How old are you?" he asked and Yisrael Meir answered "Fifteen" as his brother had taught him to say so that he would not meet the fate of the other children his age.

The Czech doctor narrowed his eyes suspiciously. After asking his brother the same question and getting the same answer, the Czech turned to Naftali and pleaded: "Please tell me the truth. I am not one of them and you must tell me how old the boy is. If I administer an adult dose of the serum he could die from it, and I am not a murderer."

Naftali looked closely at the doctor's pleading face to ascertain if he was telling the truth. Finally, he decided that the man was indeed serious. He then revealed his brother's true age and the doctor spilled half of the serum on the ground before inoculating Yisrael Meir.

There wasn't much time to talk as the line was constantly moving under the watchful eyes of the S.S. The doctor spoke a few words of reassurance to the young boy and upon hearing that the youngster spoke fluent Polish, the doctor came up with an idea of how to improve his situation.

When he found a moment, the doctor went searching and found a pile of dead bodies in which there lay a Polish national citizen. In one swift motion, he tore off the sleeve of the dead Pole with the prominent letter "P" emblazoned on it. Then, he located the group of new arrivals, including Yisrael Meir, and attached the letter "P" to the boy's clothes. He told the Nazi guards nearby that this little Polish boy lost his parents in the bombing of Warsaw and should be put in the barracks of the Poles, which had far better conditions than the ones designated for the Jews. He was moved to block eight, where the conditions were comparatively good. Naftali cautioned him not to say he was Jewish and his fellow prisoners took this young Polish orphan under their wing.

The Talmud teaches: "Heaven has many messengers." It is incredible to think that a Czech Communist was the one sent to assure the survival of a little boy who would someday become Chief Rabbi of the State of Israel.

| REB YEHUDAH TZVI WEISS |

The Mysterious Messengers of Salvation

Near the town of Munkacs, in the Carpathian Mountains, lay the village of Keretzky. This was the home of Yehudah Tzvi (Hirsch) Weiss *z"l* and his eleven siblings, as it had been for nearly six generations.

In 1943, he was taken into a forced labor unit by the Hungarian gendarmes and later conscripted into the

Hungarian army. In the winter of 1944, he was sent to the Russian front in a last, futile attempt to stave off the gaining Russian offensive. Despite the fact that the Germans were in retreat, the Hungarians placed Yehudah Tzvi in charge of the horses they so confidently assumed they would need for a victory march.

During one of the incessant shellings from Allied bombers, Yehudah Tzvi found himself caught in the midst of a terrifying stampede of panic-stricken horses, as a shower of explosives from the nearby Russian front suddenly and relentlessly rained down upon them.

A piece of shrapnel hit him in the eye. Before he could recover from this trauma, the stunning blow of a horse's hoof sealed his fate: he was blinded in one eye. Yehudah Tzvi fell unconscious and bleeding to the ground. When he awoke, the sole trace of life, amidst the noxious stench of death, was his own belabored breathing. However, he had no time to reflect or to pay heed to his numerous wounds. Now was the time to flee for his life.

But where could he go? With the threat of capture looming at each turn, Yehudah Tzvi could only trust in the *Ribbono shel Olam*, and began to trek southward in the hope of finding other Jews. However, his bodily injuries overcame his determination, and he collapsed, only to be discovered by German soldiers who put the unconscious Hungarian soldier on a train transporting wounded S.S. officers back to Germany.

It was solely due to the fact that Yehudah Tzvi was wearing the uniform of a Hungarian soldier that he was not immediately identified as a Jew. However, lying openly in his knapsack were his *tallis, tefillin,* siddur and mishnayos to which he steadfastly clung. Somehow, these religious items were not noticed by the

Germans and his knapsack was thrown into the train together with its owner.

Yehudah Tzvi eventually regained consciousness and, realizing that he was in a veritable lion's den, gave up all hope of survival. To confirm his worst fears, two S.S. officers began to deliberately make their way towards his stretcher.

An image of his Rebbe, the last Zidichover Rebbe rose before him. He silently prayed to be killed quickly without further suffering. The officers stopped in front of him, asked for his name, and then said with emphasis, "You cannot stay on this train!"

At this point, Yehudah Tzvi intuitively knew with certainty that they recognized him as a Jew. He waited for the hammer to fall, and then miraculously and inexplicably an officer lowered his voice and asked him, "Where do you need to go?"

To be so casually dismissed without even undergoing a perfunctory search could only be attributed to an outright miracle. Yehudah Tzvi was stunned, his thoughts gravitating to the *zechus* of the religious articles lying in the bag at his side. He impetuously asked to be sent to Budapest, with the inner hope of finding some remaining vestige of Jewish life. And so, at the next station, his stretcher was transferred to a train heading for Budapest.

There, in Budapest, the German defeat was rapidly approaching, and the Hungarian Nazis were frantically killing every Jew they could find. The only safe haven was the hospital, which was under Ambassador Raoul Wallenberg's safety pass and protection. It was there that Yehudah Tzvi's stretcher was providentially sent and where he spent the last weeks of World War II.

Whether the S.S. officers who saved him were actually angels, or even Jews in disguise, he would never know. But

Yehudah Tzvi Weiss' story of salvation bears brilliant testimony to the ever present *yad* Hashem which guides every Jew's life.

| IRVING BUNIM |

A Shabbos Ride to Save Lives

I t was a brisk November Shabbos afternoon in 1940, and Irving Bunim *z"l*, one of the foremost lay leaders of the American Orthodox community and the Va'ad Hatzalah, had just sat down to a relaxing Shabbos meal. Suddenly, his front door burst open and two Jews ran in, breathlessly.

"Mr. Bunim, quick," one of the men said, his hands shaking, "there is no time to waste. Rav Shlomo Heiman received a telegram from the *roshei yeshivah* who escaped to Vilna. We have to rescue a thousand rabbis and their students from the Mirrer, Slabodka, Lubliner, Lubavitch, and other *yeshivos* or the Russians will kill them. We must help these Jews now. We have to raise $50,000 - today! They have to get permits, secure visas and book passage."

No one spoke as the young rabbi gulped for air. "Please. We still have time. We can get them out - to Japan. But the Russians will not let them go from Vilna to Vladivostok without the cash. G-d forbid, if we do not send them the money immediately, they will never escape!"

The second man gestured to the taxi waiting at the curb. "Rav Shlomo Heiman, Rav Moshe Feinstein, and Rav Shraga Feivel Mendlowitz sent us to you. They said we have to make a *'geruder'* (commotion) in Flatbush. Now! There's no time to wait until after Shabbos. Every day, every minute that we waste can mean the loss of lives."

Mr. Bunim sat in his place stunned. The mere thought of riding in a taxi on Shabbos repelled him. He knew the Torah law, that saving a life supersedes all of Torah law, but Shabbos is the core of Torah life. Yet here were two young *rabbanim*, speaking in the name of three *gedolim*, commanding Mr. Bunim to violate the same Shabbos he would give everything to preserve.

Mr. Bunim sprang into action. Bidding his family farewell, he jumped into the cab and headed straight for the areas he felt would yield the most money. Then, with a plan formulated in the cab, he began knocking on the doors of the wealthiest and most philanthropic Jews, coaxing, pleading and explaining the gravity of the situation in a way that moved all those who he approached. Mr. Bunim understood these men and knew how to talk to each one in a personal, yet effective, manner. By the next morning they had what they needed; $50,000 in pledges, donations and loans.

With Hashem's help, their Shabbos afternoon efforts paid off. Within a short time, the yeshivah refugees were permitted to travel and they began their journey through the Soviet Union, across the Sea of Japan and into the port of Tsuruga, Japan.

But then, a hitch made its way into the works. To their dismay, the refugees quickly discovered that they were stuck. Their Japanese visas were only temporary and would soon expire. It did not appear as if they were going to make it in time and they were in jeopardy of being sent back. On top of that, Japan was an ally of Nazi Germany and the Germans were pressuring them to change their policy of allowing Jews to settle in their territories.

More intervention was necessary, but this time, it was the Japanese themselves who made the ultimate decision. The Japanese high command gathered top-ranking military leaders to interview representatives of the Jewish refugees who had already reached their land, to determine if they should be allowed to remain or if Japan should concede to the German government's incessant demands.

Those scheduled to be interviewed included the Amshinover Rebbe, Rav Shimon Sholom Kalish *zt"l* and the Lomzer Rav. While the others were told to remain outside, the interview with the Amshinover Rebbe went on for some time. When they finally emerged, though, both the Rebbe and the Japanese were smiling.

"What happened inside?" the others asked, curious. "What did they say? What did you say?"

The Rebbe looked amused. "Don't worry, everything is all right." But the group pressed him.

Finally, he responded with great equanimity. "They asked me why the Germans hate us so much," explained R' Shimon. It was a legitimate question, one upon which the fate of thousands depended.

"And ... what did you say?" they asked.

The Rebbe's eyes twinkled. "I told them the Germans hate Jews because they consider us Orientals too!" He laughed.

The Shabbos ride had been a success; the yeshivah students had been saved. They traveled by boat to Shanghai, where they remained studying Torah until the war ended. Among the rescued *gedolim* from that fateful Shabbos ride, were: the Amshinover Rebbe; Rav Aharon Zalman Sorotzkin *zt"l*, Lutzker Rav; Rav Eliezer Yehuda Finkel *zt"l*, Mirrer Rosh Yeshivah; Rav Shaul Yedidyah Taub *zt"l*, Modzhitzer Rebbe; Rav Reuven Grozovsky *zt"l*, Kaminetzer Rosh Yeshivah; Rav

Avraham Yaffen *zt"l*, Novaradok Rosh Yeshivah; Rav Yechezkel Levenstein *zt"l*, *mashgiach* of the Mir Yeshivah.

Torah from the European *yeshivos* would continue to grow on distant shores.

| BELZER REBBE |

A Four-Cornered *Shemirah*

As his name and reputation were widespread as a *tzaddik* and Rebbe of thousands of chassidim, the Nazis *ym"s* included the holy Belzer Rebbe, Rav Aharon Rokeach *zt"l*, on a list of "wanted" individuals. From Belz to Przemyslan, to the Krakow, Bochnia and Budapest ghettos, the Gestapo made his capture a priority among their overall hideous agenda to hunt down and destroy the leaders, and ultimately, the entire multitude of European Jewry. Consequently, the Belzer chassidim established a network of escape routes with which to whisk the Rebbe away to escape harm.

In late 1943, on one of his last stopovers before leaving the European continent behind, the Belzer Rebbe, together with his brother, the Bilgoray Rav, Rav Mordechai Rokeach *zt"l*, secretly arrived in Budapest and were set up in an apartment for a short time. Although he had hoped to remain anonymous so the Germans would be unable to track him down, this noble concept became impossible to achieve. His new home became an unending stream of humanity; chassidim bringing *kvitlach*, lay leaders wanting to discuss urgent communal matters, and even Hungarian officials and non-Jews paying their respects to the great "*wunder-rabbiner*." Eventually, the chassidim managed to arrange for R' Aharon to have his own private apartment in an isolated area of Budapest. They hoped to steer any attention away from the Rebbe's apartment and were very careful in how they came and went.

This arrangement lasted a short time before R' Aharon suddenly advised his *gabba'im* that he would like to change apartments. His attendants looked at the Rebbe in surprise; it was so convenient and comfortable where they were. Why should they move? But the Rebbe was adamant; he even gave them a general area of the city that he would like to move to. In a very short time, an apartment was found and the Rebbe was surreptitiously transferred to the new apartment.

This accommodation did not last long. Scarcely a month passed before the Rebbe called his *gabba'im* in and again requested a change of apartments. Just like previously, he indicated a different district where he would like to settle and the chassidim carried out his wishes with the utmost speed and discretion.

A few weeks later, it happened again. R' Aharon asked to move a fourth time to a particular location. The attendants had no idea or understanding of the Rebbe's intentions, and were surprised each time R' Aharon made his request. However, not willing to question the motives of the holy Belzer Rebbe, they carried out his wishes each time with alacrity, efficiency and dependability.

Not long after, the Rebbe was whisked out of the ghetto and continued on his escape route, which eventually led him out of the European inferno and into the confines of Eretz Yisrael, where he reestablished the Belzer dynasty as it exists today.

Much confusion and misunderstanding swirled around the limited stay of the Rebbe and his mysterious requests to switch apartments on three separate occasions. It was not until after the war that people began to somewhat understand.

In March 1944, after the stunning invasion of Hungary by their one-time ally Germany, the order to concentrate all of Hungary's Jews into six zones was implemented. The Jews of Budapest were herded into one large ghetto. Amazingly enough, the four apartments that the Belzer Rebbe insisted on moving to, albeit for the short period that he spent in each, were found to be situated on the four outermost corners of the hastily established Budapest ghetto. Each apartment, in all four corners of the ghetto, contained the holy specter of the Belzer *tzaddik*. His immense spiritual elevation, and no doubt, his heartfelt *tefillos* of salvation, protected the residents of the entire ghetto. In all, over 100,000 Jews managed to survive, until liberated by the Russians.

This was the Rebbe's manner of protection for the inhabitants of the ghetto. In this historical light, it is widespread knowledge that from all the ghettos that Jews were forced to live in under horrible duress and deplorable conditions during World War II, the only ghetto in the entire Europe that the majority of people survived was the Budapest ghetto.

A Comfort That Wouldn't Come

One spring day in 1944, a young girl and her mother were deported from their ancestral home in Czechoslovakia to the threshold of death - the Auschwitz platform. After passing the initial selection, they remained together. Livia Bitton and her mother lived for each other. They did not part for a second; they shared their food and their clothes. They constantly encouraged one another that one day it would all be over, they would he freed and reunited with their loved ones. Somehow, they managed to survive.

One night, one of the three-tiered, flimsily constructed bunk beds in the Auschwitz barracks gave way under its human cargo and twelve girls came crashing down on Livia's mother and the other women who slept on the lowest tier. Livia's mother suffered severe back and neck injuries and became partially paralyzed. Livia's despair was beyond words, yet she would not succumb, and nursed her mother back to health.

After four weeks in the camp infirmary, and with the constant attention of Livia, her mother regained her ability to walk. That day, Livia arranged for her mother to be discharged from the infirmary, for there were rumors of an impending selection. Yet, her back and neck pains persisted with full intensity. She was unable to bend down or to stand upright, unsupported. Livia did not leave her mother's side. She supported her at *zeil appell* (call-up), helped her dress, and did for her whatever was humanly possible.

One winter's day in the midst of a blizzard, a group of girls were ordered to clear snow. The girls pleaded with the overseer, explaining that shoveling the snow in those conditions was useless, but to no avail. The girls refused to shovel the snow and disobeyed orders. They were punished. For twenty-four hours they worked in the factory without food or even water. Livia was among them.

When she returned to her barracks, her mother was waiting for her with a bowl of soup that she had saved, her own soup portion. She had held it under the blanket to keep it warm. "I kept it especially for you."

Knowing how sickly her mother was, Livia refused to eat the soup. "Mother, I will not touch it. It is your soup and you need it more."

Her mother shook her head. "My child, I would rather spill it on the floor than let it touch my lips after you have fasted for twenty-four hours."

But Livia still refused. "I will not touch it," Livia insisted stubbornly. The mother spilled the soup. Mother looked at daughter; daughter at mother, while between them laid the empty, miserable camp soup bowl. They fell into each other's arms and started to cry. They cried the entire night. Despite the many hardships they endured together, the grief that overcame them that night was the most painful of their concentration camp experiences until the final day of liberation.

One day, years later, they met a man who had been with Mr. Bitton in the concentration camps, and later on the death march to Bergen Belsen. He told them everything, including the fact that Livia's father was shot near the gates of Bergen Belsen when his feet refused to carry him any longer.

They asked if he remembered the exact date of death. "Yes. It was bitterly cold," he replied and gave the date. It was on the same night when the incident with the bowl of soup took place, that same night when Livia and her mother were overcome with grief, the night when there were no words of comfort, only tears.

| KLAUSENBERGER REBBE |

Purifying Death With *Teshuvah*

The Klausenberger Rebbe, Rav Yekusiel Yehudah Halberstam *zt"l*, lived through the pain and torture of more than a few concentration camps during the

Holocaust. He managed to not only keep his physical presence alive, but also his belief in Hashem and his spiritual integrity intact. The Rebbe relates that in one of the camps, he was forced to sleep on the dirty, rat-infested floor of the barracks, together with about forty-two other men. Most of them did not survive their horrible ordeal.

It happened one night that the Rebbe found himself on the ground, lying next to a man from Budapest. He struck up a conversation with him and learned that he had been the president of the Hungarian National Bank. This was the most important financial position in Hungary. Unfortunately, the man had traded his faith in the pursuit of his lofty position; he had converted to Christianity and married a non-Jewish woman. Now, though, the Nazis revoked any possible non-Jewish status associated with him and he was a bedraggled prisoner in a hideous concentration camp.

The Rebbe looked pityingly at the man. "Tell me," he asked, "did your wife join you here?"

Angrily, the man responded, "My wife? Why should she have come here? To suffer as much as I am?"

Innocently, the Rebbe responded, "Doesn't a good, devoted wife follow her husband wherever he goes? Would a loyal woman leave her husband alone in this state? How is it possible that after so many years she is only willing to share the good times with you? In hard times like this, she leaves you to deal with it alone?"

Silence followed. The night passed and in the morning they all went out to work. The next night, the Rebbe struck up a conversation again. "So, did you accomplish important things for the Hungarian government?"

"Certainly," the former banker responded. "When I was hired to manage the National Bank, the economy was very depressed. The Forint's value had gone way down. I made it into a real currency, a strong currency. Hungary became prosperous, thanks to my hard work. I accomplished great things in the fields of finance and business. To this very day you won't find a single gentile in Hungary who doesn't recognize my name."

"Then how is it that you were sent here and the Hungarian nation did not protest? After all, you did so much for them. How can a person as accomplished as you be forced into a concentration camp without any legitimate reason?" The banker was ready to explode, but the Rebbe continued. "I just don't understand it. You converted to Catholicism and became a complete non-Jew in order to be liked and accepted by them - and they ignored it all?"

A long period of silence followed as the man stewed inwardly.

But the Rebbe wasn't finished. "Okay. What about your children? Did you provide well for them?"

"My children? Are you kidding? I sent them to the best schools so that they would be well educated. One is a doctor, the other a lawyer, and the third is a successful businessman." He managed a miserable half-smile.

"Really?" asked the Rebbe. "And why did your children not come after you? Even when a person dies his children follow the casket to the cemetery. But your children have left you to be exiled in shame, not bothering to even follow you. Not a single one has come to see where their father is and what is happening to him."

The man turned red. "Rabbi, you are hurting me very much with your words. Why do you want to hurt me?"

"I don't want to hurt you, G-d forbid. I just want you to understand how bitter your situation is." Again, silence.

On the next night, the man initiated the conversation. "You know, Rabbi, I've been thinking about your words all day. I realize, now, that you are right!" He expressed genuine regret for having converted, for having married a non-Jewish woman, for spoiling his children. Absolutely nothing from his previous pathetic life remained with him.

"I made a mistake," he cried in a choked voice. "I made a terrible mistake with my life."

On the fourth night, the banker was no longer among the living. The pain in his heart, coupled with the misery of his plight, was too much for him to bear. The Rebbe was grateful for the opportunity that had been sent his way. For, wherever he was, the man had at least done *teshuvah* and regretted his deeds a day before his death.

A Soldier's Miracle

Karl (Kalman) Alexander was an enlisted Jewish soldier from London during World War II, stationed in the Western Desert of North Africa with the British Eighth Army, under the command of the legendary Field Marshal Montgomery. Although he was the only religious Jewish soldier in his unit, he had been fortunate enough to be able to join the catering corps. This meant he was able to observe kashrus easily. He knew what food there was, and had even been able to kasher utensils.

It was Yom Kippur morning, 1942, and Karl was in his tent *davening*. Suddenly, his sergeant walked in. "Corporal Alexander," he shouted. "Please collect your things and come with me. You'll be leaving camp immediately. Another unit 15 miles away is short of kitchen staff, so you and a number of other kitchen workers are being assigned there."

Karl tried to persuade the sergeant respectfully to possibly hold off the order for a few hours. He knew that walking 15 miles in a desert while fasting would be difficult, if not impossible. But the sergeant would have none of it.

"Unless you want to find yourself court martialed, you must follow orders. Be ready to leave in 10 minutes," he was told.

Karl and his companions set out on their journey. Karl made a deal with one of his companions that if he holds his backpack, Karl would do three of his night shifts. Thus, he was able to avoid carrying on Yom Kippur.

After walking for some time, though, Karl's throat became very dry and he was getting weaker. While he watched the others taking sips from their flasks, he tried to concentrate on other things. He tried reciting the Yom Kippur prayers by heart, whatever he remembered.

"How much farther do you think we have," Karl asked his fellow soldier.

"At least eleven miles, I'd say," was the reply. Karl groaned.

"That much? I thought we were almost there." Karl was getting weaker and more tired. The heat, and most of all, the lack of water, had begun to affect him and he found it difficult to keep up with the others.

A wave of nausea swept over him and now he was barely shuffling along. He began to fall behind, but he was determined to keep fasting on this holy day. After a while, his weakened state became such that he found himself considerably behind the others. The sergeant turned around and noticed that Karl was a distance behind them.

"Corporal Alexander ...!" he shouted, but never finished his sentence, for at that moment there was a terrific explosion. The force of it threw Karl back several meters. He lifted his head and noticed his shirt was ripped and he was bleeding profusely. With his good arm he picked himself up and realized, in horror and disbelief, what had just taken place. There in front of him, lay his three companions, motionless and dead, across the sand where moments ago they had been marching together. "They must have stepped on a landmine." he thought before he passed out.

It was touch and go for a few days before Karl woke up in a military hospital in Cairo, Egypt. It was during his recovery that he registered the enormity of his miracle. Had he not fallen behind, he too, would have been blown to bits by the force of the explosion! In the *zechus* of his strict adherence to the mitzvah of fasting on Yom Kippur which had caused him to become so weak, he was saved!

| REB SHIMON ZRICKEN |

The "Elder Spokesman" of Hohenstein

On the evening of December 24, 1944, in the Hohenstein concentration camp near Kaminetz, something unusual occurred. Many in this camp were in the infirmary, sick and weakened from the slave labor and lack of proper nutrition. Just like in every other Nazi concentration camp, if the inmates had more food, more of them could survive. And then, without any warning, on the eve of the gentile holiday the camp's inmates were given double portions of bread, sugar, margarine, and sausages.

It wasn't their holiday, but the Jews would not turn down this offer of more food. As they stood on line to receive their extra rations, a young man by the name of Shimon Zricken had an inspiration. If everyone would donate a small portion of this extra ration that they were unexpectedly receiving, some of the sick people in the infirmary could be nourished with a little extra food, which would prolong their lives.

He got up on a box at the head of the line and spoke. "We have a great opportunity to save some of our people. My brothers, there are sick people in the infirmary who are starving. Let us join together in this great mitzvah of saving lives. Everyone should give something from these rations in order to save our starving brothers." Immediately the collective soul of the Jews was awakened and they gave away part of their rations to save these weakened people.

The next day after work, Shimon was abruptly called into the office of the Nazi camp commander. On his way, he met another man, the camp secretary, who told him that he'd been sentenced to death because he'd organized a "Communist gathering" and called for a rebellion of the inmates.

When he entered the office, the Nazi demanded to know by what right Shimon had organized the gathering and what kind of ideas was he was bringing into the camp, speaking publicly as though he were in the Kremlin?

Shimon was petrified but still managed to ask the Nazi for permission to say his last words, before being executed. The words that came out of his mouth were like thunderbolts from Heaven.

"We Jews are forgotten from the world. No one cares about us. The only ones who can take care of us are ourselves. Only we can understand the pain of one another here. I know that there is nothing wrong with our sick friends except the lack of food. And if we won't have pity on them, who will? We share a common destiny. You have made us collectively responsible. Not only are we brothers in faith, but also in our pain and affliction. I did what I did for the sole purpose of saving lives, Jewish lives, and in that way they would be able to work for the Reich."

He spoke this way for a long time and miraculously, the Nazi devil began to soften. Suddenly, the officer looked up and said one word: "Out."

Shimon ran as fast as his legs could carry him. Word got around that not only had he been acquitted from death, but that he was going to become "an elder spokesman of the Jews." This sadistic Nazi removed the previous elder who had reported him for his "crime" and installed Shimon in his place.

However, the victory was short-lived. The next day, he was called back to the office. The Nazi commander handed him a whip and said, "From now on, you will be in charge. With this whip you will hit the Jews hard and make them work!"

Shimon felt miserable. Hit another Yid? How could he? Once again, he begged the Nazi for permission to speak. "Sir, I cannot hit the prisoners. They are my brothers, brothers of one destiny, and brothers of pain. I cannot hit people from my own nation, but I guarantee that the quota of work will be done."

For the second time in two days, a miracle occurred and the Nazi appeared almost normal. Then he looked at Shimon in wonder and barked, "Get out, you dirty Jew!" Shimon was saved from two horrors, one worse than the other - his own death paled in comparison to torturing his poor brethren.

| REB YOSEF FRIEDENSON |

"G-d Has Not Forsaken Us; Not Totally and Not Forever!"

After being a prisoner and slave laborer in numerous concentration camps, in 1943, Yosef Friedenson was transported to a steel factory labor camp in Poland where armaments were made for the German war effort. There he met Akiva Goldstoof, a 40-year-old Jew from Krakow. The two became close friends. Despite the difficult circumstances, they exchanged *divrei* Torah and thoughts of faith and belief.

A few weeks before *Pesach*, Akiva called Yosef to the side and said, "I think we should ask the factory chief if he would allow us to bake matzah for the holiday."

"You must be mad," replied Yosef. "Bruno Papeh has been kind to us in certain circumstances, but he would never allow us such a luxury!"

Akiva was insistent and Yosef finally agreed to go along with him and ask the factory chief for permission to bake matzos.

When Papeh heard their request, he was incredulous. "Don't you have any other worries? Is this all that is on your minds?" he asked in disbelief. "Yes," replied Yosef. "This is what we are concerned about, and it would mean a great deal to us if you granted permission."

Papeh thought about it for a moment and then said, "All right. If you have the flour, go ahead. Just talk to the Polish workers who are in charge of the ovens and tell them I gave consent."

They didn't have flour, though, and it took a further bribe to Bruno to organize a kilo of flour. Within a day, Yosef and Akiva were called into Papeh's office where he clandestinely gave them the flour for the matzos. The two thanked him profusely, but secretly worried that he could rescind his permission at any moment.

Several women, including Yosef's wife, Gittel, kneaded the dough and baked the matzos in the large melting ovens that had a temperature of 2,000 degrees. There was an air of controlled ecstasy in the barracks as the matzos emerged from the ovens, ready for any who wanted.

On the first morning of Pesach, Papeh walked into the factory and suddenly became furious. He looked around at the people eating matzah and realized that they had purposely declined their ration of bread. "Your G-d has forsaken you, and you are still loyal to Him?" asked Papeh.

Papeh scanned the room and then said, "Friedenson! Eat your bread or you will starve!"

Everyone froze. None of the people moved as they waited to see what he would do. Papeh walked directly over to Akiva and yelled, "Has your G-d not forsaken you?!"

Akiva, standing erect and ready to accept the worst, replied softly but with certainty, "No sir. Not totally and not forever."

Papeh was taken aback by the answer. He could not comprehend such conviction. He knew well the suffering and torment of the Jews. "Not totally?" he demanded, raising his voice.

"You let us bake matzos, didn't you?" Akiva replied. In the midst of pain, there was a glimmer of consolation. In the dark hours of night, the light of dawn eventually appeared.

| KLAUSENBERGER REBBE |

Water Rising From the Ground

In the early morning of Friday, July 28, 1944, the 8th of Av, Nazi S.S. guards ordered a block of prisoners from a labor battalion in Warsaw to prepare to leave on foot, heading toward the concentration camp known as Dachau. This was the dreaded death march.

The Germans imposed a goal of 35 kilometers to be covered every day, quite a distance for even a healthy and strong person. The prisoners, among them Rav Yekusiel Yehudah Halberstam *zt"l*, the Klausenberger Rebbe, were beaten, hungry, thirsty, and weakened from years of forced labor. Nevertheless, they were forced to maintain a rapid pace.

Many did not have footwear worthy of being called shoes, the sun beat down upon them vigorously, and they were not allowed even a drop of water at any time. Along the way they passed rivers and streams, but the S.S. soldiers would not allow them near the water. Anyone seen approaching the water would be immediately shot. Just the sight of the water caused greater thirst and made walking more difficult. Many people were driven by their thirst to delirium. They could not control themselves and risked approaching the water to obtain some moisture. The Germans, true to their word, immediately shot anyone who came near the water.

They marched on like that all day Friday, Shabbos and Sunday (the fast of Tishah B'Av). On Sunday, the Germans cruelly drove them to exhaustion in order to cover the allotted number of kilometers as quickly as possible. This was so that they might reach a town quickly, where the officers could take the day off and get drunk.

Because the day was Tishah B'Av, the Rebbe had removed his leather shoes and had been walking barefoot all day. An S.S. guard noticed this and sadistically forced him to walk - and then run - on the shoulder of the road so as to tread on as many stones and thorns that littered the roadside. At one point, the Rebbe had tried to hide and not only was caught, but was shot in the arm for his efforts. He was forced to rejoin the marchers and stanched the wound with dried leaves. (Later, in 1980 at a cornerstone laying for the Sanz Medical Center in Netanya, Israel, the Klausenberger Rebbe recounted that he had decided at that moment - the moment he was shot on the death march - that if Hashem would let him survive, he would establish a medical institution for Jewish patients.)

Greatly stricken by the terrible thirst and the real threat of death that the Germans were imposing on their prisoners, the people looked to the Rebbe for moral support. The Rebbe kept warning people around him not to risk their lives by going out of line to get water. He asked them to pass on this warning to others. He was certain, he said, that Hashem would not forsake them and that they soon would have water.

Approximately two hours before sunset on Sunday afternoon, the haggard survivors arrived outside the town of Lovitch, between Sochatchov and Kutna. The Nazi guards ordered them to halt in a wheat field whose crop had already been harvested. The stubble protruding from the ground stabbed the prisoner's bodies and made it extremely painful to follow the order to be seated on the ground.

The Nazis began screaming and soon all the Jews had sunk to the ground, another dimension of suffering added to their repertoire.

The Klausenberger Rebbe was lying on the ground but his mind was absorbed with another matter. Surreptitiously, he whispered to those sitting closest to him that perhaps there was some water in the ground. If they would dig down beneath the surface, they might come upon some water.

Soon the word spread, "Dig for water!" All over the wheat field people began clandestinely digging - one with a rusty spoon, another with a stick, most with their bare fingers. A large contingent of physically fit Greek Jews, former longshoremen, dug with their considerable strength. Every centimeter they dug cost energy they so desperately needed. Yet, here was an opportunity for survival, and the people clutched at it with all their will. For over two hours people pushed themselves relentlessly to try and find some water.

As night fell and Tishah B'Av came to an end, some of the prisoners were disheartened. But suddenly a stream of water some 30 centimeters high shot up into the air. Someone had found an underground water pocket! Soon the whole field seemed to be full of water fountains.

The S.S. guards came running, furious. They barked and screamed but it was to no avail. They watched helplessly as the spouts spread throughout the field and the Jews drank their fill. The Rebbe, too, drank his fill and broke his fast on the wonderful water shooting out of the ground.

Ultimately the German sadists were awed. They could do nothing about the spouts but fill their canteens from them.

The Certificate of
Rav Yitzchok Isaac Herzog

Once the Gerrer Rebbe, Rav Avraham Mordechai Alter *zt"l*, was ingeniously sneaked out of the city of Warsaw from right under the nose of the Gestapo, he managed to cross over the border from Poland into Italy, where the escaping group was able to rest in the port city of Trieste. But they were not totally "out-of-the-woods", so to speak, yet.

In Trieste, the *Imrei Emes* and his family had to wait for British immigration certificates that would allow them entry into Palestine - documents that should already have arrived. However, a month after the outbreak of the war, the British had halted the granting of certificates to Jewish immigrants coming from Nazi-held territory. Their absurd pretext was that such immigrants might be Nazi spies.

Two days after their arrival in Italy, on Erev Shabbos, Rav Yitzchak Meir Levin *zt"l*, son-in-law of the Rebbe, sent a telegram to a group of rescue activists in Yerushalayim informing them that the certificates for passage had not been received. The telegram arrived on Shabbos, and the Gerrer chassidim who received it walked to the home of the Chief Rabbi of Palestine, Rav Yitzchak Isaac Herzog *zt"l*, and asked him to do what he could on behalf of the *Imrei Emes* and his family.

The following day, R' Herzog went to the home of the British high commissioner for Palestine and, with great emotion, explained that his teacher, the Gerrer Rebbe, a leader of hundreds of thousands, had escaped from Nazi-occupied Poland and was at present in Italy. R' Herzog requested that the high commissioner make an exception and issue the ten entry certificates needed for the Gerrer Rebbe and his entire family.

The high commissioner listened sympathetically to R' Herzog and said that if it was up to him he would issue the certificates immediately. However, since it was Sunday, the office was closed and there was no one to type the certificates. First thing Monday morning, he said with a patronizing smile, he would be glad to do whatever he could to help.

R' Herzog smiled back and said, "That's not a problem. If you don't have anyone to type up the certificates, I'll type them out myself!" And, to the utter astonishment of the high commissioner, the dignified-looking Chief Rabbi sat down at the desk and, for the next hour, proceeded to peck at the typewriter keys until all ten certificates were completed.

It was no easy feat to get the certificates to Italy under the precarious conditions of that time. During the next two weeks, many telegrams were sent back and forth between Trieste and Jerusalem, as information was exchanged about the whereabouts of the entry certificates.

Finally, just before Pesach, several of the visas arrived, including the one for the *Imrei Emes*. It was decided that any further delay was dangerous, and those who had received their immigration certificates should board the next ship and leave, immediately. Even the fact that the next ship, the Marco Polo, was scheduled to sail on Chol Hamo'ed Pesach, and that it was small and uncomfortable, did not matter.

Thus, the Gerrer Rebbe and all those who already had immigration certificates boarded the Marco Polo during Chol Hamo'ed. Twenty-four days after leaving Warsaw, the *Imrei Emes* reached the shores of Eretz Yisrael.

Mishloach Manos in the Bunker

The amazing story of Rav Michoel Ber Weissmandel *zt"l*, and the way he survived the war, is truly inspiring. Being a well-known presence and guardian of Slovakian Jewry, he was also a prime target of the Nazis. He was able to avoid capture for some time but eventually the Nazi sadist in charge of Slovakian deportations, Alois Brunner, made it his prime goal to capture Rabbi Weissmandel. Eventually, he was indeed caught and placed on a cattle car to Auschwitz.

R' Michoel Ber came prepared and snuck a small saw with him which he used to cut through the wooden boards of the train doors. When he opened up a hole large enough for a person to fit through, he begged his family and the other Jews on the train to jump out. They were petrified at the thought of hurtling from a speeding train and, in the end, only R' Michoel Ber jumped off, saving himself. He was sure that his wife and children would see his example and follow him, but when he realized that they were not coming, his heart was torn asunder and he never fully recovered from the pain of his loss.

He had heard of a secret bunker set up for Slovakian Jews by a kind Slovakian gentile and by the time R' Michoel Ber reached the confines of the bunker, seventeen Jews, including the holy Stropkover Rebbe, Rav Menachem Mendel Halberstam *zt"l*, were living there. It was said that when the Rebbe came to the bunker and asked to be let in, the people there would only do so if he blessed them and "guaranteed" that they would all survive. He did so and not one person from the bunker was killed!

Life in the bunker was menial and at times interminable. The men used their time to learn Torah, and the women took care of the cooking and laundry. The kind Slovak provided them with food and tried to acquire whatever they requested of him. It was hot and stuffy inside and there was nothing to do in the bunker.

There were a few teenaged girls among the others and R' Michoel Ber noticed that some of the girls had some inappropriate reading material which they were surreptitiously looking at. Apparently, they had asked the Slovak to procure them some reading material to while away the long hours of boredom and he had brought them whatever he could. How could he know what was appropriate and what was not?

The holiday of Purim was upon them and the Jews inside the bunker were determined to keep the spirit of the holiday and its *mitzvos* as best as they were able. There was one single cube of sugar in the bunker and everyone took turns passing it to the next person. In this way, they fulfilled the mitzvah of *mishloach manos*.

Suddenly, R' Michoel Ber thought of an idea. Turning to the girls, he said, "We have given each other a 'gift' with this cube and have done our best to fulfill the mitzvah of *mishloach manos*. Now let us give *mishloach manos* to the One Above, *Hakadosh Baruch Hu*. Let us offer Him a gift as well. If we were to get rid of these books and papers which a Jewish daughter has no business reading, surely Hashem will look favorably on this 'present' to Him. Maybe this merit will see us all through to the end of this bitter war."

The girls agreed and the books were tossed.

An Unscheduled Stop on the Way to Freedom

Day after day inside the Slovakian bunker became grueling. One day, the inhabitants were surprised to receive a visit from the prominent Hungarian Zionist leader, Dr. Rudolph Kastner, the same Kastner who had negotiated with the Nazis to release hundreds of Jews in the famed "Kastner Transport", including the esteemed Satmar Rebbe. He had received information that Rav Michoel Ber Weissmandel was hiding there and he had come to the bunker to tell R' Weissmandel and the rest of the Jews that he had reached a deal with the Germans. All Slovakian Jews hiding in bunkers would be freed as part of a prisoner exchange. They were to be driven by truck to Switzerland.

Doubt and indecision crept into the minds of the hiding Jews, but they were soon convinced and prepared to leave. A truck appeared, driven by a Gestapo officer, and all the doubts returned. The Jews feared a hoax and were reluctant to get on board. The Stropkover Rebbe, Rav Menachem Mendel Halberstam zt"l, however, allayed their fears and urged everyone to get onto the truck.

They finally set out and the tension was palpable. Constant Allied shelling in the area made for ear-splitting accompaniment and the thought that at any moment the German driver could turn on them forced them to never let their guard down. The driver never stopped driving and the truck wound its way to the Swiss border.

The Stropkover Rebbe motioned to the driver and asked if he could stop for a moment and allow him to relieve himself in the nearby forest. The driver refused to stop. It was bad enough that he was given the distasteful task of transporting Jews to safety, but if he was stopped by other Nazi agents, they wouldn't look upon him kindly and he would personally pay. Besides, they needed to keep moving in the event an errant shell found them on the road.

But the Rebbe persisted. He adamantly announced that he must get off the truck immediately and if the people refused to wait for him, they could go on without him. Even his fellow Jews argued that it was crazy to stop right here in the middle of the road, but the Rebbe dug his heels in.

A few more tense moments went by until the people gave in to the Rebbe's request. They were not going on without him and they urged him to be quick. They told the driver to stop and he finally relented.

The Rebbe got off the truck and walked calmly into the dense foliage. The people waited nervously and their nervousness soon turned to impatience. Five minutes went by, then ten. Where was the Stropkover Rebbe? Had he wandered too far and gotten lost? Another argument broke out inside the truck and some people wanted to leave - they couldn't just stand there on the side of the road for so long.

The German driver, too, had lost his patience, if not his temper, and he was emphatic about leaving. Just then, the Rebbe emerged from the forest and, once again, walked calmly toward the truck. One man stuck his hand out to help hoist the Rebbe up but he refused.

"I need water," he intoned sincerely. "I must have a bit of water to wash my hands before we continue our trek."

This was becoming ridiculous. The Rebbe had already wasted so much valuable time - now he wanted to waste even more time by searching for water. But the Rebbe continued to insist and one man jumped down and began rummaging through the luggage. It took another few minutes but he finally found some water and gave it to the thankful Rebbe. They were now a full thirty minutes behind schedule.

Once on board, the truck continued to drive smoothly and uneventfully until they reached the border. A few, short minutes later, the truck stopped inside Switzerland's border and the German driver got out and went back across.

A Swiss official came out to greet the relieved passengers. "You must surely have had Someone watching over you from above," said the friendly border guard. "You just missed running right into a disaster."

The man explained that literally thirty minutes earlier, Allied planes came swooping in and began shooting at the few buildings and vehicles on the road leading up to the German side of the border. Explosions erupted and German soldiers were cut down as they attempted to shoot back at the incoming planes. It all lasted a few seconds but almost nothing remained from the German side of the border.

Thirty minutes earlier! Had they reached the border right on schedule, they would have been there exactly thirty minutes earlier. However, due to the emergency stop on behalf of the Stropkover Rebbe, they came in unharmed and avoided the carnage that took place.

Children of Hunger

The Janowska concentration camp was smaller than some of the more famous Nazi death camps, but no less lethal. Very few survivors of that camp were able to bear witness to the atrocities that took place there.

In the camp, there were twin brothers who had been born after thirteen years of a childless marriage. Their *bris milah* was celebrated joyfully by the entire *shtetl* of Vorshtein and its vicinity.

The boys' father was a devout Polish chassid. It was his custom to travel to Rav Yehoshua Spira *zt"l* of Ribatich for every holiday. The chassid was sure that he was given his twin sons in the merit of the Rebbe's blessing. After the death of the Ribaticher Rebbe, the chassid began to travel to his son, Rav Yisrael Spira *zt"l*, who later become known as the Bluzhever Rebbe.

When World War II engulfed European Jewry in flames of destruction, the family was separated. The twins, then about eleven years old, found themselves in Janowska, along with their father's Rebbe, who was also an inmate in that horrible place.

The boys were inseparable, as close as brothers can possibly be. The Bluzhever Rebbe felt especially close to these two sons of his former follower, and the three helped each other whenever it was possible. The Rebbe constantly assured the S.S. guards and their local assistants that the boys were older than they appeared to be. The twins kept the secret that the tall, shaven inmate with the comforting voice was a renowned and beloved Chassidic leader. In Janowska, being a child or a Jewish leader was a crime punishable by immediate death.

One day, all the inmates were taken out to work. Three people were left behind to sweep up the barracks: one of the twins, the Bluzhever Rebbe, and a third Jew. They were not alone, however, as a German guard was left to watch over them.

The sick and sadistic guard decided to have some fun with his young captive and ordered the boy to bring him water. In no time, the boy returned with the water. The German took out his revolver and for no reason shot the child in the leg. The boy collapsed and spilled the water.

"Get up, dirty Jew," shouted the Nazi monster and the boy somehow managed to stand up on one leg. Then, the guard shot him in the other leg. The boy fell hard and writhed in pain as blood flowed from his wounds. To the horror of the two onlookers, the German continued to taunt the little boy and then, as the monster soon lost interest in his brutal game, he finished off the child with one last bullet.

"Take him away!" the guard now roared at the rabbi. R' Yisrael took the boy into his arms and carried him away as his tears washed over the lifeless boy's face.

"How will I tell the other twin about his brother's death?" R' Yisrael wondered. How will he break the terrible news to one of two souls that were so close to each other?

"Tell him that his twin brother is very sick," the other Jew advised the Rabbi.

Evening came. The inmates returned to camp. "Chaim'l, your brother is very sick," said the Bluzhever Rebbe, "his life is in mortal danger. It is quite possible that he is no longer alive." The Rebbe tried to avoid the boy's eyes.

Instantly, the brother began to cry: "Woe unto me! What am I going to do now?" The Rebbe tried to comfort the boy, but he refused to be comforted. Looking into the Rebbe's face, he cried, "Today was his turn to watch over the bread. I left all the bread with him; now I don't have a single piece of bread left!"

R' Yisrael was shocked, but continued his ruse, saying that the other twin had sent Chaim'l his share. With a trembling hand, he took a small piece of bread from under his jacket, which was his ration for the day, and gave it to the boy. Chaim'l glanced at the stale piece of bread and said, "It's missing a few grams. The piece I left with him was a much larger one."

"I was hungry and ate some of it. Tomorrow I will give you the rest of the bread," replied R' Yisrael.

When the Bluzhever Rebbe finished telling the story, he said, "Only on that day in Janowska did I understand a *passuk* in *Eichah* (4:9): "They that are slain with the sword are better than they that are slain with hunger.""

Heroism in the Face of Death

The city of Zhichlin, in the upper portion of Poland, had the dubious distinction of being considered a part of the "Third Reich" due to its proximity to the German border. The Germans, however, still felt it was foreign enough to "merit" having its own ghetto. It was there that the entire Jewish population of the city and the surrounding villages were packed into a small area, under intolerable conditions. This ghetto didn't last very long as it was just a temporary measure until its inhabitants were sent out to concentration camps.

In 1941, my grandmother, Rachel (Rushka) Grizak, and her sister Bronchia *hy"d*, were separated from the rest of their family in the Zhichlin ghetto and sent to a small working camp called Inowroclaf. They remained there until 1943 when they were taken to Auschwitz.

Rushka was put to work in a factory called the "Union" where the inmates assembled hand grenades. Being from among the youngest of the prisoners, she was assigned to the "*kindertisch-kontrol*" table, where it was the job of the young girls to examine the finished grenades by inserting long metal screws into the pin hole to see how tight or loose it was.

Each girl had three boxes in front of her: the good grenades went into the box marked "*Gut*", the ones that were too loose and couldn't be fixed were marked "*Auschutz*", and those that were a bit tight but needed a little more work to be loosened were considered "*Nach-Arbeit*". The boxes marked "*Nach-Arbeit*" were then brought to a different area of the factory where two men had the extremely difficult and dangerous job of loosening the pin holes using fire.

These two men were brothers and were very friendly people. On one occasion, when Rushka was depositing her box of "*Nach-Arbeit*" grenades by their work area, one of the brothers looked at her and in guarded tones asked, "You look familiar. Are you by any chance a "Zhichliner *einekel*"?"

Surprised, she answered that she was and they proceeded to carry on a hushed conversation about their families. The next time she came by their area, one of the brothers secretly passed her a small parcel containing bread, two hard-boiled eggs and a note. "This is from Fulek Zlatkin," he said.

Raphael (Fulek) Zlatkin was himself a "Zhichliner *einekel*" and he constantly looked out for the welfare of his townspeople. Fulek managed to obtain a job in the "magazine" - or storage area, where the kitchen supplies were located. At tremendous risk to himself, he would "organize" bits and pieces of valuable food items and smuggle them into his barracks. There, he had compiled a kind of "help list" and he selflessly divided up his booty to be distributed to those he could assist.

In the note he sent to Rushka, my grandmother, Fulek wrote that he would help her as much as he could and if she knew of any others who needed a little more food, she should inform him. Most importantly, he told her to be positive, have hope, and that they would live through this terrible ordeal. My grandmother told me that this encouragement was truly a life-saver. It wasn't just the extra food rations that made her feel better but the fact that someone she knew still cared about her and believed that they would survive this horrid ordeal.

Fulek continued to send extra food and soothing words, using couriers such as the two brothers and a kind young man, by the name of Salek Atlas for most of the last year of the war.

One day, in late 1944, as the girls sat by their table sorting the grenades, one of the German *obermeisters*, or overseers, happened to pass by on a routine inspection. The girls always felt pressured and tense when he came by, and Rushka accidentally placed an *"Auschutz"* grenade into the box marked *"Gut"*.

Immediately, the *obermeister* began barking orders for her to get up from the table and screamed menacingly, "For sabotage, you are to be punished!"

He checked the number on her arm with the number on his clipboard and, without a thought, crossed it out, thus sealing her fate. No amount of apologies or begging would change the evil man's mind and he forcefully pushed her to the door where she was to wait until a wagon would come by and take her away.

Standing there, knowing that she was to be taken to her premature death in the gas chambers, the young girl began crying. All hope seemed to fade. Her time had come.

Some time had passed, when out of nowhere, Salek Atlas happened to walk by the doorway where she was standing. Why he had just happened by at that exact moment, my grandmother will never know, but Salek recognized her and asked what had happened. Through her sobs, she told him what had happened and what was to be her fate. She cried and cried as Salek attempted to comfort her. Then, he said he had to leave, but he'd be back as soon as he could.

Salek had obtained a carton of cigarettes from Fulek, who was a master at bartering, and this was considered the most precious commodity in the camps. The Nazis had no need for the scraps of food that Fulek organized, but cigarettes were rare enough in wartime and, for this, even they could be bribed. He would give out these precious items to people who would use them as was necessary to compensate the German soldiers for favors rendered. A carton of cigarettes was an enormous ransom, but saving a life was of utmost importance and Salek knew what he had to do.

Salek found the *meister*, and after brief negotiations and an exchange, he saw to it that Rushka's number was reinstated on the list. As the wagon was nearing to take her away, he ran over, took her by the arm, led her away from the doorway, and helped her back to the table. Not to worry, everything was taken care of, he said, thanks to Fulek.

Just as the war was nearing its end, Fulek was put on a death train to be taken to an unknown, yet deadly, destination. My grandmother was told after the war that he somehow managed to pry open the door and jump off the moving train but a Nazi soldier saw him and shot him right there. She was under the impression that he had perished and she was truly grief-stricken.

Two years later at the Jewish Committee building in Munich, she, along with my grandfather, Reb Alter Kurz *z"l* whom she had recently married, came across Fulek's brother, Duvid, who told them that Fulek was alive. He was extremely sick and was in a hospital in Vienna, and they were able to make contact with him.

He was overjoyed to hear from my grandmother and soon after his recovery, traveled to Munich to see her and be reunited with her. It was a bittersweet reunion, as were most reunions at that time, for both of their families had been almost entirely wiped out and only a handful of "Zhichliner *eineklach*" survived the war. He stayed with them for just a short period of time, as not long after that, my grandparents were issued visas and immigrated to the United States.

It was not until 50 years later that, through a strange set of circumstances, my grandmother Rushka met up again with the man who saved her life, Fulek Zlatkin.

Fulek had married, and he and his wife Gertie moved to Montreal where they were blessed with a beautiful family. He was a respected member of the community and, through a mutual friend, Chayale Makover Sherman, he and my grandmother met in Miami Beach, Florida. Thereafter, they became good friends once again. He would come in from Canada for family celebrations and he would relate stories of how he helped my grandmother during those dark days of the war. He was 76 years old when he passed away in Montreal.

Some people's actions are recognized universally and they become very well known and popular because of it. Fulek

Zlatkin was not this type of person. His extraordinary acts of heroism, the multitude of people he helped and gave hope to through his "network" of helpers, and his overall attitude of placing the lives and needs of others before his own, were not for the purpose of self-aggrandizement or a need to "look good" in the eyes of others. Rather, it was a sense of purpose that fueled Fulek. He recognized that by being in a position where he could ease someone else's hunger or save a fellow Jew by bribing a guard infused him with a feeling of responsibility that caused him to jump into action. It wasn't important that every man or woman, boy or girl he helped knew from where the help was actually coming. If that person needed a little bit of extra food to tide him over, Fulek made sure to provide him with it. If someone's belief and strength were ebbing, Fulek took it upon himself to provide extra encouragement, a note or brief message that would see the person through the difficult period.

Fulek was a "war hero"; but not the kind of war hero that books are written about or films are made of. He was an unknown hero to the outside world, but he literally meant the world to those unfortunate Jews inside the camps who were assisted by and had the merit of knowing Fulek Zlatkin. May his many deeds of kindness allow his pure soul to rise to a lofty position from where he can once again assist his brothers and sisters, helping to bring Mashiach speedily and in our days.

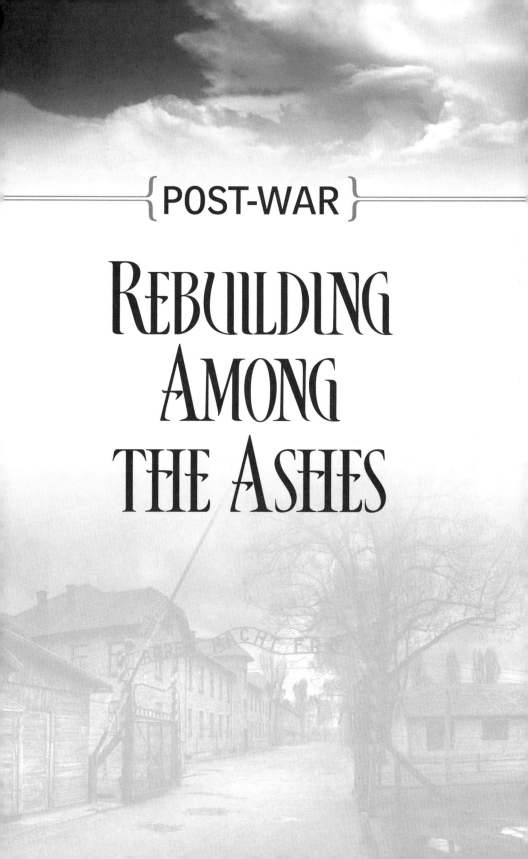

REBUILDING
AMONG
THE ASHES

A Child of Faith

by Raize Guttman

Strife in life seems overwhelming,
Giant waves crash upon the shore,
In vain, the pain, I try to muffle,
The heart so crushed, can bear no more.

Were I but a tiny child,
Cradled in my mother's clasp,
Sheltered, warm and unafraid,
Of things too great for me to grasp.

The bombs explode, the fire glowed,
A burning sun upon my head,
The children ask, "Remove the mask,"
The nights are long and filled with dread.

Hashem, You hold me as I roam,
This world of lies, from place to place,
For nestled at Your heart is my home,
To view the splendor of Your face.

Indeed, I am Your tiny child,
My faith is real, my trust is pure,
I do not fear the waves, the sun,
For in Your arms I am secure.

| RAV MICHOEL BER WEISSMANDEL |

Kiddush Hashem in the Upper Spheres of Heaven

Having miraculously survived the war, Rav Michoel Ber Weissmandel *zt"l* made his way to the United States and settled in the Williamsburg section of Brooklyn. He would go from shul to shul crying out in anguish over the failure of world Jewry, especially American Jewry, to do anything to save their brethren from extermination. While he continued to bemoan the terrible misfortune of his people, he involved himself in re-establishing the great Nitra Yeshivah in the Mount Kisco farm settlement, north of New York City. He later wrote a book entitled *"Min Hameitzar"* (From the Depths) which included a scathing condemnation of all those who refused to place the rescue of their fellow Jewish brothers as the top priority in Jewish activity.

R' Michoel Ber rebuilt his life from scratch. After losing his wife and five children in Europe, he remarried and was blessed with five sons, who became great scholars and leaders of the Jewish people in their own rights.

At the festive occasion of the *bris* of R' Michoel Ber's fifth son in Mount Kisco, he got up to speak to the assembled. Immediately, though, everyone could see that his mind was elsewhere, harking back to a darker period in his life.

"*Rabbosai*," he began solemnly, "*Hakadosh Baruch Hu* has brought us all here today to celebrate this wonderful occasion, the *bris* of our son. This morning, during Shacharis, as we were reciting the *Kedushah* prayer, a thought occurred to me which I now want to share with you."

The assemblage waited expectantly to hear the words as they poured forth from R' Michoel Ber's anguished soul. "We say, '*Nikadesh es shimcha b'olam* - Let us sanctify Your Name in this world', '*K'shem shemakdishim oso b'shmei marom* - Just as they (the angels) sanctify the Name in the upper spheres of Heaven.' That is *pashut pshat* (the simple explanation)."

R' Michoel paused for a moment. "But I thought of a different understanding." With a sigh and a heartrending sob, he cried out, "'Let us sanctify Your Name on this world,' - Hashem, my goal is to sanctify Your holy Name with these five children that I have been blessed to bring into this world, this life that Hashem has allowed me to create after the atrocities of the Holocaust; 'Just as they sanctify Your Name in the upper spheres of Heaven' - Just as I was blessed by the Almighty to sanctify His Name with my previous five children who died *al kiddush Hashem* during the war, and are now sanctifying His Name each and every day in Heaven!"

A Lesson to Walk Away With

After the passing of the Klausenberger Rebbe, Rav Yekusiel Yehudah Halberstam *zt"l*, during the *shivah*, a woman who was not known to the family came to the Rebbe's house. She certainly looked out of place and for awhile she sat quietly, biding her time. She listened with great interest to the many conversations that went on about the Rebbe and his greatness, but she did not speak and had nothing to add.

Eventually, someone asked her what her name was and what her connection to the Rebbe was. In response, she pulled out a pair of black socks from her bag and held them up. At that moment, everyone understood that a great story was forthcoming. Then, she related the following:

Immediately after the Second World War, the Klausenberger Rebbe was in a D.P. (Displaced Persons) camp in Fehrenwald, Germany. Conditions were extremely difficult and for some people, even basic necessities were hard to come by. The Rebbe was everyone's father, brother and teacher. His objective was to strengthen the broken survivors as best as he could. A never-ending stream of despondent Jews trailed to and from his lodgings and the Rebbe even made "house calls" - going to those people who he knew would not come to him.

One day, as the Rebbe walked along the street, he saw an Orthodox Jewish girl who was obviously not keeping to the highest standards of modesty; she was walking in public with no socks or stockings. There were many Jews who had let themselves go as far as religious observance but this girl was different; she was obviously religious, yet she was not covering her legs.

The Rebbe could not understand how a *frum* and righteous Jewish daughter could walk around like this, and he said to the girl in Yiddish, *"Mein kind, vi kumpt dos az a Yiddishe maidel gayt un zuken?"* ("My child! How can a Jewish girl walk around without stockings?")

"Rebbe!" answered the girl, more than a little embarrassed, "what can I do? I simply don't have any." She turned her head modestly away from the Rebbe's towering presence.

R' Yekusiel Yehudah thought about this for a moment. Then, without another word, he bent down, removed his shoes and began taking off his own black socks. As he did so he said to the young girl, "Please, I'll give you mine!"

The Rebbe removed his socks and was about to hand them to the stunned and bewildered girl. She shied away and was blushing effusively. How can she take the Klausenberger Rebbe's socks? What, then, would he wear? Noticing her expression, the Rebbe smiled kindly and added by way of explanation, "It is because I am permitted to go without socks, but the Torah demands that a Jewish girl must have her legs covered!"

With this he gave his socks to her, although he, a highly-respected Rebbe would now have to walk around with bare legs.

The young girl that day in the D.P. camp was the very same woman who came to visit the family during the *shivah*. She had held onto and cherished these socks for fifty years and now brought them along to the *shivah* to show the family the incredible righteousness and *tzidkus* of their father, the Klausenberger Rebbe, even under the most trying of conditions.

A Match Made in Heaven

One of the most famous of the Chassidic Rebbes of Lithuania was the Stoliner Rebbe, Rav Yisrael Perlow *zt"l*, who was known as the "*Yanuka*" - "young child," or "babe" of Karlin-Stolin. He became the rebbe of thousands of chassidim at the tender age of four when his father, the great Rav Asher of Karlin *zt"l*, passed away.

R' Yisrael was a *tzaddik*, a fine composer, and had a commanding understanding of worldly affairs. He traveled extensively, seeing to the needs of many communities. He died in Frankfurt am Main during one of his many travels and was buried there. After his death he was sometimes referred to as the Frankfurter Rebbe but he was most endeared to the masses through his title, "*Yanuka*." Despite the desecration of many Jewish cemeteries in Nazi Germany, incredibly, the Rebbe's grave was never vandalized.

After World War II, Frankfurt, Germany became a center for displaced persons. Most of these tortured souls were people who had been liberated from the concentration camps; others came to find possible survivors of their families; while yet others believed that in Frankfurt, they would be able to find ways to immigrate to Eretz Yisrael or America. Among the many refugees were a handful of chassidim from Karlin-Stolin. For them, the Frankfurter's grave was a source of strength and solace.

One day a chassid of Karlin-Stolin who, along with his son, had been fortunate enough to survive the war, came to pray at the Rebbe's grave. He placed a stone on the gravestone, as is customary, and said a few chapters of Tehillim. He then poured out his heart before the holy grave, begging the Rebbe to intercede on his behalf with the Almighty, so that his son would find a proper mate, befitting a pious young man. When he finished, he wrote his son's name and his request on a piece of paper, folded the paper or "*kvittel*" neatly, and placed it in one of the crevices of the tombstone. The chassid left the Frankfurter's grave in high spirits, sure that his prayers and request would be answered.

A few days later another Chassidic Jew, also a Stoliner chassid, found his way to the city of Frankfurt and to the *Yanuka* of Stolin's grave. Like the thousands before him, he told his bitter tale and asked for the Rebbe's blessing. He too, was fortunate, more than many others. Though he had lost almost his entire family, one daughter of marriageable age survived. He prayed now, on his daughter's behalf, that she should meet a fine Jewish boy, who if possible, should also be a chassid of Karlin-Stolin.

As he was about to write his request, he realized that he did not have anything to write on. He felt around in every pocket but he had no slip of paper. Just then, a gentle wind blew and a piece of paper fluttered to his feet. He picked up the paper and wrote his request in the customary manner. As he was about to fold the "*kvittel*", he noticed that the other side also had writing on it. It was the "*kvittel*" of none other than the first chassid of Karlin-Stolin who had appeared earlier. His eyes widened in astonishment as he read the other chassid's request and he knew that this was, undoubtedly, the instant answer to his prayer.

A few days later, a wedding took place in a D.P. camp in Germany. The two young people whose fathers had prayed at the *tzaddik's* grave were united in matrimony. A new generation of devout Stoliner chassidim began under the ever-vigilant eye of the *Yanuka* of Stolin, the Frankfurter Rebbe.

| RAV ELIEZER SILVER |

Chief Rabbi of the United States ... and Canada!

While feeding thousands of Holocaust survivors who were dispersed throughout Germany and abroad in Displaced Persons camps, the Va'ad Hatzalah rescue organization did not forget their original stated mission: to bring *roshei yeshivah*, their *talmidim*, and other Torah scholars to freedom. The Va'ad labored to secure entry visas to the United States or Palestine for hundreds of surviving scholars who made their way into Poland and Western Europe. In July, 1946, a pogrom in Kielce, Poland took the lives of forty-two Jews and wounded hundreds more. The Va'ad responded with herculean - and often improvised - relief efforts to evacuate the scholars as quickly as possible.

Rav Eliezer Silver *zt"l*, acting as a Va'ad representative and president of the *Agudas Harabbanim*, was urged to travel to Europe to assess the rescue effort there. He spent three months visiting Holland, Belgium, France, Czechoslovakia, Germany and Poland. Wearing a surplus American Army uniform purchased for this mission, he moved about freely, distributing funds to build *mikvaos, yeshivos* and kosher kitchens. He gave out money at such a frenetic pace, that he was forced to cable back to the Va'ad's New York headquarters requesting more funds. He also located children who had been in hiding throughout the war, including his famous encounters with church and monastery leaders who refused to relinquish - and often even acknowledge - the Jewish children within their walls.

R' Silver never seemed to rest. He distributed money so quickly that, after depleting Va'ad funds, he raised additional cash against his own IOUs (all of which he redeemed, personally). He gave everything he had brought with him to the needy Jews of Europe - everything but the clothes he wore. The desperation was frightening. In Lodz, R' Silver opened a relief office in a private home. Shortly thereafter, he had to escape through the roof because the enormous crowd had become dangerous, as everyone clamored for help.

"He is living on Torah, not food," a religious U.S. Army chaplain wrote about R' Silver in August 1946, "and he is comforting and lecturing beyond the capacity of any five humans half his age!"

This bearded rabbi in uniform did experience some awkward moments, as well. Once, when an Allied soldier saluted him, R' Silver did not recognize the gesture and did not respond in kind. The soldier's surprise soon turned to suspicion, causing the soldier to doubt the bearded man in uniform's credentials. He immediately got in touch with American occupation officials and expressed his concerns.

The officials confronted R' Silver and demanded to see his military identification - after all, he was a man in uniform. R' Silver stared defiantly and proclaimed, "I don't need papers. I am the Chief Rabbi of the United States and Canada!" (It came out "United Shtates" in R' Laizer's characteristic accent.)

Understandably, the American authorities did not believe him and were not inclined to let him go. Chagrined, R' Silver pointed to the telephone and barked, "You shtill don't believe me? Call Shenator Taft. Tell him Shilver's here!"

The officials looked at each other. They didn't know that the small man, seething with almost comical anger, enjoyed a personal and political friendship with the powerful senator from the great state of Ohio, Robert Taft.

After lengthy delays the exasperated American occupation officials finally managed to get through to Senator Taft's Washington office. They started describing the rabbi who was there with them.

"What?" Taft shouted when he learned whom they were holding. The Senator knew that if his friend remained in the occupation office much longer, the rabbi - not the army - would be running Germany. Such was the magnitude of R' Laizer's personality and leadership capabilities. He quickly vouched for R' Silver's mission and credentials.

"Get him out of there as soon as possible," Senator Taft added, laughing, "before he takes over!"

| RAV MOSHE TEITELBAUM (YISMACH MOSHE) |

A Legacy of *Mesiras Nefesh*

A number of years ago, a tour group of about thirty men traveled to Eastern Europe, to visit and pray at the graves of the great men buried there, the *kivrei tzaddikim*. They chartered a bus and drove for four days through parts of Hungary, Austria, Slovakia and the Czech

Republic, stopping at the graves of many of the great *gedolim* of yesteryear who were buried in the various towns and cities. At every stop, they learned about the *tzaddikim*, their accomplishments, and often learned from the *sefarim* that they wrote. Then, they would recite Tehillim and move on to the next site.

One of the men on the trip was a bit older than the rest, a middle-aged man, who felt truly inspired to stand and say Tehillim at the grave of each *tzaddik*. Yet, one place was different. When the group arrived in Uhel and stood in front of the gravestone of the holy *Yismach Moshe*, Rav Moshe Teitelbaum *zt"l*, the man felt more than inspiration. In his own words, "I couldn't stop crying. I could barely breathe!" He hadn't felt this way by any of the other *kevarim*, and could not understand what brought about this subconscious emotional reaction, specifically in Uhel, which caused him to become short of breath.

When he arrived back home, he mentioned this unusual phenomenon to his elderly father, a man of ninety-three years, who spent his entire life steeped in Torah and *avodas* Hashem. At once, the sharp and alert man replied, "I know exactly what happened. I have no doubt!"

A great story was sure to follow and the man waited expectantly to hear his father's words. "I probably should have told you this story earlier but now I am certain that you must hear this." The elderly man looked wistful and continued. "I was a student learning in yeshivah when the terrible war finally hit us in Hungary, in 1944. The German army plowed through Hungary with incredible speed and there was little time for any of us to get away or escape. A friend of mine and I managed to slip out of the Nazis' evil grasp and we began a trek that took us through village after village all along the

Hungarian countryside, hoping to remain out of sight and away from the advancing Nazis.

"One night, we came to the small town of Sembaty and what we saw was heartbreaking. The Germans deported all the residents and destroyed anything and everything that was Jewish within the town. The synagogue was totally wrecked, all the benches overturned and the *sefarim* thrown about, haphazardly. As a final insult to the Jews, the Nazis removed one of the large Torah scrolls, unrolled the parchment and stood it up outside the door of the main synagogue for everyone to see. It was as if they were taunting us with the way they dealt with our holy and precious items: "We have made this town *Judenrein*! The Jews will have no need for these scrolls anymore!" It was an absolute disgrace to behold the *sifrei* Torah in that state and my friend and I decided right then and there, that we could not allow this desecration of a *sefer* Torah to remain.

"Although it weighed us down heavily, we struggled to lift the desecrated Torah and we carried it in our arms as we continued on our trek. The Torah was torn into two pieces; I carried one half while he carried the other. We walked this way for many miles throughout the rolling Hungarian countryside.

"For a while we managed to elude the Germans and, believe me, it wasn't easy. Finally, however, we realized that there really were no more places for us to hide. The Nazis were all around us and our capture was inevitable.

"We continued to walk a bit more until we reached the town of Uhel. There, we made a decision: Since our capture was imminent, we wanted to do one final mitzvah with extreme *mesiras nefesh* and devotion. At least, we would give up our lives with the knowledge that we had accorded a holy *sefer* Torah its proper honor and respect. We went straight to the cemetery in Uhel and began digging with our bare hands in the dirt right next to the grave of the *tzaddik*, the *Yismach Moshe*. Then, we took the two pieces of the rescued *sefer* Torah that we had been carrying with us and laid it to rest in that shallow grave. After the terrible destruction and desecration that the Nazis did to our people and to our Torah, this one final act of *mesiras nefesh* was to be the restoration - however small - of *kavod haTorah* - the honor of the Torah. We buried the *sefer* Torah with tears streaming down our cheeks and covered over the shallow grave. From there we ran away and, with the miraculous assistance of Hashem, somehow survived."

After a moment of stunned silence, the father concluded, "*Chazal* tell us that when Avraham Avinu led Yitzchak to the *akeidah*, he raised his eyes and 'saw the place from a distance.' The place he saw was the holy site of the Beis Hamikdash and he felt the spirituality and *kedushah* emanating from there, not just for himself, but 'from a distance' - for the many distant generations of Klal Yisrael that will come to pass and will, likewise, be nurtured and contained by the holiness therein."

The elderly man looked fondly at his son and said, "I have no doubt that what you felt standing there in front of the grave of the *Yismach Moshe* was the electric current derived from the mitzvah of *mesiras nefesh* that I performed over sixty years ago!"

| THE SATMAR REBBE AND RAV YAAKOV KAMENETZKY |
Diligence and Truth

In the early days of Mesivta Torah Vodaath, the yeshivah was located on South Third Street, in the Williamsburg section of Brooklyn, before it eventually moved during the 1960s to its present location in Kensington. Rav Yaakov

Kamenetzky *zt"l*, the famed *rosh yeshivah*, would customarily walk from his house to the yeshivah during the warm summer months, accompanied by one or more of his students. They would discuss issues of Torah learning as they walked, and it was deemed quite an honor to walk with the *rosh yeshivah* on his occasional strolls.

On one of these walks, R' Yaakov and a *talmid* walking with him encountered the renowned Satmar Rebbe, Rav Yoel Teitelbaum *zt"l*, who was likewise strolling with a group of chassidim to his nearby *beis medrash* in Williamsburg. It was quite a sight to see, as the great chassidishe Rebbe and the great *Litvishe rosh yeshivah* stopped and greeted one another with the highest respect and regard. However, after a moment, R' Yaakov was able to discern that the Rebbe, R' Yoilish, as he was fondly called, whose countenance was usually extraordinarily bright, did not look well that day.

R' Yaakov inquired about this and the Satmar Rebbe remarked, "These days are especially difficult for me." He was referring to the time of year when he and many of his congregants observed the *yahrtzeits* of their martyred families and neighbors who had been deported from their hometown in the Hungarian city of Satmar, to the Nazi death camps in 5704 (1944). As the memories were still quite fresh in the minds of R' Yoilish and a considerable constituency of Satmar chassidim, the pain of those tragic events was readily apparent on their faces.

R' Yaakov endeavored to steer the conversation to a happier subject matter and asked the Rebbe, "Tell me, how was the Rebbe saved from Europe?"

R' Yoilish was glad to take his mind temporarily off the melancholy thoughts of his family's death and began explaining the details of the Kastner Transport, an amazing episode in war history which allowed the Satmar Rebbe and over 1,680 Hungarian Jews to be transferred into Switzerland, as a result of the exorbitant bribes paid by Rudolf Kastner to Adolf Eichmann. R' Yoel was among a group of religious Jews chosen to be included in the transport. Although they were supposed to travel directly to Switzerland and to safety, the train was diverted to Bergen Belsen for over four months and the refugees thought they would never see the light of freedom. Thankfully, Kastner's negotiations bore fruit and the train with its passengers eventually reached the safe haven of Switzerland.

The Satmar Rebbe finished speaking, but R' Yaakov persisted in his questioning. "Rebbe, this was not my question. What I meant to ask was in what *zechus* - merit - was the Rebbe saved?"

This time the Satmar Rebbe hesitated, unsure of how he should respond to this line of questioning. R' Yaakov nudged him a bit to reply by adding with a smile, "It's fine to tell me. This is between us."

R' Yoilish was thoughtful for a moment. Then he said, "*Rosh Yeshivah*, I believe it was due to my never going to sleep." He was alluding to his well-known diligence in the study of Torah whereby he would remain in one stationary position, learning Torah until he dozed off, then continue on from where he had left off as soon as he awoke. R' Yoilish was universally known for this extraordinary trait, and in his humility, he attributed his salvation to his diligence in learning.

Then, with the usual twinkle back in his radiant eyes, the Satmar Rebbe looked at R' Yaakov and countered, "Nu, what about the *Rosh Yeshivah*? In what merit was he saved?" R' Yaakov had escaped the impending blazing inferno, coming to America in 5697 (1937) before the outbreak of hostilities. In fact, one of his major considerations for leaving Europe was his view that war was imminent. In this regard, R' Yaakov was unlike many other notable individuals who either believed that the brewing tempest would soon simmer down, or that they must remain with their congregations and *yeshivos* no matter what was to happen.

This time, R' Yaakov hesitated somewhat and was reluctant to reply. In a spirit of kinship, the Satmar Rebbe objected good-naturedly saying, "Look, I revealed my thoughts to you!" He was obviously expecting R' Yaakov to do the same.

Whereupon, the great *rosh yeshivah* of Torah Vodaath responded in a humble voice, "I think it may be due to the fact that as far back as I can remember, I never in my life uttered a lie!"

| REB ELIMELECH (MIKE) TRESS |
Finding the Stoliner Rebbe

As President of Agudas Yisrael and one of the most influential builders of Orthodox Judaism in America, the famed *askan*, Reb Elimelech (Mike) Tress *z"l*, was granted a commission with the U.S. Army allowing him to tour the Displaced Persons (D.P.) camps in Europe immediately after World War II. This notable honor afforded him the opportunity to travel through war-torn Europe, providing supplies, comfort and support to the many survivors he encountered. The refugees, on the other hand, were thrilled to see an Orthodox Jew outfitted with a U.S. Army garb who adhered to the strictest measures of religious practice. Here was an American who spoke fluent Yiddish, sympathized with their plight and gave them money and food to keep them going. Most of all, though, Mike gave them what they needed most: much needed encouragement and solace.

One of the emotional high points of Mike's trip was his discovery of the Stoliner Rebbe, Rav Yochanan Perlow *zt"l*, in the Feldafing D.P. camp. Son of the previous Stoliner Rebbe, the "Holy *Yanuka*" (so named because he became Rebbe at the tender age of four after the sudden passing of his father), who was famous for his Torah genius and the miracles attributed to him, even after his death, R' Yochanan suffered through the horrors of the Holocaust, never divulging his illustrious heritage. He survived the Nazis through sheer will, determination and *bitachon* in Hashem, and with little fanfare, he continued to serve Hashem after the war. It was rumored that he had survived, but no one knew for sure. Before he left for Europe, Rav Yaakov Perlow *zt"l*, the Stoliner Rebbe in Williamsburg, told Mike Tress that he believed his brother R' Yochanan was in Feldafing but that he was, almost certainly, concealing his identity.

Indeed, a few of the survivors had noticed a fellow survivor who had somehow managed to retain his beard and still wore a *kapote*. The man was extremely quiet and always kept to himself, leaving no one with a clear idea of who he really was. When the "mystery man" was asked how he had avoided having his beard cut off by the Nazis, the man replied cryptically, "I was a partisan. Some partisans fire with a gun while others shoot in another way. Everyone shoots in his own unique fashion."

Even so, people recognized an aura of spiritual greatness surrounding the mysterious stranger and, over the course of the winter, a few younger men attached themselves to the bearded Jew, who referred to himself only as "Yochanan the partisan." There were suitable living quarters for him available, however he chose to reside in a cold and damp basement which lacked the most elementary comforts, even by the primitive standards of Feldafing.

Thus, it came about that no one in Feldafing had any idea who R' Yochanan really was nor his famous lineage. Around Rosh Hashanah, a letter addressed to "Yochanan Perlow" arrived in Feldafing and when some of the chassidim from Warsaw noticed that his last name was Perlow, they asked, excitedly, if he was related to Rav Areleh Perlow *zt"l*, the Stoliner Rebbe of Warsaw (another son of the *Yanuka*, and one of five brothers). His only comment was, "What does it matter?"

When Mike Tress arrived, however, he made it his mission to find the *tzaddik*. His first question upon arriving in Feldafing was: "*Vu voint duh der Stoliner Rebbe? Far allem vill ich gein tzum Stoliner Rebbe?*" ("Where is the Stoliner Rebbe? Before anything, I want to meet the Stoliner Rebbe"). No one was sure who he was talking about, but people guessed that it might be the mysterious partisan living in the basement.

During a reception for Mike in the office of the Agudas Yisrael branch in the D.P. camp, Mike asked someone to go down to the basement and tell R' Yochanan that the visitor from America was very eager to meet him and would come down to see him. R' Yochanan, however, was not anxious to have visitors and finally agreed to come up.

As soon as he entered the room, Mike immediately recognized his face, for he looked very much like his brother, the Stoliner Rebbe of Williamsburg. Rising with great deference, Mike called out for all to hear, "Shalom aleichem, Stoliner Rebbe. Shalom aleichem. I have regards from your brother." After that, R' Yochanan was unable to hide himself from the masses and soon took on his role as successor to his father, the Stoliner Rebbe.

| RAV AHARON KOTLER |

The "Civility" of Berliners

Many of the leading *roshei yeshivah* and *baalei mussar* from the previous generation found their humble beginnings in the hallowed halls of the Slabodka Yeshivah. When the holy Alter of Slabodka, Rav Nosson Tzvi Finkel *zt"l*, would deliver his regular *shiur* in the yeshivah, some of the brightest luminaries of the day sat at his feet, eagerly drinking in the words of their *rebbi*. The Alter had a knack for knowing just what to say, to whom it must be said, and precisely when it needed to be heard. No wonder then, that the Slabodka Yeshivah not only produced tremendous Torah scholars, it created wholesome and well-rounded leaders of the next generation.

One day, as the *talmidim* sat awaiting their *rebbi*'s arrival for the daily *shiur,* a discussion ensued involving some of the assembled, including Rav Avraham Kalmanowitz *zt"l* (later the *rosh yeshivah* of Mir), Rav Eizek Sher *zt"l* (who became *rosh yeshivah* in the Slabodka Yeshivah in Eretz Yisrael) and Rav Aharon Kotler *zt"l* (the esteemed *rosh yeshivah* of the Lakewood Yeshivah). The argument was whether a Jew had anything of value to learn from the gentiles. After all, the *Shulchan Aruch* spells out clearly every action during the day that a Jew must follow and adhere to. There was nothing that halachah did not prescribe for a Jew to live his days by. If so, what could possibly be learned from the *goyim*?

One *bachur*, a young *illuy* - genius - born and raised in Berlin, Germany, was the sole dissenter. He passionately maintained that there were indeed practices and ideas that a Jew could gain from the gentiles, although one must elevate those concepts and use them properly in the service of Hashem.

His great mind and ability to grasp ever difficult concepts earned him the respect of his peers and they listened to what he had to say.

"Look," said the young genius, "at the sophistication and moral clarity of my fellow Berliners. They are precise not only in their timing but in their every action, and their well-mannered polish is known to all. Surely, there is what to be learned from them, even for a religious Jew." He argued his position while the others disagreed with him. This went on for a bit until their *rebbi*, the Alter himself, entered the room.

Without preamble, the Alter launched into a *shiur*, discussing the greatness and holiness of the Jewish people. As if he had been present during the discussion before the *shiur*, he clearly outlined the greatness of every single individual Jew and how a gentile has nothing from which a Jew needs to learn! Those in attendance were amazed at the "prophetic" clarity of the Alter, who seemed to be addressing the question they had posed right before the *shiur*.

As the students were filing out of the *shiur*, the student from Berlin sidled up to R' Aharon Kotler and insisted that, notwithstanding the great master's lecture, he still believed that the civility and etiquette of the courteous Berliners was worth emulating. Is this not an ideal worth encouraging amongst us *Yidden*, he asked? Not wishing to enter into an argument, R' Aharon shrugged and left it at that.

Troubling times came to the world, and European Jewry underwent a period of devastation unlike any ever experienced before in the annals of history. Six million European Jews gave their lives *al kiddush Hashem* at the hands of the Nazi beast; while countless others survived physically, although it would take years - if ever - to mend their emotional wounds, shattered hearts and broken souls.

Many years later, on a sunny morning in Lakewood, New Jersey, a visitor appeared on the steps of the great *yeshivah gedolah*, waiting to talk with the renowned leader of American Jewry and *rosh yeshivah*, R' Aharon Kotler. He refused to come inside and preferred to stand outside on the steps of the yeshivah.

R' Aharon finally arrived and was making his way inside in order to give his daily *shiur.* The man came over to the *Rosh Yeshivah* and asked, "R' Aharon, do you remember me?"

R' Aharon looked at him carefully, and vaguely recognized the man's face, but he just couldn't place it.

"Rosh Yeshivah," he said evenly, "I was with you in Slabodka. We learned together by the Alter. I was the *bachur* from Berlin, who so vehemently insisted that the civil practices of my fellow Berliners were worth emulating. And even after we heard a *shiur* from our holy *rebbi*, I still insisted that there was what to be gained from the gentiles."

R' Aharon nodded indicating that he did remember the man. The man's face clouded over as he began to remove his jacket. "Well, let me show you what the civility and graciousness of my fellow Berliners did for me." He took off his jacket, revealing a stump where his hand had once been. The people standing around gasped in horror.

"I was caught up in the insanity of the war. My fellow Berliners, the people I so vociferously defended, what did they do to me? They cut off my hand in cold blood, while a cheering crowd egged them on with encouragement! I was forced to learn the hard way what a Jew has to gain from the 'civil' practices and ideas of the gentiles! Our *rebbi* understood this years before, but I was too foolish and obstinate to believe him!"

He broke into bitter tears and continued to sob as R' Aharon attempted to console him.

"A Sorrow Shared is a Sorrow Halved"

When the Lakewood *rosh yeshivah*, Rav Shneur Kotler *zt"l* lost his young beloved son, the Bluzhever Rebbe, Rav Yisrael Spira *zt"l*, though well advanced in years, traveled with one of his devoted chassidim from his home in Brooklyn to New Jersey, to show respect and pay the customary condolence call during the *shivah*.

When they entered R' Shneur's house, the Rebbe was shocked at what he saw. R' Shneur, as prescribed by halachah, was sitting on a low mourner's stool. Sitting around him were about sixty men - rabbis and yeshivah students - and no one uttered a single word or sound. A pervasive sentiment of gloom and despair hung heavily in the room.

The flickering candles continuously played with the lingering shadows on the walls, while the deafening silence could practically be felt. As the Bluzhever Rebbe entered, a chair was immediately placed for him next to that of R' Shneur. All remained silent, in deference to the mourners' law that the mourner must open the conversation. When R' Shneur continued his tortured silence, R' Yisrael decided to speak.

"I envy you, R' Shneur," began the Rebbe in a soft voice. "Your son passed away, yet he left a young wife and child to carry on his name. *Baruch Hashem,* you know the place where your son is buried. Hashem blessed you with other children, and so many people are coming to comfort you in your sorrow. Not everyone has the same situation."

R' Yisrael closed his eyes and a pained expression came over his face. "I had but one daughter whose face brightened the world, a son-in-law who was a most promising young *talmid chacham,* and a grandchild who was the absolute delight of my heart. Nothing made me prouder and happier than my family. Then came the bitter war years, the Holocaust; years of separation, torture, pain and sorrow. I don't even know the day my family was murdered, nor have I any idea where the sites of their graves lie, if they even have one at all. And believe me, no one came to comfort me because we were all being murdered. Everyone experienced the same emotions and suffered through the same torturous existence." The Rebbe looked up. "R' Shneur, how can I not envy you?"

All those present remained still - there were no words to be spoken - and the Rebbe continued to talk. "The Sages tell us, 'A sorrow shared is a sorrow halved.' So many people, *rabbanim,* students, friends, and neighbors, have come to share your sorrow. R' Shneur, you must be comforted! I beg of you, Rosh Yeshivah, please be strong, for in a strange way, you are privileged."

A few days later, after the *shivah* was over, R' Shneur called the Bluzhever Rebbe and thanked him for his heartfelt words of solace which had given him the courage and strength to overcome the most difficult days of his life.

|RAV ELIEZER SILVER|
Making a *Mikvah*

During World War II, the American government, under great pressure from various organizations, created a rescue commission known as the War Refugee Board. In many respects, it failed to fully understand and encompass the necessary action needed to rescue the multitude of survivors and refugees fleeing Europe. Not having a Jewish "soul", the men who ran this government agency carried out their operations in the manner of just about every governmental body, past and present: with the bureaucratic pace of drying paint. History will attest to the fact that the WRB had the potential and intention, but lacked the wherewithal, alacrity and direction, to achieve its stated objective.

To be perfectly fair, the WRB did achieve some notable results, including the rescue of over 100,000 Jews and the distribution of vital relief services when the war ended. Of those 100,000 Jews, however, only a handful came to the United States during the war. In one unique instance, roughly 1,000 refugees, many - but not all - of them Jewish, were brought from Italy to Fort Ontario, an abandoned army base near Oswego, New York.

The Va'ad Hatzalah, the Orthodox relief organization, offered a wide range of support services, a model for its postwar efforts. Among the refugees were 300 Torah-observant Jews. The Va'ad promptly met their basic needs: kosher food, *tallis, tefillin* and a shul in which to pray. At first, only Orthodox refugees registered for kosher food. Yet, as word of its superior quality spread, the number of registrants doubled. How could the Va'ad refuse? After all, Jews wished to eat kosher. The Va'ad was delighted. In time, a second kosher kitchen was established, and a Talmud Torah for the children.

The camp's needs increased daily. The refugees requested an *eruv* in order to carry on Shabbos, and the Va'ad had no problem taking care of that need. The next request, however, was not as simple: the Jews insisted that they need a *mikvah*, to ensure spiritual sanctity in their homes. The Va'ad was happy to oblige but before they could do anything, they needed to explain the concept and importance of a *mikvah* to Joe Smart, the Quaker camp director. Without his approval, nothing could be done.

Rav Eliezer Silver *zt"l*, who had come to visit the refugees and offer them encouragement, represented the Va'ad in their attempt to receive permission for this venture. The word *mikvah* needed to be translated into English, and one way to do this was to use the word, ritualarium, which had been coined earlier while building Boro Park's first *mikvah*.

"A ritualarium," R' Silver explained in his heavily accented English to Joe Smart, "is a bath where Jewish men and women immerse themselves for religious purposes, separately, of course."

Smart nodded knowingly. "What you need is a swimming pool," he said chirpily. R' Laizer shook his head indicating that a swimming pool was not acceptable. He decided to try to explain the concept of a *mikvah*, by showing Smart how to build one.

"Okay. First," he said, "the Talmud requires that a *mikvah* must have at least 40 *se'ah* (a minimum of 648 liters) of water."

Smart shrugged unknowingly. He had never heard of a "*se'ah*." But R' Laizer didn't notice. "Also, the space is measured in *amos* (cubits)." The camp director looked around, helplessly lost in the terminology, searching desperately for a translator.

But R' Laizer would not let him go. "*Amos* ... you know, forearms, forearms. It's measured in cubits - about the length of a forearm." He stretched out his right arm as if to demonstrate the exact dimension in true life. Joe Smart immediately agreed, taking the matter on faith.

"Rabbi, it's okay. *Amos* - cubits - that's fine." Joe realized that this diminutive rabbi had already drawn a crowd. And he still had no idea what the man was talking about!

"Okay," R' Laizer nodded, "now the water. A *mikvah* needs natural water." R' Laizer began making flowing gestures with his hands. Smart thought he understood this one. Displaying enormous patience, he smiled and said, "All water is natural. You want us to pump water in for your *mikvah*, right?"

"No, no," R' Silver shouted, arms flailing in all directions, "natural water. A *mikvah* cannot have water collected from a pipe. The water must be obtained from the sky or a river. It has to be still and natural."

Joe Smart sighed and gave up. He could not grasp the details and really had no clue what this eminent rabbi was talking about. Shrugging, he motioned to a couple of army engineers standing nearby. "Do whatever the rabbi says," he said, and slowly backed away.

The engineers had not been part of the conversation before and now ambled over to the short man with the top hat and long coat. Before they had even reached him, R' Laizer launched into a discourse on *amos*, forearms and natural water, to the utter surprise and bewilderment of the new arrivals.

R' Eliezer Silver persevered, and in two weeks there was a *mikvah*!

"All I Need is a Gemara!"

A number of years ago, there lived a Chassidic Jew in Brooklyn by the name of Cohen, who owned a grocery store and was perceived as a simple Jew. He had survived the ghetto and concentration camps during World War II, lost many loved ones, yet his *emunah* and faith in Hashem was never shaken. He spent any available spare time sitting and learning his beloved Gemara.

When a seminary girl who boarded at the Cohen home received a letter with an enclosed picture of her family back home in the Midwest, she showed the picture to Rabbi Cohen who studied the image of the girl's brother. "This young man," he remarked, "looks very much like a man I once knew in Italy."

"Oh, my father spent some time in Italy," said the girl. "He was a chaplain in the United States Army and was with the troops that ran the displaced persons camps after the war." Rabbi Cohen was dumbstruck.

Some time later, the Cohens were blessed with a baby boy. The girl's father flew to New York for the *bris* and, after spending some time talking to Rabbi Cohen, he related the following at the *seudas mitzvah*: One of the chaplain's responsibilities was to determine each survivor's most urgent needs. He would climb onto an army truck and, using a bullhorn, would instruct the people to line up.

The survivors would file past the truck and tell the chaplain what they needed. One of those who stood on line was Rabbi Cohen. When his turn came, he looked up at the chaplain and said, "I need a gemara *Bava Kamma*."

The chaplain did not understand. He looked down at the frail, battered Jew and said kindly, "I'm here to try to get you clothing, medical supplies, whatever you need to become healthy again. So how can I help you?"

The young survivor looked up and responded, "Five and a half years ago, I was learning *Meseches Bava Kamma*. Then the Nazis came. I have not seen a Gemara since that time. Now, baruch Hashem, I am free to learn again. I want to resume my learning of *Bava Kamma*. That is what I need most. Please get me a Gemara!"

The chaplain had heard that in an old mansion near the camp, the Nazis had dumped the contents of a Hebrew library. He went to the mansion, searched throughout the heaps of books, and found a gemara *Bava Kamma*. Rabbi Cohen now truly had everything he needed.

| KLAUSENBERGER REBBE |

"A Ropshitzer *Einekel* Doesn't Wear a Ring"

Immediately after the war ended, many of the survivors who had lost their parents, brothers, sisters - entire families that had been wiped out by the Nazi's failed plan of Jewish extermination - felt that it was their obligation and duty as Jews to defy the Germans and repopulate the Jewish people. Many youngsters, teenagers who had witnessed so much horror in their lives as to be equal in this area to elderly individuals, looked to settle down and get married. In fact, within a few short months after liberation, the city of Munich, Germany already contained a sizable population of Jewish couples. Many who were brought to the DP camp in Fehrenwald after the liberation were now branching out and moving to Munich since Fehrenwald was, after all, still a camp. Every Shabbos and Yom Tov, people came to Fehrenwald to be with fellow survivors or family members there, and also to be near the Klausenberger Rebbe.

The Rebbe breathed life into thousands of survivors after the war. He had personally lost his wife and eleven children to the Nazi murderers, yet, despite his tremendous personal suffering, he continuously encouraged and uplifted those around him. He injected faith and trust in Hashem into the hearts of so many. It was an inspirational experience to speak with him, or even just to see him. So many downtrodden Jews owe much of their spiritual rejuvenation to the Klausenberger Rebbe.

My grandparents, Alter and Rushka Kurz *a"h* were among those young couples who had married soon after the war. As soon as he arrived in Germany, Alter had heard that some of his relatives were alive and well and residing in Fehrenwald, and he had been anxious to be reunited with them. Alter and Rushka felt at home in Fehrenwald as soon as they arrived, and Alter's family was extremely good to them. They spent every holiday and many *Shabbosos* in Fehrenwald after that first reunion. It was Alter's relatives who advised them to go in and speak with the Klausenberger Rebbe, whom Alter had met on many occasions on his visits to Sanz before the war.

The Rebbe knew the entire Kurz family quite well. Alter traced his lineage back to the holy Ropshitzer Rebbe, Rav Naftali Tzvi Hurvitz *zt"l*, and the Kurz family maintained familial connections to many of the leading Chassidic dynasties, including Bobov, Sanz and Ropshitz. When Alter and Rushka entered the Klausenberger Rebbe's room, they were immediately struck by the special kindness radiating from his holy face. He greeted them with so much love; they felt as if they were his own children.

Alter introduced himself (as he had been a young *bachur* when he had last seen the Rebbe) and the Rebbe grasped his hand tightly. The Rebbe spoke with the two for quite a while, inquiring after their well-being and pouring strength and inspiration into their broken souls. All the while, the Rebbe was grasping Alter's hand warmly. They had not realized that the Rebbe had noticed a gold ring on Alter's finger, a trinket that a friend had recently given him and he had worn ever since, without much thought about it. The Rebbe, with his piercing perception and deep sensitivity, was gently working the ring off of Alter's finger while they were speaking.

When he finally let go of Alter's hand, the Rebbe held up the ring and said, "*Ich hub kein nisht gevist az a Ropshitzer einekel trugt a ringel!*" ("I never imagined that a descendant of the Ropshitzer wears a ring!") The Rebbe smiled and handed the ring back to a surprised and embarrassed Alter, who quickly slipped it into his pocket.

Alter and Rushka left the room feeling very warm, uplifted and inspired by the Rebbe. He had shown them, through his words and actions, that he truly understood and cared about them as individuals. From his personal example, they gained the courage to rebuild, and strength to continue to serve Hashem with devotion.

When they arrived home in Munich, Alter took the ring out of his pocket and stared at it for a few moments, absorbing the Rebbe's message about his stature as a *chassidishe* Yid. Then he put the ring down on their small table and went to sleep with the vision of the holy Klausenberger Rebbe filling his thoughts. When he awoke, inexplicably, the ring wasn't there. He never found it again.

Wiesenthal and the "Half-Empty Cup"

Towards the end of the Second World War, the renowned Nazi-hunter, Simon Wiesenthal, was confined in a concentration camp. A new arrival had smuggled in a siddur and Wiesenthal admired his courage, for by risking discovery of a Jewish prayer book, he was risking his own death. His admiration soon changed, however, when he discovered that the courageous smuggler was not doing his heroic deed for the sake of doing good. Rather, he was bartering fifteen minutes rental of the siddur in exchange for one-fourth of a day's meager rations from each renter. Although the inmates were emaciated, they willingly gave up their food to make the exchange. In time, the owner of the siddur died before anyone else, for the huge quantities of soup and additional rations he ingested were too much for his shriveled system to handle.

After the war, the great Rav of Cincinnati, Rav Eliezer Silver *zt"l*, visited many displaced persons camps on behalf of the Va'ad Hatzalah. He arranged prayer services and gave words of encouragement to the survivors. After noticing that one man, Simon Wiesenthal, did not come to any of the prayer services or addresses, R' Silver decided to visit him.

R' Silver was a small man and close to 75 years old, but his mind was sharp and his voice was youthful. "So, they tell me you are angry with G-d," he said in Yiddish, as he smiled and put his hand on Wiesenthal's shoulder.

Wiesenthal looked at him and replied, "Not exactly with Him, but with one of His servants." He told him the story of the siddur smuggler.

R' Silver's smile never broke. "And that's all you have to tell me?"

"Isn't that enough, Rabbi?" asked Wiesenthal cautiously.

"You silly man," he said warmly, "So you look only at the man who took something? Why don't you look instead at all the men who gave something?" He squeezed Wiesenthal's hand and left.

The experience made a tremendous impression on the young Wiesenthal and he began attending services the very next day. In the words of Simon Wiesenthal: "Ever since, I have always tried to remember that there are two sides to each and every situation."

| RAV YISRAEL ZEV GUSTMAN |
A Belated *Shivah*

From his early years as a child prodigy until he reached the respected position of *dayan* - judge - in the rabbinical court of Rav Chaim Ozer Grodzenski *zt"l* at age 20, the life and times of Rav Yisrael Zev Gustman *zt"l* are recounted with awe in the yeshivah world. It is said, that a singular brilliant insight which R' Yisrael Zev shared with his fellow students as a young man, was later repeated to R' Chaim Ozer, who was so astounded by its brilliance, that he invited the young student to repeat this same insight the following day in his office in Vilna. Unbeknownst to the young genius, the insight clinched an argument in a complex case that had been debated among the judges in R' Chaim Ozer's court, allowing a woman to remarry. R' Yisrael Zev was soon asked to join the court himself, a distinguished honor of the greatest kind.

While a long productive career in Vilna could have been anticipated, Jewish life in and around Vilna was obliterated by the pain and fear of World War II. R' Gustman escaped, though not unscathed. He hid among graves. He hid in caves. He hid in a pig pen. He somehow survived.

After arriving in Eretz Yisrael and establishing Yeshivas Netzach Yisrael Ramailles, R' Gustman taught a small group of loyal students six days a week. His yeshivah never ranked among the large institutions of the time, yet this no less diminished the *rosh yeshivah's* stature amongst the *rabbanim* of his time.

On Thursday afternoons, however, for a few short hours, Yeshivas Netzach Yisrael became the center of the Torah world. At precisely noon, the *beis medrash* would fill to capacity: *rabbanim, roshei yeshivah, dayanim,* intellectuals, even a Supreme Court justice and various Orthodox university professors, would disrupt their busy daily schedules and participate with those who sought a high-level Talmud class offering a taste of what had nearly been destroyed. When R' Gustman delivered a gemara *shiur,* Vilna was once again alive and vibrant. One could almost feel the air of "Yerushalayim of the West" - a term with which the city of Vilna was affectionately referred to - permeating throughout the jam-packed study hall. Not even the maze of ceiling fans could whisk out this feeling of pre-war Torah. Who wouldn't want to be a part of this lofty and intellectual ideal?

One of the regular participants was a professor at the Hebrew University of Jerusalem, Robert J. (Yisrael) Aumann. Once a promising yeshivah student, Aumann had eventually decided to pursue a career in academia, and on December 10, 2005, he was even awarded a Nobel Prize in Economics. Yet, his weekly participation in R' Gustman's *shiur* was part of his weekly schedule which he refused to give up, together with many other illustrious residents of Jerusalem.

The year was 1982. Once again, Israel was at war. Soldiers were mobilized, reserve units activated. Among those called to duty was a reserve officer, a university student who made his living as a high school teacher. His name was Shlomo Aumann, Professor Aumann's son. On the eve of the 19th of Sivan, in particularly fierce combat, Shlomo fell in battle.

When the unfortunate news hit the streets, R' Gustman mobilized his yeshivah: each and every one of his students joined him in performing the mitzvah of burying the dead. At the cemetery, R' Gustman was agitated. He surveyed the rows of graves of the young men, soldiers who died defending the land. On the way back from the cemetery, R' Gustman turned to another passenger in the car and sighed, "They are all holy - every single soldier."

The Aumann family had just returned from the cemetery and would now begin the week of mourning, seven days of *shivah*, for their loss. R' Gustman felt that he needed to be there and asked a student to drive him to the *shivah* house.

When R' Gustman walked in, all those present rose in his honor and a seat next to the professor was immediately placed for him.

"*Rebbi*," said Professor Aumann when he sat down, "you have a yeshivah to see to. I truly appreciate your coming to the cemetery and sharing in my grief, but now is time for the rosh yeshivah to return to his yeshivah."

R' Gustman nodded gravely but indicated that he would like to say a few words. He spoke, first in Yiddish and then in Hebrew, so that all those assembled would understand. "I am sure that you don't know this, but I had a son named Meir. He was a beautiful child. During the Holocaust, he was taken from my arms and executed before my very eyes. Through the grace of G-d, I escaped. I later bartered my child's shoes so that we would have food, but I was never able to eat that food - I gave it away to others. How could I?" R' Gustman paused, "my Meir is a *kadosh* - he is holy - he and all the six million who perished are holy."

The room was still and spell-bound. R' Gustman turned to the mourners and continued. "Let me tell you what is transpiring now in the World of Truth, in Gan Eden. My Meir is welcoming your Shlomo into the *minyan* and is saying to him 'I died because I am a Jew - but I wasn't able to save anyone else. You, on the other hand, died defending the Jewish People and the Land of Israel.' My Meir is a *kadosh* - but your Shlomo is a *shliach tzibur* - a *chazzan* in that holy, heavenly *minyan*!"

Then to the awed group, R' Gustman added, "I never had the opportunity to sit *shivah* for my Meir. If you don't mind, please allow me to sit here with you just a little longer."

There was not a dry eye in the room. Professor Aumann finally spoke. "I thought I could never be comforted, but *Rebbi*, you have comforted me." R' Gustman did not allow his painful memories to control his life. He found solace in his *talmidim*, his daughter, his grandchildren, and in every Jewish soul.

| KAPYCZNITZER REBBE |

Peace at all Costs

Rav Avraham Yehoshua Heschel of Kapyschnitz *zt"l* (1888-1967) was named after his paternal ancestor, the renowned Apter Rav *zt"l*. He was especially regarded as an "*ohev* Yisrael," a lover of his people, and even called his classic *sefer* by that name. His descendant, the Rebbe of Kapyschnitz, surely inherited this love for his fellow Jew and was no less an "*ohev* Yisrael" than his illustrious patriarch.

The Rebbe managed to get out of Nazi-controlled Vienna, and not a minute too soon. He re-established his Chassidic court on the Lower East Side and worked tirelessly to rescue as many Jews as he could from the Nazi inferno.

In post World War II America, he carried the pain and suffering of countless individuals on his weak and frail shoulders. Indeed, often when he heard the problems of others, he would break down in uncontrollable weeping. The grief of his fellow Jews tormented him much more than his own afflictions, and, countless times, the Rebbe put his name and honor at risk in an attempt to help others.

A great example of his empathy for his fellow refugees occurred soon after the war. A broken survivor of the Nazi regime showed up at the Rebbe's door. He had just arrived from Europe and was hoping to settle in America. His wife, however, had been refused entry into the United States due to her ill health. She was stuck on Ellis Island, in limbo, awaiting imminent deportation. Believing that coming to America was a way of putting the gruesome past behind them, the man was inconsolable and indicated that, should his wife indeed be deported, he had nothing left to live for. He wouldn't think twice about giving up his own life.

The Kapyschnitzer Rebbe began to shake. "Don't worry, please don't worry," he implored. "I promise you that by next week your wife will be here together with you!"

A promise from the Rebbe; this is what the man needed to hear. Upon hearing the Rebbe's words, an immediate feeling of calm overtook the distressed man and, greatly relieved, he went away a new person.

One of the Rebbe's Chassidim had witnessed the entire scene with the distressed man. The Rebbe's words were out of character; he could not remember when the Rebbe had ever made such a bold statement - effectively guaranteeing a miracle! He gathered up the courage to ask the Rebbe how it was possible for him to make such an extraordinary promise like that. The chance of this poor, ill woman being allowed into the country was slim to none. This amounted to no less than promising a miracle!

The Kapyschnitzer Rebbe sighed. "You saw how desperate the poor man was," the Rebbe replied. "My first concern was to calm him down and, *baruch* Hashem, I succeeded. At least for the next week he will feel better. If after a week he sees that I was wrong and his wife was deported, he will say, 'Avraham Yehoshua is not a real *rebbe*, Avraham Yehoshua is a liar.' But at least for a week I succeeded in bringing some peace into his life."

With that the Rebbe began to recite the *pesukim* of Tehillim with intense emotion. As tears streamed down his face, he was overheard pleading softly, "Please Hashem, please see to it that Avraham Yehoshua didn't say a lie. I was only trying to help a Jew in a dismal situation. Please don't let me be a liar." In this fashion, his prayers continued long into the night.

The Almighty heard his prayers. Through a wondrous turn of events, the woman was granted permission to stay in America and was reunited with her husband. A liar he was not; Hashem would make sure of that!

The Safety of Flight

To understand the greatness of our *gedolim*, past and present, one must recognize the concept of *"daas Torah"* that these towering personalities, as a direct result of their total immersion and supreme knowledge of Torah, are imbued with. It includes a unique understanding of the workings of the world as they view every event and occurrence exclusively through the lens of Torah, often with startling insights.

A famous incident occurred that became well-known and widely publicized. Just after World War II had ended, during those uncertain days in Europe and beyond, time and resources were of critical importance to assist untold numbers of Jews to move on in their shattered lives. The Va'ad Hatzalah, the Orthodox rescue organization, led by Rav Aharon Kotler *zt"l*, the Lakewood Rosh Yeshivah, and other great personalities, worked tirelessly to this effect. As busy as they were during the war years trying to rescue thousands upon thousands of Jews from annihilation, the aftermath of the war presented a whole new host of issues that were no less needy and exceptional in their importance.

One of these issues came up suddenly and it was necessary to send a representative of the Va'ad Hatzalah to Paris on an emergency rescue mission. R' Aharon requested that a certain rabbi drop everything and fly to Paris immediately. Of course, the man agreed and a flight was arranged.

The flight that this rabbi was to have taken to Paris was scheduled to leave at night and everything seemed to be on schedule. However, at 3:00 in the morning, R' Aharon was awakened by a call from the rabbi's wife. Sobbing hysterically, she told him that she had just been informed that her husband's plane had crashed over the Atlantic Ocean, and everyone on board was reported killed. Her hysterical cries were heart wrenching.

R' Aharon was silent for a moment, collecting his thoughts. Finally he spoke in a calm and soothing voice. "Don't worry," he said, "your husband is alive. He was not on that plane."

This did not help to calm the sobbing woman. "It's not possible," the woman cried, saying that she had seen the plane tickets with which her husband was traveling and it matched the flight number that was reported crashed over the ocean. "He's dead," she wept in a loud voice, nearly out of control. "My husband is dead. I know he is."

"No," R' Aharon said, a bit more firmly this time. "He cannot be dead. I am telling you that he was not on that flight."

The woman was taken aback at the firmness in his voice and asked how the *rosh yeshivah* could be so sure. He explained, "It says in the gemara that harm will not come to those on a mission to perform a mitzvah. Your husband was traveling for the sole purpose of saving Jewish lives - an enormously important mitzvah for the Jewish people. Therefore, he could not be hurt, and you are not permitted to observe *shivah* - the seven day period of mourning."

The woman listened to the *rosh yeshivah's* words, and it calmed her. R' Aharon promised to look into the matter and hung up.

Early that very morning, R' Aharon called the airline directly about the flight in question. He was told that it had indeed crashed and unfortunately all aboard were killed.

R' Aharon seemed puzzled; how could this be? The words of *Chazal* are immutable. It simply wasn't possible that the Sages should be wrong. The phone was quiet for a moment.

Then, R' Aharon inquired about the passenger in question. This time, there was a short delay.

"Good news," explained the airline representative. The rabbi in question had not been on that flight; he had missed his connecting flight and was forced to travel with another airplane. But not to worry, the representative assured him, the second flight had arrived safely.

R' Aharon immediately called the rabbi's wife to tell her the good news. The woman wept - this time for joy - at the news that her husband was indeed safe.

"The Torah spells it out quite clearly," R' Aharon explained, "so your husband could not have been injured in any way."

Don't You Think It's Time?

Shlomo Rosenberg and Maurice Schechter glanced at each other as they completed the long check-in procedure at El Al's boarding gate in Heathrow International Airport in London. Shlomo walked right behind Maurice through the jet-way to the plane. Thankfully, they had been assigned adjacent seats.

The plane departed London for Tel Aviv at 6 a.m. As the plane lifted off, it appeared that it was flying directly into the morning sun. It flew across the English Channel, heading eastward over Germany, while Maurice Schechter sullenly stared at the ground below. He did not encourage conversation between himself and his seat companion.

Shlomo took his *tallis* and *tefillin* from the overhead bin and slowly inched his way to the back of the plane where a *minyan* was forming to *daven* Shacharis. When he returned to his seat, he tapped Maurice on the shoulder and said gently, "We just finished *davening*. Maybe you didn't feel like joining the *minyan*, but would you like to borrow my *tallis* and *tefillin* before I put them away?"

Maurice glowered. "Let me tell you something! I don't need your, or anybody else's *tallis* and *tefillin*. I have nothing to do with Him. When they," he slowed his speech and pointed to the earth below, "when they took my youngest son, when they told me to go to the right and shoved my son to the left, from that time until this day, I have no use for Him!"

Momentary silence prevailed. "You are right," whispered Shlomo. "It was presumptuous of me to interfere with your private thoughts. You don't have to explain anything. But we can still be friends and talk about other matters. After all, we are both going to Israel. But let me ask you just one more question: If you are so angry with G-d, why are you going to Israel?

"What do you mean, why am I going to Israel?" Maurice sputtered, "I am angry with G-d, but not with His people. I love the Jewish people, and I want to spend time with them, especially during this season of the year. Now, on condition that we don't talk about Him, we can be friendly."

Soon, the big jet touched down at Ben Gurion Airport, and Shlomo and Maurice had become friends. Clearing customs, they agreed to share a cab to Yerushalayim.

Shlomo anxiously watched pedestrians as the cab zoomed down King George Street, turned on two wheels at Gershon Agron Street, and sped down Dovid Hamelech Street before stopping in front of the King David Hotel. Breathlessly, he alighted, paid half the fare, and the cab lurched forward without giving him an opportunity to ask Maurice where he was staying.

This was Shlomo's fifth annual trip to Yerushalayim for Rosh Hashanah, Yom Kippur, and Sukkos. Six years ago, when his wife passed away, he decided to spend these holidays in the holy city. On his first trip, he found a small shul up the street from the hotel, tucked behind a tall wooden fence, where a middle-aged *chazzan* with a sweet voice *davened* with great fervor. He loved that *chazzan* and therefore, returned each year.

Between Rosh Hashanah and Yom Kippur, he walked the streets of Yerushalayim, always keeping his eyes open for his new friend, Maurice, but to his distress, they never met.

During a break in the service after Yizkor on Yom Kippur, Shlomo walked toward Liberty Park. It was not far from the shul, and he thought that he would be able to rest under a shady tree. Usually, the din of children playing resounded throughout the park. On this day, it was nearly empty. Instead of children, though, sitting right there on a bench, shaded by a large, broad-leafed tree, he recognized Maurice, who was munching on a sandwich.

A sandwich? On Yom Kippur? He walked over and sat down next to Maurice. "My friend, I know that you are angry with G-d and that you want to have nothing to do with Him. The fact that you are eating on Yom Kippur is your business ... but your son, what did he do that you refuse to recite a prayer in his memory?"

Maurice turned sullenly away. "You promised," he reminded Shlomo, and immediately scowled into stony silence.

Shlomo sat on the bench next to him, not responding. Surprisingly, after a few minutes that seemed like an eternity, Maurice blurted out, "You might be right. I thought about it. In fact, I've thought about it for a long time. It is true that I said good-bye to Him in Auschwitz, but I never said good-bye to my son. Maybe it is time to say a prayer in his memory."

Maurice tearfully turned to Shlomo and whispered, "Somehow, meeting you has inspired me to do something about it. Won't you show me where the shul is?"

The two men clutched each other as they walked back. The *chazzan* was still standing at the *bimah*, as a long line of people waited patiently for their turn for him to recite an individual "*Kel Malei Rachamim*" in memory of their loved ones.

The line grew shorter as Maurice and Shlomo inched forward. Finally, Maurice was standing face to face with the *chazzan*.

"Please, recite '*Kel Malei Rachamim*' for my son," Maurice stuttered brokenly.

"What was your son's name," asked the *chazzan*, gently.

"His name was Pinchas ben Moshe, and he was murdered in Auschwitz." The *chazzan* paused for a moment and looked up from his siddur. "Tell me again," he insisted, "what was your son's name?"

"Pinchas ben Moshe."

"And the last name?"

"Schechter."

The *chazzan* heaved a sob. Then he grabbed Maurice in a loving embrace and cried, "*Tatte, Tatte*, I've been waiting for you!"

Torah Will Never be Forgotten

After World War II, a young Hungarian *bachur* named Shlomo was among a group of Auschwitz survivors who successfully reached the Land of Israel. With no designated destination in mind, he ended up in the city of Bnei Brak. Once there, he heard of the Ponevezher Yeshivah and decided that he would like to be a part of it.

When he entered the halls of the *beis medrash*, the sound of Torah learning warmed his heart, bringing back fond memories of the years he learned in yeshivah and an aching reminder of all that he had lost. He asked somebody who the *rosh yeshivah* was and was led to him.

The Ponevezher Rav, Rav Yosef Kahaneman *zt"l*, welcomed the new arrival. "I would like to learn in the yeshivah," said the Hungarian boy earnestly.

"Have you ever learned in yeshivah before?" asked the Rosh Yeshivah.

"Yes," said Shlomo, "before the war, I was learning in a yeshivah in the town of Veitzun, Hungary."

Suddenly, the Ponevezher Rav stood up excitedly. "Did you go through the war?" he asked. "Were you in Europe the entire time or did you get out before?"

The boy's face took on a pained look. "My entire town was sent to Auschwitz and almost everyone died. My entire family was wiped out and I have no one left and no place to go. But I want to learn here in the yeshivah, if that's okay."

"First, can you tell me something that you learned in Europe?" breathed the Rav, "anything, a line from the gemara, a *machlokes* (disagreement) between Rashi and *Tosafos*?"

The *bachur* could not understand the excitement of the Rosh Yeshivah; how he was practically jumping with anticipation. After a moment of thought, he recalled a gemara in *Maseches Chullin, perek Eilu Treifos*, and recited a famous argument that was discussed on that page. As he spoke, he could see the emotion growing on the Rav's face until he literally could not contain himself anymore.

Suddenly, without warning, the Ponevezher Rav grabbed Shlomo and emotionally kissed him on the forehead. He grabbed his hand and shook it forcefully and wouldn't let go for quite some time. Then, he began pulling the young boy out of the yeshivah and onto the street. Shlomo was bewildered but could not - perhaps would not - release his arm from the Rav's grasp. Shlomo could feel the electric current of warmth and love that had been missing for so long in his life coursing from the great man's arm directly into his fragile body. As much as he was being pulled along, he didn't want to let go.

As they half-walked, half-ran down the street, the Ponevezher Rav would call out to every person they came across, "Do you know who this is? This *bachur* went through the horrors of Auschwitz and carried a *machlokes* Rashi and *Tosafos* with him all throughout!" He repeated these words to just about every person on their route and the people responded in kind, with an other-worldly awe that Shlomo had never seen before. Meanwhile, the Rav did not stop hugging him and squeezing his hand.

Finally, they arrived at their destination, the home of the great *posek* and leader of the Jewish people, the Chazon Ish, Rav Avraham Yeshaya Karelitz *zt"l*. Apparently, it was not unusual for the Ponevezher Rav to come to his house at all hours, so when the Rav burst into the house pulling along a young emaciated yeshivah *bachur,* the Chazon Ish did not hesitate to talk to him.

Without preamble, R' Kahaneman told the Chazon Ish about the boy; how he lost his entire family in the Nazi death camps and barely managed to survive, himself. He recounted how the young boy had known the gemara in *Chullin* and how he had little difficulty recalling the argument between Rashi and *Tosafos.*

At once, the Chazon Ish stood up and took the boy's hand in his. He, too, appeared to be full of excitement and, in a voice laden with emotion, said, "My son, you are proof that the Torah will always have an existence forever and ever, a '*kiyum l'netzach*'! It will never be forgotten from Klal Yisrael. Never!"

| RAV YITZCHAK DOVID GROSSMAN |

The Parchment Wallet

In the Book of Kings (2-22) a story is related regarding King Yoshiyahu, who sent emissaries to renovate the Holy Temple which had become badly damaged. During the restoration, they discovered a Torah scroll which was rolled to *Parshas Ki Savo* and, specifically, to the portion of the *"Tochachah"* - the words of harsh criticism that were leveled at the Jewish People. The King took this as a Heavenly message that the Jews should repent in order to prevent grave suffering. He gathered together all the Jews and encouraged them to destroy all remnants of idolatry, and to serve Hashem according to the commandments of the Torah.

Recently, a ceremony in honor of the 25th anniversary of the twin cities pact between the Lower Galilee Regional Council of Israel and the Hanover district of Germany was held in Germany, and a number of dignitaries from both Israel and Germany were in attendance. The pact was to celebrate the mutual cooperation and exchange of ideas, commerce and social understanding between the two provinces.

After the ceremony, German Bundestag (Parliament) member, Detlev Herzig, of the S.P.D. party, approached the head of the Lower Galilee Regional Council, Mutty Dotan, and related a passionate story. His father had just recently passed away and, before his demise, he tearfully confessed to his son that he had been a part of the terrible Holocaust perpetrated against the Jewish People. He explained that since there are many Holocaust deniers today, he wanted to present irrevocable evidence of the truth. He told his son that he had been an officer in the German air force, the Luftwaffe, during World War II, and handed him an envelope which contained the proof.

Upon opening the envelope the astonished son found a Wehrmacht Army Officer's certificate, wrapped in a strange wallet made of parchment. His father explained that while under orders to destroy a Jewish synagogue, he had found a scroll made of parchment and cut out a piece to use as a wallet. Later he discovered that the scroll was something very holy to the Jews and regretted having desecrated so holy an item.

On his deathbed, he now told his son to give over the evidence, including the parchment wallet, to the first Jew he would meet, and ask him to deliver it to a holy Jew in Israel who would know how to use it properly. His father had died, but not before fulfilling one last act of repentance. Detlev Herzig then asked if Mutty Dotan would serve as his emissary and bring the parchment back to Israel, to be delivered to a great rabbi. Mutty said it would be his honor.

Upon returning to Israel, Mutty decided to bring the parchment to Rav Yitzchak Dovid Grossman *shlit"a*, Chief Rabbi of Migdal Ha'Emek. As exciting as the story was, R' Grossman was curious to see which part of the Torah the Nazi "happened" to cut out.

His whole body trembled as he read aloud the following words from the *parshah* containing the *Tochachah*: "If you will not be careful to perform all the words of this Torah that are written in this book to fear this honored and awesome Name, Hashem your G-d. Then Hashem will make extraordinary your blows and the blows of your offspring, great and faithful blows and evil and faithful illnesses. He will bring back upon you all the sufferings of Egypt of which you were terrified and they will cleave to you. Even any illness and any blow that is not written in this book of the Torah, Hashem will bring upon you until you are destroyed ..."

"The Nazi could have cut out any section of the Torah," exclaimed a shaken R' Grossman. "Yet Hashem led him specifically to this *parshah*. It is something which must make us reconsider our ways."

The Menorah in the Window

At the end of World War II, a young Jewish soldier in the U.S. Army found himself marching through Western Europe, liberating towns and villages from German control. At one point, Private Winneger's unit was assigned to a small German village with orders to secure the town, search for any hiding Nazis, and help the villagers in any way they could.

One night, out on patrol, Winneger saw a slim figure running through a field just outside the village. He gave chase and shouted, "Halt or I'll shoot." The figure ducked behind a tree. Winneger waited and eventually the figure came out and looked around to see if he was still being pursued. Figuring that the soldier was no longer nearby, he went to a spot near a large tree and started to dig. Winneger waited until the figure had finished digging and removed an object from the ditch. Then, he was once more on the move. Winnegar stepped out from a nearby patch and again shouted, "Halt or I'll shoot!" The figure ran. Winneger decided not to shoot but to try to catch the furtive figure. He shortly caught up and tackled him to the ground.

To his surprise, he found that he had captured a young boy. An ornate menorah had fallen from the boy's hands in the scuffle. Winneger picked up the menorah.

The boy tried to grab it back shouting in an unfamiliar dialect, "Give it to me. It's mine!" Winneger assured the boy that he was among friends. Furthermore, he told the boy, he himself was Jewish. The boy, who had just survived several years of the Holocaust and had been in a concentration camp, was distrustful of all men in uniforms. He had been forced to watch the shooting of his father. He had no idea what had become of his mother.

Winneger calmed the boy down and brought him back to his barracks. In the weeks that followed, he took the young boy, whose name was Dovid, under his wing. As they became closer and closer, Winneger's heart went out to the boy. He had lost everything in the war and he needed a stable home in which to grow up. The soldier offered Dovid the opportunity to come back to New York City with him after his tour of duty and Dovid gladly accepted. Winneger went through all the necessary paperwork and officially adopted Dovid.

After the war, Winneger settled down and became active in the New York Jewish community. An acquaintance of his, a curator of the Jewish Museum in Manhattan, once happened to see Dovid's precious menorah. He told Dovid it was a very valuable, historic, European relic and should be shared with the entire Jewish community. He offered Dovid $50,000 for the menorah, but Dovid refused the generous offer saying the menorah had been in his family for over 200 years and that no amount of money could ever make him sell it.

That year, when Chanukah came, Dovid and his newly adopted father lit the menorah in the window of their home in New York City. The candles burned bright and, for Dovid, the memory of this family heirloom put to use in happier times was an emotionally draining experience for the young boy. Afterwards, he went upstairs to his room while Winneger stayed downstairs in the room with the menorah.

Suddenly, there was a knock on the door and Winneger went to answer it. Standing by the door, he found a woman with a strong German accent who said that she was walking down the street when she saw the menorah in the window. She said that she had once had one just like it in her family and had never seen any other like it. Could she come in and take a closer look?

Winneger invited her in and said that the menorah belonged to his adopted son who could perhaps tell her more about it. Winneger went upstairs and called Dovid down to talk to the woman.

Dovid walked down the steps and abruptly stopped short. Then he shrieked, "Mama!" She, in turn, began crying hysterically as she was reunited with the son she thought she had lost forever. The only surviving members of their family, mother and son had both come to these shores independently, yet, through the miracle of the precious menorah, they found each other once again.

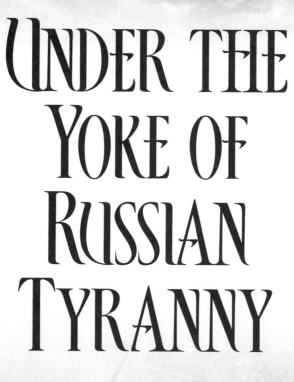

Under the Yoke of Russian Tyranny

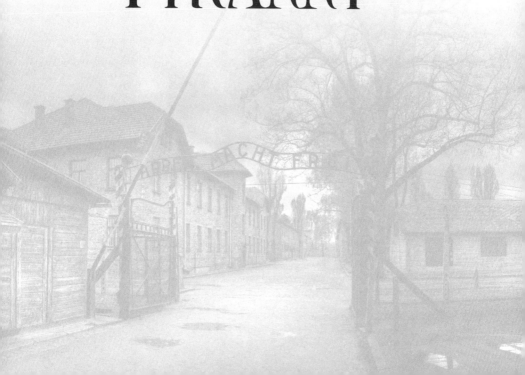

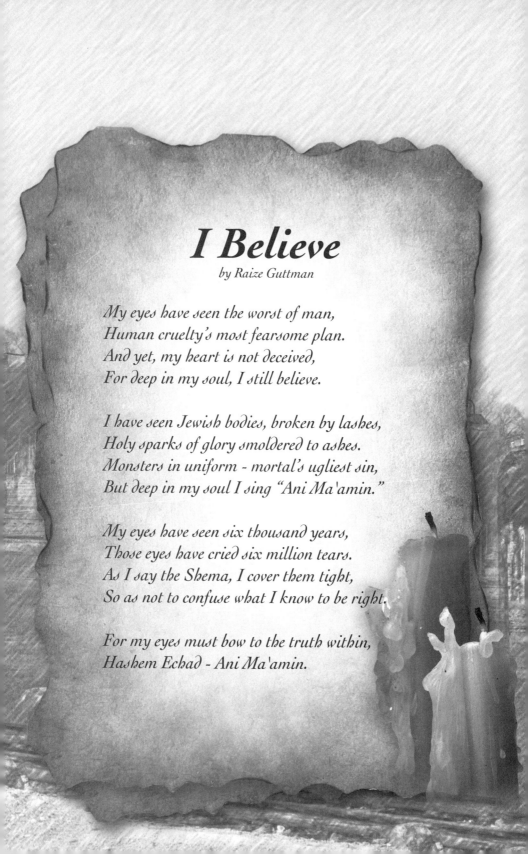

I Believe

by Raize Guttman

My eyes have seen the worst of man,
Human cruelty's most fearsome plan.
And yet, my heart is not deceived,
For deep in my soul, I still believe.

I have seen Jewish bodies, broken by lashes,
Holy sparks of glory smoldered to ashes.
Monsters in uniform - mortal's ugliest sin,
But deep in my soul I sing "Ani Ma'amin."

My eyes have seen six thousand years,
Those eyes have cried six million tears.
As I say the Shema, I cover them tight,
So as not to confuse what I know to be right.

For my eyes must bow to the truth within,
Hashem Echad - Ani Ma'amin.

| RAV MOSHE FEINSTEIN |

Jewish Education is Paramount

At the tender young age of twenty-five, Rav Moshe Feinstein *zt"l* accepted the mantle of *rabbanus* in the city of Luban, Russia. This was a difficult time for the Jews in Russia, as the Communist government of the U.S.S.R. was doing its utmost to root out any vestige of religious practice. If the ordinary Jews found life difficult, the rabbis and community leaders were put through all manners of torture, both physically and mentally, to try to dissuade them from practicing their religion.

The *shochet* was first banned from ritual slaughtering and later deported to Siberia. The *shamash* of the main synagogue, with his wife and seven children, was forced to live in a one-room shanty adjacent to the shul, and, within a short time, was required to take in the newly evicted rabbi and his family, in that same tiny shack.

The rabbi's salary was continually slashed year after year, to the point where it became nearly impossible to support himself and his family. Late night visits from the Russian secret police were intentionally done to spike the family's growing tension and fear. The *mikvah* was shut down and it took a great deal of R' Moshe's ingenuity to maintain a kosher, working *mikvah* for the townspeople, right under the Soviets' noses.

Through it all, however, R' Moshe soldiered on. For sixteen arduous years, he bore the brunt of the authorities' manipulations, but never once wavered in the performance of his communal duties. He was wont to remark: "A Jew is but a soldier in the midst of battle, and a soldier never deserts the ranks!" The community loved him for his ferocious dedication; he loved them in turn.

Thus, when the news hit town, it came as a bombshell that tore through the hearts of the citizens of Luban: The rabbi is leaving! R' Moshe is moving to America! Not only that, but even the local Russian officials were facilitating the processing of his papers, so happy they were to rid themselves of this unrelenting foe!

The community leaders came rushing to his house. Why was he leaving? How could he leave them? Of course life was hard, but it was hard for all of them and they were all in it together.

R' Moshe looked at their worn faces. It was a difficult decision. "Believe me," he said, "it's not because I fear the Russians, nor is it the danger. I've dealt with that for so many years."

"Then what is it?" they cried. "What did they do to you to finally cause you to break?"

"Nothing caused me to break," replied R' Moshe. "It's just that the situation has changed. Like I've always said, 'A Jew is but a soldier in the midst of battle.' But the most important battle that a Jew must fight - and win - is the battle of *chinuch habanim* - educating our children. My children are growing up and it is impossible for me to raise them to be G-d-fearing and observant Jews here in Russia. Although I want to remain here and guide you, my first responsibility is to my children, to ensure that they receive a true Torah education."

Indeed, R' Moshe taught his children - and the rest of Klal Yisrael - for the next fifty years!

| RAV MEIR SIMCHA HAKOHEN |

Never Put All Your Eggs in One Basket

A non-religious lawyer was very open with his praise and unbounded respect and admiration for Rav Meir Simcha Hakohen *zt"l*, of Dvinsk, the renowned *rosh yeshivah* and author of *Ohr Samei'ach*, *Meshech Chachmah*, etc. It was unusual to see such effusiveness from this man, especially for a religious rabbi and an observant Torah Jew. The lawyer himself had no connection with Orthodox Jews and certainly none with religious practice, so when he was once asked what had made such a strong impression on him that he spoke of R' Meir Simcha in such glowing terms, he responded with the following story:

During World War I, a committee was organized to care for Jewish refugees who were fleeing from the battlefront into the depths of Russia. This committee was convened in St. Petersburg and decided, among other things, to try to rescue the *sifrei* Torah from those areas where the fighting was fiercest.

Soldiers on both sides of the battlefield shared a hatred for Jews, and whichever side conquered a town often made the desecration of the local synagogue their first priority. Therefore, the committee sought to gather all the *sifrei* Torah in a central location in St. Petersburg. This way, it would be safer and easier to keep track of all the *sefarim* and avoid a catastrophic loss and desecration.

The committee decided to approach R' Meir Simcha for approval. Without R' Meir Simcha's backing, who, even as a young man of 25, was already considered one of the greatest scholars of the generation and was greatly respected by all segments of Russian Jewry, there was little likelihood of communities relinquishing their *sifrei* Torah.

To the committee's surprise, however, R' Meir Simcha did not approve of the plan. The committee members could not understand how ordinary people like themselves could be so eager to protect the *sifrei* Torah while the *gadol hador* was not equally concerned. They questioned him about his reluctance to grant approval to their plan.

R' Meir Simcha explained his objection: "We Jews have a long history in these matters. Our holy father Yaakov Avinu taught us the foolishness of such a strategy. His preparations before meeting his brother Eisav, and the division of his camp, teach us a profound lesson: Experience belies the need to become too concentrated in one place, so that if one area comes under attack another one will always be spared. *Chazal* tell us that for this reason, 'Hashem did a favor for Yisrael when he scattered them among the nations' (פסחים פז:). It would be foolhardy for us not to heed the words of *Chazal* and follow the example of Yaakov Avinu."

In the end, R' Meir Simcha's words proved to be prophetic. St. Petersburg, indeed, fell into the hands of the Communists, who closed the *batei medrash* and confiscated all the *sifrei*

Torah they found. After the war, however, the cities from which the committee wished to remove the *sifrei* Torah came under Polish rule, and it was there that the communities of Torah and some of the great European *yeshivos* survived and flourished until the Holocaust.

"When I saw this with my own eyes," concluded the lawyer in awe, "I realized that this was no ordinary man. We truly see the extent to which a wise man can anticipate the shifting tides of history."

| CHAFETZ CHAIM |

"Communism is All Your Fault!"

A well respected man, a leader and overseer of a large and thriving Jewish community, once came to visit the holy Chafetz Chaim, Rav Yisrael Meir Hakohen Kagan *zt"l*. Expecting to be welcomed with honor and respect befitting an important man such as himself, he was shocked when the *tzaddik* took one look at him, turned away and had him unceremoniously escorted from his presence. Such a thing was rare, if not unheard of, especially for a community leader who was widely recognized throughout Poland and its environs. Even more than being insulted, though, the man was frightened at the reaction of the *gadol hador* to his presence. What had he done to bring on such a reaction, to incur the wrath and ire of the great man? He searched his memory for any sort of incident but he came up empty-handed. Trembling, he decided that he could not leave Radin without finding out the source of the *tzaddik*'s displeasure with him.

With a faltering step, he timidly knocked on the Chafetz Chaim's door and begged to be given one more chance to talk with the *tzaddik*. He finally managed to ease his way inside and once again came face to face with the *tzaddik*. "*Rebbi*!" he cried, "What have I done? What was my sin, that you pushed me away and removed me from your home?"

The Chafetz Chaim's gaze turned steely. Then, he spoke in an icy tone: "You should just know that it is all your fault, all your responsibility! The fact that more than three million of our Jewish brethren are suffocating under the harsh yoke of the Communists, the entire affliction, all the oppression, all the pain and suffering – it's all your fault!"

All your fault! All your fault! The Chafetz Chaim's words rang out with the force of a locomotive train! The fate of millions of suffering Jews was on his shoulders! How can that be? What had he done?

"But *Rebbi*," he began, a stifled sob of protest erupting from his lips - but the Chafetz Chaim cut him off.

"Now? Now you cry? Of course, now you lead a large *kehillah*, you oversee the workings of your community and surely you wouldn't want any harm to come to it. But what about then? What about all those years ago?"

The man was unable to open his mouth. He truly had no idea what the *tzaddik* was talking about.

"Surely you remember," continued the Chafetz Chaim, "many years ago when you worked as the administrator of the local Talmud Torah, there was a young boy in your yeshivah, a small child who had lost his father and lived with his struggling mother. With those unfortunate circumstances, it was no wonder that the boy tended to act out and make trouble. He was wild, sharp-tongued and difficult to control. In the end, you lost patience with him and had him thrown out!"

The man thought long and hard. Then he asked cautiously, "What was the boy's name?"

"Laibel," said the *tzaddik*. "His name was Laibel. Since the yeshivah wouldn't keep him, his mother had no choice but to put him in a non-Jewish school. But the boy was smart; brilliant perhaps. He may have even become a *rosh yeshivah,* given the proper guidance. Instead, his sharp mind absorbed secular knowledge and he grew to become a leader among the *goyim.* This young Jewish boy Laibel - Leon Trotzky - became one of the founders of Communism and the supreme commander of the Red Army during the Bolshevik Revolution, an ideology he spawned after being spurned from your Talmud Torah. How many countless *neshamos* have suffered due to this dangerous ideology?"

"Now I ask you," concluded the Chafetz Chaim, "who is to blame? On whose shoulders is the enormous weight of history's unforgiving irony placed if not yours? Leave me! I can't bear to even look at your face!"

A postscript to this story is the action the Chafetz Chaim took to counter the nefarious plans of Trotzky. He was staying at Dugalishok, a health resort in the vicinity of Radin, and he summoned his prized disciple, Rav Elchanan Wasserman *zt"l hy"d* by telegram, to come there without delay.

Upon R' Elchanan's arrival, the Chafetz Chaim revealed to him, in the utmost secrecy, that he had decided to pronounce a ban (*cherem*) and curse on Trotsky for his role in the religious persecutions and for all the misdeeds of the *Yevsektsia* (the Jewish Communists).

"As for the gentiles," he declared, "we have no control over them. But Trotsky is a Jew. I have already determined his and his mother's names in Warsaw, and it lies within our power to frustrate his designs."

At the behest of the Chafetz Chaim, a number of Jews were summoned in secret to the local synagogue, and were instructed not to utter a word. They lit candles, took a *sefer* Torah from the *aron kodesh*, blew a shofar and, in that awe-filled assembly, placed a *cherem* upon Laibel Trotsky, cursing him with all the terrible curses recorded in the Torah.

History will reflect that from that point onwards, Trotsky's fortunes began to decline. He was expelled from the ruling cabinet and forced to flee from Russia. Finally, an assassin murdered him in far-off, Mexico City.

| RAV ELAZAR MENACHEM MANN SHACH |

The Voice of *Chizuk*

I n 1982, when the Soviet Union, with its tyrannical and treacherous policies against religious expression, was still in full force, an underground movement, backed by many of the *gedolei* Yisrael, was formed to strengthen the existing Russian Jews. This included delivering to them the basic necessities of *Yiddishkeit*. At that time, a delegation was received by the venerable *rosh yeshivah* of Ponevezh, Rav Elazar Menachem Mann Shach *zt"l*, to discuss the many issues that pertained to Soviet Jewry and what could be done to assist them.

R' Shach agreed to record a message of inspiration and *chizuk* to be played at secret and informal gatherings in Russia. This short message in Hebrew, not more than three or four minutes long, was infused with a love of his Jewish brethren suffering the torment of religious persecution. It was the *rosh yeshivah's* message and in it, he encouraged the people to view themselves as Avraham *Halvri* - standing apart from the entire world in defense of his firm belief in the One True G-d Above, which eventually led him on the path of creating the religion of Klal Yisrael. *"Ashreichem, ashreichem* - praiseworthy are you, who are able to stand firm in the midst of the terrible decrees of the Communist regime, and continue to serve *Hashem* as best as you can. Be strong until the coming of Mashiach, speedily and in our days."

Two *avreichim* were responsible for bringing this tape and its message into the Soviet Union, and although its contents would most definitely be considered incendiary against the State, causing anyone with whom it would be found on their person to be placed in grave danger, they took it with them willingly and without thought to their own safety.

Arriving at the airport in Russia, they immediately fell under the suspicion of the KGB who singled them out as Jews, and had their luggage confiscated and searched. Eventually, after emptying all the contents of their luggage, the authorities found the little white tape and demanded an explanation. When no satisfactory response was forthcoming, they took out a tape recorder and decided to listen to it themselves. They pressed play and waited - but nothing was heard. They forwarded the tape a bit and again nothing. They turned it over and pressed play at small intervals but nothing was there, and with no reason to hold onto it, they gave the "blank" tape back.

A bit disappointed that their precious message from R' Shach would not be heard, they nevertheless brought the tape with them when they met with a number of Russian Jews. This time, when they tried the tape in one of the local's tape recorder, R' Shach's voice came through loud and clear. In pure astonishment, they continued to play the *rosh yeshivah's* message of inspiration over and over, at every gathering that they attended, and indeed, the heartfelt words, spoken in a *Litvishe* Hebrew accent, were felt in such a powerful way. The once "lost" Jews of the Soviet Union could now hear with their own ears, that the *gedolim* and rest of Klal Yisrael, were thinking of them and praying for their continued success and elevation in *Yiddishkeit*.

Until this very day, the two young men who risked their lives to carry that precious tape have no words to explain what happened. The miracle, they insisted, is not so much that the tape did not work when the KGB tried to play it in their tape recorder, but rather, in those underground meetings, with hard-pressed and downtrodden Jews looking for a glimmer of hope and inspiration, R' Shach's words came through loud and clear on old and well-worn players, delivering his all-important message of *chizuk*.

A *Yiddishe* Mama in Life and Death

At the turn of the twentieth century, mass emigration from Russia to the golden shores of the United States was in full swing, with many of the Jewish refugees inevitably finding themselves in the teeming and constricting tenements of the Lower East Side.

The Cohen family was no exception, and although life was hard, with the struggle to make a living nearly insurmountable, they retained their Jewish identity and distinct *Yiddishe* flavor. To a large degree, this achievement was due to the tireless efforts of the warm and loving matriarch of the Cohen family who embodied the ideals of a true *Yiddishe* mama; always there for her children, exhorting them to never lose their identity as Jews. *Chessed* to anyone in need was a mainstay in the Cohen household and the first question asked to every visitor was, "Is there anything that you need? Can we do something to help you?"

This legacy of true *Yiddishe chinuch*, however, did not start there; this was a heritage in the Cohen family that had been passed down for many generations.

Many years earlier, the great-great-grandparents of the Cohen family resided in a small town situated almost directly on the Russian-Polish border. During the terrible years of the Cantonists, when young Jewish children were snatched off the street in broad daylight and forced to serve extended terms in the Russian Army, a network of smugglers was necessary to transport children in imminent danger of being drafted across the border into Poland and away from the Russian spies.

A leader of this daring network was an elder of the Cohen clan, a man who singlehandedly transported many children hidden in his carriage past the unknowing guards, at great risk to himself and the children. Week after perilous week, he would journey with his precious cargo, and in the face of constant perilous danger, persisted in his holy work. Many, many Jewish children were thus saved from the terrible decree of the Cantonists and the reputation of Cohen as the one to turn to in a time of need gained fame.

Unfortunately, this distinction was not lost on the Russian border guards. They had heard the whispers and they realized something was up. Then, at one of Cohen's border crossings, one of the guards became suspicious. He reported his concerns to his superiors and an ambush was set up to catch Cohen in action and arrest him.

On his next attempt at the border, he realized something was amiss. As he approached the border in his wagon, he saw an unusual delegation of guards descending upon him. That was all he needed to see. Without another moment's thought, he quickly jumped out of his wagon, and flung open the inner compartment, urging the kids hiding inside to run for their lives. With precious few moments to spare, he led as many children as possible to safety, but when he saw the hordes of soldiers coming after him, he took off in the opposite direction to buy some time for the kids to escape.

Running with every ounce of strength, he made it to the edge of the nearby woods, where dense foliage provided him with a measure of cover and security. Frantically searching in every direction, he saw a large stone in the distance, overgrown with weeds and brush. He needed to hide and this was his best cover, for the moment. He dropped down behind it and covered himself with the undergrowth.

Huddled and shivering, he began praying in earnest that *Hashem* should protect him from this danger. The soldiers meanwhile, with their bayonets poised on the tips of their rifles, fanned out to search, poking and prodding the underbrush with deadly thrusts, hoping to spear their prey and kill him. For quite some time, they continued their hunt and, all the while, Cohen's heart was thumping so hard, that he was sure the guards would hear it. Miraculously, though, they never did.

After some time futilely searching, the guards gave up. Their man had escaped, and as the shouts and screams of the guards slowly receded, Cohen lifted his head above the foliage.

It took a few more minutes before he felt safe enough to stand up fully. Looking around, he realized that he was in a cemetery; in fact, he was in the old Jewish cemetery with many gravestones inscribed with Hebrew text. Curious, now, as he recognized the place, he brushed away the branches and dirt that covered the large stone which had served as his cover to read the name written on it. He read the name in sheer astonishment: it was the name of his own dear mother, who had died many years earlier, and was buried in this exact spot in the cemetery. In his haste, his legs had carried him, unknowingly, to his mother's grave and it was his dear mother who was had shielded and protected him from the soldiers and their deadly bayonets.

A *Yiddishe* mama, in life and in death; looking after her children and safeguarding them from harm.

| RAV MEIR CHADASH |

Never Give in to Despair

The First World War ended in January 1919, yet chaos swept through Russia. The army was in disarray. The Bolshevik Revolution was still in its early stages. Troops scattered in every direction on their way home, while lawless individuals roamed the villages, plundering the helpless inhabitants. Various powers vied for control of the country, one rising as the other fell. The government kept changing hands and battles between the Bolsheviks, Cossacks and White Russians were fought in every city and in every region.

In the city of Kremenchug, a unit of Cossack soldiers took control of the city. The terrified Jews hid behind their locked doors. Few brave souls ventured outside. Rav Meir Chadash *zt"l* was then a young man studying in the *beis medrash* of the exiled Slabodka Yeshivah and although he understood the danger of venturing outside, he thought that he could perhaps slip away quickly and get to the yeshivah safely. Stealthily, he walked along the silent streets, hoping to go unnoticed. He had managed to get as far as the corner, when, suddenly, there were Cossacks blocking his way. Frightened, he turned to run but soldiers quickly came up behind him as well.

"There's a Bolshevik Jew!" they yelled, closing in on him. "Show us your papers!" they ordered, rifles pointed his way. R' Meir didn't have his papers with him. That was a crime punishable by death!

The soldiers seized him and began to drag him toward a courtyard, right next to the building which they were using as their headquarters. A deathly fear fell over R' Meir and he began to recite the *vidui* (prayer before death) over and over.

The Cossacks stood him up against the wall. One of them aimed his rifle at R' Meir. "Stand up straight!" he shouted, taking aim at R' Meir's heart. "Straighten up!" He accompanied the order with a flurry of curses.

But R' Meir, paralyzed with fear, was unable to move. The soldier was having trouble with his aim and again shouted for R' Meir to stand straight, in order to give him a clearer shot. Suddenly, a window a few floors above R' Meir's head opened and an annoyed official stuck his face out. "Who's that shouting down there?" the commander called angrily.

"It ... it's a Bolshevik," the soldier began to stammer. "I caught him in the street!" One after another, his fellow soldiers slowly began to slip away, not wanting to be caught by the irate commander.

"Stop babbling!" the commander shouted. "Get out of here, and stop ruining my rest! Do you understand? Get out of here now!"

The soldier hastened away before his commander's fury could grow greater.

R' Meir stood alone in the courtyard, stunned, hardly able to believe his own eyes. Raising himself up from his slumped position, he quickly recovered his wits and ran out of the courtyard as fast as his legs could carry him.

As he ran, still trembling from head to toe at his miraculous brush with death, he recalled the words of *Chazal* and played them over and over in his head: "Even if a sharp sword is resting on a person's neck, he must not despair of (Hashem's) mercy."

Exactly ten years later, in August of 1929, R' Meir Chadash, who had immigrated together with the Slabodka Yeshivah to the holy city of Chevron four years earlier, found himself trapped inside the yeshivah's building during the infamous riots that nearly wiped out the ancient community of Chevron. As R' Meir lay among the dead and wounded while the Arab murderers still rampaged through the building, he forcefully stopped one of his friends from standing up. He whispered urgently, "Lie still and hope!"

Later, when it was all over, his friend asked in astonishment, "Where did you find the strength to lie quietly and continue to hope at that awful time?"

It was then that R' Meir related the story of the miracle that had happened to him in Kremenchug. He was certain that it was the power of that miracle, and the resolutions he had undertaken in its wake, which gave him the strength he needed years later.

A similar story is told about Rav Yaakov Yitzchak Ruderman *zt"l*, *rosh yeshivah* of the renowned Yeshivas Ner Israel in Baltimore, who once found himself in a similar dangerous situation. During those uncertain and dangerous times, young

Yaakov Yitzchak was captured by a gang of Cossacks who threatened to kill him unless he gave them a huge amount of money as ransom.

Overwhelmed with fear, he directed them to the home of his *rosh yeshivah*, Rav Moshe Mordechai Epstein *zt"l*. When the Cossacks made their demand, those present in the house attempted to collect the desired sum, penny by penny, but the total was far beyond their means.

The thugs left the house, dragging the terrified child along with them as they took him outside to kill him.

R' Moshe Mordechai acted quickly. He ran out of his house and chased after the marauders, shouting on the top of his lungs, "*Gevald*, help!"

Suddenly, as if on cue, people came swarming out of every home, joining the *rosh yeshivah* in a kind of impromptu mob, all of them screaming and carrying on. The Cossacks took one look at the oncoming parade of angry men and became frightened. With all this noise and rabble, perhaps the Bolsheviks would hear and come out to aid the victims. Leaving their young captive behind, they ran for their lives.

In this way, the Jewish people merited an illustrious *rosh yeshivah*, a pioneer of Torah in the United States.

| RAV YECHEZKEL ABRAMSKY |

"The Bolsheviks Didn't Accomplish Anything!"

I n Elul 5690 (August 1930), Rav Yechezkel Abramsky *zt"l* author of Chazon Yechezkel and formerly *Av Beis Din* of Slutsk, later of London, was sent to prison by the Bolsheviks. His "crime" was that he engaged in religious activities. He was tried and sentenced to five years of hard labor in Siberia.

Friends outside Russia, and especially the great *gaon* and *posek*, Rav Chaim Ozer Grodzenski *zt"l* of Vilna, made various protests to the Communist authorities, and diplomatic pressure was applied to secure his release, but all the efforts were to no avail. For almost fourteen months, R' Yechezkel was persecuted in a Siberian prison. Then, in a sudden miraculous turn, the Soviets changed their minds. On September 20, 1931, Erev Yom Kippur, the Russian authorities came to him and informed him that he was to be freed that very day and that he must leave Russia within one month.

Aside from his miraculous release, there was another miracle involved in this story. When R' Yechezkel escaped from the Siberian death trap and traveled by train from Moscow to Riga, the first person to greet him in the railroad car was Rav Elchanan Wasserman *zt"l hy"d* of Baranovich, the prized pupil of the holy Chafetz Chaim, who fell onto him with tears of joy. What R' Elchanan was doing there at that time was not immediately known to R' Abramsky. After he had settled in London, he was privileged, once again, to meet R' Elchanan, who was there in the interests of his yeshivah. This time, they met on the platform of the railway station. While they were standing there they talked Torah and R' Elchanan spoke of the Chafetz Chaim.

Then R' Elchanan told him: "On Erev Yom Kippur of the year that you were released from captivity, I was staying in the Chafetz Chaim's home. We were studying Torah together. Suddenly, my *rebbi* interrupted the discussion, and without any connection to what we had been talking about beforehand, announced again and again, triumphantly, raising his hands, 'The Bolsheviks didn't accomplish anything; the Bolsheviks didn't accomplish anything. They were forced against their will to release the Slutzker Rav.' Then, without another word, he resumed his studies with me."

R' Elchanan looked at his watch and noted the time. Years later he learned that this was the very moment when R' Abramsky was granted his freedom!

This story was related by veteran students of Slabodka in Bnei Brak, who heard it from R' Abramsky when he recounted the story of his imprisonment and release. He would speak about it each year on Erev Yom Kippur, the anniversary of his release. His son, R' Mordechai Abramsky, also added that during the entire period of his imprisonment, the Chafetz Chaim would recite eight chapters of Tehillim each day after Shacharis to pray for his release. On the day of the release itself, however, he did not.

A Spy Wearing *Tefillin*

A Jewish student in Moscow University clung to his religious observance with incredible determination and tenacity. A recent *baal teshuvah* whose spirit and longing for a life of Torah and *mitzvos* was profound, Valentin (Velvel) would attend secret classes in Judaism, right under the ever-vigilant eyes of the KGB and university informants. Eventually, he was caught, finding himself in serious trouble. Retribution was swift, and soon Valentin was expelled from the university. He was now an able-bodied man without a university exemption, and there was only one place for him to go - the Soviet army.

Within weeks, Valentin had been drafted and shipped out to a small Siberian town, far, far away from gemara classes, kosher food, and fellow Jews. All the *mitzvos* that he'd so recently taken on had become impossible to observe. But Valentin was determined to hold onto one thing at the very least; each and every morning, he told himself grimly, he would perform the mitzvah of *tefillin*; no matter what. It wasn't easy dragging himself out of his bed on those frigid Siberian mornings, but yet, Valentin managed to be up half an hour before reveille, don his *tefillin*, and pray to his Creator.

One day, one of his fellow soldiers who had woken up early was astonished to see Valentin standing quietly in a corner, carefully winding straps around his arm, and placing a box upon his forehead. The next morning the soldier, his suspicions aroused, again awoke early, and again witnessed this mad - or possibly traitorous - behavior.

By the third day, the soldier had decided that he was required to do his patriotic duty. He informed his superior officer of the unusual practices of this young man in his regiment, and when Valentin roused himself from his all-too-short night's sleep the next morning, there were two officers on hand to witness the event. The officers surprised Valentin in the middle of his prayers and were not impressed with his protestations that the *tefillin* were religious objects. Prayer they could understand, although they didn't like it, but these straps? Clearly, Valentin was a spy, and the straps and boxes were some sort of transmitting device.

Their first step was to confiscate the dangerous transmitter. Valentin, still protesting, insisted upon accompanying the *tefillin* to the lab where they would be examined. Curiously enough, the officers agreed, though insisting that a military guard escort him.

In the lab in a small Siberian town, the technicians had never seen such a device. The boxes, they agreed, served as transmitters, while the straps must be antennas. As Valentin watched, horrified, they actually opened up the *tefillin* boxes. Gleefully, they pulled out the writing. A secret code!

"It is Hebrew," he protested.

"A language that has been dead for 2,000 years," they answered admiringly, "it's pure genius! What a perfect code!"

Now Valentin became nervous and angry at the same time. With surprising authority in his voice, Valentin instructed his captors to contact the small, local Jewish community in the city of Novosibirsk to corroborate what he had told them. In an attempt to display their fair-mindedness, they agreed. The next day, bright and early on Saturday morning, the investigators duly visited the synagogue. They looked around and observed the few older men who had ventured out to the synagogue that morning. But within a short time, they returned unimpressed; not even one person had been wearing the straps and boxes!

Eventually the president of the synagogue heard about the hapless Jewish soldier and came forward to validate his story and explain that no Jew puts on his straps on Saturday. At this point, the officers had a choice: They could either charge

Valentin with espionage, although it would look bad on their unit's records, or they could simply look away.

In the end, they told Valentin he would be discharged on psychiatric grounds. "Because, if you're not a spy, you certainly must be crazy" - was their halfhearted response.

Instead of two harsh years in the employ of the military of the U.S.S.R., Valentin finished his army service in just two months, and soon was ready to rejoin his family and friends - Jewish friends - back in Moscow. Later, because he hadn't spent much time in the army, he was allowed to leave Russia and immigrate to Israel, without having to undergo the ordeal of being a *refusenik*. Valentin never lost sight of where his "good fortune" came from: his devotion to the mitzvah of *tefillin*.

| RAV CHAIM BERLIN |

The Last Shofar in Moscow

Life under the rule of the Russian Czar was difficult, made all the more harder for the Jews of Russia by the constant decrees that never seemed to stop coming. Many edicts were issued against the practice and observance of Judaism, a number of notorious policies against Jewish education, and monetary decrees were almost routine to the already impoverished people. Many Jews were forced to flee their homes, and Moscow, which eventually became the capital city of the U.S.S.R. under the Bolsheviks, even forbade Jews to reside there. Only certain worker permits were issued to Jews in special cases.

The Rav of Moscow had been the renowned Rav Chaim Berlin *zt"l*, son of the famous Netziv, Rav Naftali Tzvi Yehudah Berlin *zt"l*. As thousands of Muscovite Jews fled the city, R' Chaim remained behind, determined to see that every last Jew found a place to resettle.

That very same year, as Rosh Hashanah approached, only a few dozen Jews were left in the city. One of the remaining members produced a shofar, the only one left in the city, and was preparing to blow it on the holy day. To his horror and dismay, however, he noticed a long crack along the length of the shofar, which invalidated it. Yom Tov would soon be upon them and there was no time to procure a second shofar. R' Chaim and the remaining Jews of Moscow realized that this would likely be the first time in their lives that they would be unable to perform the mitzvah of *tekias* shofar on Rosh Hashanah.

With a heavy heart, R' Chaim resigned himself to the situation. "Well," he thought sadly, "If I cannot hear the sound of the shofar, at least let me study the *halachos* of shofar. Maybe in that merit, it will allow me to somewhat 'make up' for the loss of the mitzvah."

On the first night of Rosh Hashanah, R' Chaim stayed up all night in the *beis medrash* studying any and all the *halachos* pertaining to the mitzvah of shofar. At the crack of dawn, he left the *beis medrash* and headed towards the large shul for the early morning prayers. As he looked up, he couldn't believe his eyes: driving down the empty street, right in front of him, was a horse-drawn wagon adorned on all sides with unusual crafts, historical artifacts and an assortment of musical instruments, including a ram's horn which looked exactly like a ... shofar!

The stunned Rav hastily ran over to the coachman and asked, "Where did you get this horn from?"

The coachman had been enjoying the peaceful stillness of the early morning and jumped up startled. Looking directly at the Rav, he began sputtering incoherently, until he finally blurted out, "Honored Rabbi, I didn't know it was yours. I would have never stolen it had I known it was yours."

Slowly, the story came out. The gentile coachman had a hobby of collecting all sorts of horns, trumpets and wind instruments. When the Jews of Moscow left the city, he went rummaging through the old deserted synagogues looking for anything of value. It was there that he came across this ram's horn and it became one of his valued collectibles.

"But rabbi," the gentile pleaded, hoping the rabbi would not report his theft, "take it. It's yours. It's the only one I found, but I want you to have it."

R' Chaim's joy knew no bounds. That year, the Jews of Moscow merited the fulfillment of the mitzvah of *tekias* shofar, and it would be quite some time before such a sound would be heard again in the city. The selfless act of staying up all night studying the laws of shofar was the merit that allowed R' Chaim to obtain and fulfill the mitzvah of shofar.

| SKULENER REBBE |

Knocked Down But Not Out

At the end of World War II, the Skulener Rebbe, Rav Eliezer Zusha Portugal *zt"l* was living in the city of Chernowitz, which was then under Soviet dominion. Although the authorities had their eyes on him at all times, he never ceased his religious and rescue activities on behalf of his fellow Jews. He founded a number of institutions for orphans of the Holocaust and he personally cared for at least three hundred orphaned children, all of whom called him "*Tatte*". Most of these children eventually settled in Israel and remained observant Jews.

R' Eliezer Zusha's determination to help his fellow Jews was legendary. Nothing stood in the way of his self-appointed mission to rescue Jews who were in need. The city of Chernowitz was relatively close to the Romanian border and the Rebbe remained there in order to be able to smuggle as many Jews out of the Soviet Union and across the border into Romania. From there, it was much easier to get papers to enable them to go to America or Israel.

The man in charge of the border guards was a certain colonel who lived in Chernowitz. He was a true-blooded Soviet who felt no love for the Jews and little compassion for the Skulener Rebbe. Yet, on more than one occasion, the Rebbe was able to break through his hardened exterior in order to help his fellow Jews in trouble. The colonel was generally a difficult man and he warned the Rebbe not to impose on him. But the Rebbe didn't take heed and continued to come to him when he thought he could help.

Finally, the colonel had had enough. He warned the Rebbe that he was through putting his neck on the line for these Jews and he refused to assist anymore. "Enough is enough," said the colonel after he helped the Rebbe one last time, "Do not come here and do not bother me anymore. I'm not interested in helping you and I don't want to see your face. If you come to me again on behalf of your Jews - I will kill you!"

It wasn't long, though, before the Rebbe was notified about a family of nine souls which had been captured trying to smuggle across the border. He immediately sprang into action and undertook the daunting and dangerous task of rescuing them. He knew that their punishment was to be imprisonment in Siberia and he refused to sit still. "I must get these people out of prison here in Chernowitz before they are sent off to Siberia. I will get them out - regardless!" he exclaimed.

Nothing worked, not even a hefty bribe. The Soviets were adamant; these people were to serve as an example for others.

There was still one avenue to be tried. The Rebbe would go to the colonel and beg, regardless of the imminent personal danger involved. Jewish lives were at stake and that was more important than his life.

His family pleaded with him not to go. "How can you risk your life like this?" they asked. "He said he would not help you anymore and that if you came to him again, he would kill you!"

The Rebbe shook his head. "I must go. It is not clear that he will take out his anger on me. But one thing is for certain, the fate of those nine people is surely sealed unless I am able to do something on their behalf."

The Rebbe approached the colonel's house with trepidation, climbed up the steps and, with a prayer on his lips, knocked on the door. When the Soviet officer saw who stood on his doorstep, he was overcome with anger.

"I told you not to come back here, didn't I," he roared. Without warning, he grabbed the Skulener Rebbe and threw him down the stairs. Then he turned and slammed the door.

R' Eliezer Zusha was badly hurt. Bleeding profusely and in somewhat of a daze, the Rebbe collected himself and stood up. Then, with extreme difficulty and the little strength he had left, he once again climbed the stairs and knocked on the colonel's door.

The colonel swung open the door and could not believe his eyes. There stood the rabbi, dirty, bloodied, clothes torn - but with defiance in his eyes.

"I must speak to you, Colonel!" the Rebbe said, with tears streaming down his face.

This time, the colonel listened - it was the least he could do.

The Rebbe began to speak and burst into tears. He begged, he cried, and he tugged at the heartstrings of this Soviet officer as he depicted the bitter plight of this helpless family. Even the colonel's hardened heart could not possibly ignore the selfless pleas, the heartfelt emotion of the Rebbe. His devotion to others at the expense of his own health was too much to ignore. The colonel promised to help the family and in a short time, they were freed.

| RAV ASHER SOSONKIN |

The Russian's Secret

Life in the Siberian labor camps was always difficult for the Jewish prisoners, but during the holiday season it was even more so, as it was nearly impossible to perform the *mitzvos* of each holiday under those terrible conditions.

Rav Asher Sosonkin *zt"l* was exiled to Siberia for the "crime" of spreading Torah throughout Russia. Even under the harsh conditions of the work camp, he did his best to continue to observe the Torah and *mitzvos*. With him was a Jew by the name of Nachman Rosemann. He was an ardent Communist who had risen in the ranks of the Russian army. He was arrested for illegal business dealings, and was sentenced to twenty-five years of hard labor in Siberia. It was there in the work camp that Nachman felt a renewed interest in Judaism, and he befriended the devout R' Asher. Nachman was determined to learn all he could from R' Asher, and do the *mitzvos* as carefully as possible.

Chanukah was approaching and R' Asher asked Nachman to obtain a tin can to use as a menorah in order to fulfill the mitzvah of kindling the Chanukah lights. R' Asher emphasized that it should be small, so that their activities wouldn't be noticed by any of the labor camp officials.

R' Asher was amazed by his friend's determination. Nachman found a prisoner who happened to be a tinsmith and paid him several rubles to make a beautiful menorah. He did this knowing that if the authorities found out, he would be punished severely.

On the day before Chanukah, Nachman approached R' Asher with a big smile. In one hand he held a menorah, and in the other hand he held a bottle filled with oil.

On the first night of Chanukah, R' Asher and Nachman placed the menorah discreetly by the doorpost of their barracks and prepared a cotton wick. The other prisoners watched curiously as the two men commenced this "dangerous" act. R' Asher recited the three blessings over the lighting of the menorah, and lit the wick with tears of joy and gratitude. They continued to light the menorah successfully for the first four nights of Chanukah.

Then they ran into trouble. On the fifth night, just after R' Asher and Nachman had lit their makeshift menorah, an armed guard appeared at the entrance of the barracks, announcing roll call. The prisoners were stunned. Roll call had never been announced at this hour before! R' Asher and Nachman were sure that someone must have reported them, which would explain the unusual roll call.

When the Russian officer entered the barracks, everyone stood still, anticipating the worst. He walked around slowly looking at each inmate as he counted them off. When he approached the bed of R' Asher he suddenly stopped. Then, he noticed the menorah. He stared at it for a long moment and then looked up - right at R' Asher.

"Five?" he said in an inquisitive voice. No answer. R' Asher was too scared and in shock to reply. "Five?" the officer asked again, this time a bit more urgently.

"F-f-five," stammered R' Asher in a confused reply.

The officer nodded his head, and without another word, turned and left the barracks. The prisoners were shocked. They all wondered the same thing: Who was this officer? And why did he come to them at such an unusual hour and ask about the candles?

R' Asher understood, however, and was careful to keep this "Russian" officer's secret safe.

| RAV CHAIM STEIN |

"*Ribbono Shel Olam,* Now It's Up to You!"

I n order to survive in the harsh Siberian tundra, one needed to maintain a competitive edge. Whether it was in goods, money, or services, the ability to provide for another - for a price, of course - increased one's value and chances for survival.

During the war years, the revered *rosh yeshivah* of Telshe, Rav Chaim Stein *shlit"a*, and his lifelong friend, Reb Meir Zelig Mann *z"l* were deported by the Soviet authorities to Siberia for the crime of being Jews. They found their competitive edge amongst the lowly Russian peasants by pretending to be doctors who could heal the masses. They were fortunate enough to locate a single thermometer which they placed in an impressive doctor's bag, and when "diagnosing" patients, they made a great show of fussing over the medical gadget and discussing the patients "needs" in their own language. Herbs, roots and chicken-soup remedies from their youth were the medicine they prescribed, but their own *tefillos* on behalf of the ill patient was the actual formula that worked and prolonged their ruse.

One year, shortly before Chanukah, while "treating" a patient, their entire charade took a tragic turn: their thermometer broke! Attempting to cover up the problem, they pretended to continue with their medical visits, but the peasants became suspicious. They alerted the authorities who immediately sent out a warrant to arrest the fake Jewish "doctors". R' Chaim and R' Meir Zelig were forced to run away with nothing but the clothes on their back, with the N.K.V.D. in hot pursuit.

They eventually reached a railroad station and managed to board the first train that came into the station, not even sure in which direction they were heading.

The train was mostly deserted and, for the first time that day, they were able to relax and assess their situation. As nightfall approached, they realized that the first night of Chanukah was that evening and they had nothing with which to fulfill the mitzvah of lighting the Chanukah candles. R' Chaim was inconsolable over the thought of missing this mitzvah and immersed himself in prayer, begging Hashem for a solution to their problem.

R' Meir Zelig, always the practical one, came up with a plan. At the next train station, the two got off and walked to the edge of the platform. One of them removed his boot and began collecting the dripping grease from the back of the railroad car. When they filled it up as much as they were able, they ran back into the train and, using a piece of material from their clothing, created a wick for their oil lamp.

Amazingly, it worked! They managed to collect enough grease and prepared their portable "menorah." They excitedly began lighting the "wick" for their Chanukah menorah, but their happiness soon turned to bitter disappointment when the material refused to light. They felt crushed and defeated.

As their entire survival up until this point relied heavily on the power of their *tefillos*, R' Chaim and R' Meir Zelig sat down and began crying until there were no more tears, imploring Hashem to assist them in their time of need. R' Chaim called out, "*Ribbono shel Olam*, we have done all we can; now it's up to You!"

It didn't take but a few short minutes, when the train came to a sudden stop. An unknown station in the middle of Siberia, nowhere near civilization, cropped up seemingly out of nowhere, and the train paused to let on a single passenger. A rugged and coarse Russian peasant hopped up into their railcar. Pulling something from his pocket, he announced, "Would anybody like to buy a candle?" R' Chaim and R' Meir Zelig stared at him - and then at one another - in disbelief.

Many times, R' Chaim has revealed that he truly believes Eliyahu Hanavi himself came to their rescue that night, selling them that one candle which they cut into eight pieces for all eight nights of Chanukah.

| CHAFETZ CHAIM |

Approaching the Tree of Life

When the Bolsheviks seized power in Russia in 1917, the upheaval forced many people to relocate. The holy Chafetz Chaim, Rav Yisroel Meir Hakohen Kagan *zt"l*, who had left Radin temporarily during World War I, was forced to settle in the small village of Snovsk.

There is always a shortage of food during a war, and during the Russian Revolution, the situation was worse than during other wars. This was due to a decree issued that anyone who possessed food was required to hand it over to an official appointed for this purpose. That official would then distribute food rations to each family, at his discretion. Because of this arrangement, there were many families who did not have enough to eat. The Chafetz Chaim resolved to collect whatever extra food families might have and divide these scraps among the poorest families.

When the war finally ended in 1921, the Chafetz Chaim announced that he was returning to Radin. On the Shabbos before he left, the Chafetz Chaim invited the congregation to his house for *seudah shlishis*, the third Shabbos meal.

On the way to the Chafetz Chaim's lodgings, they came across the officer who was in charge of the city. He was a cruel man. His parents were Jewish but not at all religious, and their son had continued along the same path. At one point, he had joined the revolution against the Czar, and had been exiled to Siberia. When the Bolsheviks took over, they freed him and appointed him as the officer in charge of this city. He disliked all religious Jews, except for the Chafetz Chaim, who he deeply respected.

The Chafetz Chaim greeted the officer respectfully and then asked, "Perhaps, you could come to my house for the third meal?"

The officer answered him mockingly, "I have already eaten the 'third meal.' I have eaten a lot more than three meals!" The Chafetz Chaim ignored his sarcastic barb and once again invited the man to join him. The officer thought about it for a moment and then reluctantly agreed.

The Chafetz Chaim was careful to accord the man a great deal of respect and even seated him next to him at the table. The meal proceeded as normal and the officer made small talk at the table.

Towards the end of the meal, the Chafetz Chaim suddenly turned to the officer and said, "I want to ask you a favor, but first I must tell you a *vort* - a small bit of wisdom from the holy Torah."

"A '*vort*'?" laughed the officer. "Why do I need to hear a '*vort*'? Surely I will not understand it."

"Even a child," said the Chafetz Chaim, smiling, "could understand what I am going to tell you." He looked at the Russian and began, "The Torah states: 'Hashem, the Lord, made every tree .... with the Tree of Life in the midst of the garden, and the Tree of Knowledge of Good and Evil.' (Bereishis 2-9) The commentator Rashi explains that the Tree of Life was exactly in the center of the garden. Why? Because the Tree of Life is the focus of life. This refers to eternal life, the life of the World to Come. The Almighty wants every Jew to receive his portion in the World to Come. A person can achieve this through prayer, through learning Torah, or through giving charity. Now, perhaps a person will claim that *mitzvos* are too far from him, they are not within his reach. Therefore, Hashem put the tree exactly in the center of the garden, to show us that it does not matter where one is standing. A person can approach the tree from any direction and have the opportunity to acquire a portion in the World to Come."

"Upon you," continued the Chafetz Chaim to the Bolshevik official, "the Almighty also has mercy. Who knows? Perhaps you were placed in your position of power for the sole purpose of fulfilling the request which I am about to make of you." The officer stared curiously at the great man.

The Chafetz Chaim sighed, "During the war, I went around and collected food for the poor families of this city. Now I am going back to my own town. I am giving you a list of these poor people, and I want you to accept upon yourself to provide them with food, just as I did. You cannot say that you are unable to do so, because you are in charge and everyone here has to listen to you. Do this and I assure you that you will reach some level in the Eternal World."

This officer had a heart of stone, but words which emanate from the heart can penetrate any heart. The impassioned words of the holy Chafetz Chaim broke through a previously impenetrable barrier in the officer's heart and his soul became receptive.

"Give me the list, Rabbi," he said to the Chafetz Chaim, "and I will do it." And amazingly, he did!

| RAV AVRAHAM NETZACH |

A Siberian Kiddush Hashem

L ife in a Siberian labor camp was unimaginably difficult. For one man, Rav Avraham Netzach *zt"l*, who made a vow to never bend on his principles to keep Shabbos and remain a Jew true to the Torah, which made his difficult situation exponentially compounded. Torture, beatings and hunger were common to him and no matter what the Soviet authorities threw at him in an attempt to subjugate his will, he never did bow to their pressure. In the many camps that he was forced to serve, he was nicknamed "Subbota" or the "Sabbath" for his reputation as one who would never desecrate the Jewish holy day.

One year, a few weeks before Pesach, Avraham managed to send a letter to his wife back home asking her to send him matzos for Yom Tov. With a bit of luck, he reasoned, and the correct individual in the receiving office, it was conceivable to actually attain one's packages, and Avraham was hoping that he would receive his precious package before Yom Tov. Otherwise, he decided, he would go hungry for the full eight days, hoping that some camp official would take pity on him and provide him with fruit or potatoes, which were considered contraband for the inmates.

Every day he checked the camp office to see if any package came for him. But he was always told the same thing: nothing for Netzach. The female *natchalnik* (supervisor) who acted as censor for all the letters and packages of the prisoners, would ask him about Passover and matzos and what they meant to a Jew. He explained in great detail how important the holiday was and how Jews do not eat any bread, but only matzos for eight days straight. He reiterated his commitment to her and she nodded gravely.

Finally, Yom Tov arrived. With no matzah, potatoes or anything else worth eating, Avraham subsisted on brewed tea and nothing else. Day by day, he grew weaker and various officials came by and took pity on him. Invariably, they almost always brought fresh-baked rolls, cookies and cake which he flatly turned down, much to their chagrin.

By Chol Hamo'ed, he was having trouble walking around, and by the last days of Yom Tov, he was too weak to even get out of bed. No amount of persuasion or coercion could get him to eat *chametz* and he was semi-conscious when Yom Tov finally ended. On Motza'ei Yom Tov, a fellow Jewish prisoner managed to soak some bread and sugar in tea, and spoon-fed him until he regained a bit of strength. Miraculously, he survived and grew stronger every day.

Two days after Pesach, a Jewish inmate was released from captivity and Avraham asked him to check if a package ever came for him in the local post office. Indeed, the man reported later, a large-size delivery came for him but was returned with a written declaration from the censor that the prisoner had died. Twice, this had occurred, and now Avraham understood why he never received his matzos.

With nothing to lose, he went to the chief *natchalnik* and issued a formal complaint against the woman who censored his packages. In a rare display of Soviet justice, the *natchalnik* was incensed and confronted the woman with the accusation. She broke down in tears and confessed that she had returned the packages.

The chief turned to Avraham and demanded a formal written complaint against the censor and said he would personally see to it that she was punished. She cried and begged the chief for mercy. He, in turn, responded coldly that she shouldn't apologize to him but to the man who almost died because of her.

All eyes looked at Avraham. He turned to the weeping woman and said that he was willing to forego the charges against her on the condition that she swears never again to abuse any prisoners, Jew or gentile alike. This impressed the chief so much and caused a great kiddush Hashem, and he promised not to inform the higher authorities of her crimes. Instead she was relieved of her post and transferred out of the camp.

It wasn't until a number of years later that Avraham's incredible act of clemency on behalf of the censor proved beneficial. One night, in 1943, all the inmates were awakened and told that they were being transferred to a different camp. They found that the camp they were being moved to was a much more difficult place, with less food, harder work and horrible living conditions. The prisoners were miserable and many despaired of ever seeing freedom.

As they approached the front gate of the new camp, the chief *natchalnik* came out to greet them. It was none other than the woman who had served as the censor in the previous camp!

When she saw Avraham, she took him aside and gave him proper living conditions. She explained, "You will see that I am not as cruel as you thought. I will never forget how you treated me and I intend to reciprocate."

Her voice went soft. "Please believe me that the chief forced me to act as I did. With a threat against my children, they forced me to return your matzos and arranged for people to bring you fresh rolls each day of your holiday. You never budged and earned the respect of every person in the camp."

For the duration of his stay in that particular camp, she eased his plight as much as possible which allowed him to continue performing *mitzvos* in the camps until his ultimate liberation in 1955.

| RAV MOSHE FEINSTEIN |

A Fortuitous Ruling

I n the city of Luban, Russia lived a sinister man who made it his life's mission to inform on his Jewish brethren, gaining favors from local government officials in return for juicy gossip and dirt on the Jews of the city. As a result of his information, often fictitious and spiteful, he caused untold hardship to the residents of Luban. He was understandably a hated and feared man.

His day finally came and the informant took ill and died. The *chevra kaddisha* discovered a letter that was addressed to them wherein the deceased wrote: "My fellow Jewish brothers, I feel terrible for all that I have done to the people of Luban and I regret my actions. To complete my penitence, I hereby request that in preparation for my burial, my body be defiled and debased and that I am to be buried outside the cemetery in an unbecoming manner."

Although willing to happily accede to these requests, the members of the *chevra kaddisha* were still unsure as to how to proceed. They decided to bring the matter before the *rav* of Luban, Rav Moshe Feinstein *zt"l*, and allow him to decide the matter.

R' Moshe thought about the question for a long moment and then made his ruling. "A human being is not the possessive owner of his body and is not in any position, especially after his death, to decide what is to be done with it. Therefore, this man must be buried according to the normal standards of Jewish law, with a proper burial within the confines of the Jewish cemetery."

The *chevra kaddisha* members, however, persisted in their arguments. "But *Rebbi*, this man wants to do *teshuvah*. Why should we not take pity on him and allow his final request to be carried out?"

R' Moshe waved them away. "It is your responsibility to handle the dead according to *halachah*, and not by what the deceased writes. It is my responsibility as *rav* of this city to ensure that this is properly carried out. As for how the Heavenly Court will look upon him and his feelings of regret, that is their business!" The man was buried in the Jewish cemetery, respectfully and with little fanfare.

A number of days later, a cemetery attendant noticed a group of uniformed men gathered around the grave of the former informant. They dug out his body and unwrapped the shroud to peer closely at his body. After a moment, they rewrapped his shroud and reinterred him in his grave.

The attendant walked over and asked them what they were doing. They explained that they had just received a posthumous letter from the man in question informing them that since his Jewish brethren hated him so for his frequent negative reports against them, they would no doubt defile his body after his death and bury him with little or no respect, outside the Jewish cemetery. He had hoped, he wrote, that the authorities would not let this grievance go unpunished. They had come to determine if he was right about the Jews, but it seemed that all was in order and nothing further would be done.

The Jewish attendant ran to the synagogue and excitedly told over what he saw and how this evil man hoped to get his last laugh at the expense of the Jews of Luban from beyond the grave. If not for the tenacious conformance of R' Moshe to the letter of the halachic law, disaster would have befallen his people.

| RAV ELCHANAN WASSERMAN |

A Providential Meeting
With the Rogatchover

The Bolshevik Revolution, and subsequently the clamping down of Communism towards the end of the First World War, caused untold hardship to hundreds of millions of Russian citizens, as well as a devastating death blow, from which they never recovered, to the Jewish population who found themselves under its tyrannical regime.

Not surprisingly, *yeshivos* and its students felt the hardship more keenly. Food was in short supply and the authorities hounded the faculty of many great institutions of Torah learning in many cities, threatening them with deportation to Siberia, or worse. Many *yeshivos* were forced to disband, and others, to split up. The yeshivah in Radin, under the Chafetz Chaim, migrated from place to place and divided itself into a number of smaller *yeshivos* that spread out across the Lithuanian landscape. In 1918, Rav Elchanan Wasserman *zt"l hy"d*, the prime disciple of the Chafetz Chaim, was asked to lead a group of students and maintain the "Chafetz Chaim Branch" in the village of Smilovitz.

For close to five years, R' Elchanan carried the burden of the yeshivah on his capable shoulders and worked tirelessly to raise money. On one of his fundraising trips to St. Petersburg, R' Elchanan made the acquaintance of the well-known *baal tzedakah*, Reb Dovid Potash, a wealthy philanthropist and communal leader. During years of famine, Reb Dovid used his resources to support the poor and needy. He was also popular with the great Torah scholars of the time who all admired his nobility of spirit. They turned to him when they were in need and he supported them in many communal undertakings.

He was especially friendly with the *illuy* (genius), Rav Yosef Rosen *zt"l*, (1858-1936) renowned throughout the Jewish world as the Rogatchover *Gaon*, author of the classic "*Tzafnas Pane'ach*." During World War I, the Rogatchover was forced to flee from his hometown of Dvinsk. He took up residence in St. Petersburg and he spent many days in Reb Dovid Potash's home. Since so many individuals presented themselves to Reb Dovid as *roshei yeshivah,* rabbis and scholars to solicit donations, he adopted the following procedure: Each was invited first to present himself to the Rogatchover and discuss

Torah topics with him. The sum he would receive would be based on the Rogatchover's stated opinion of him.

When R' Elchanan appeared to request a contribution for the Smilovitz Yeshivah, Reb Dovid introduced him to the Rogatchover. R' Elchanan was much younger than the famous *gaon* and his reputation had not yet spread throughout the Torah world. The two great men began a lively discussion on some halachic topic, one asking and the other answering, one posing some difficulty and the other offering a solution, one demolishing a concept, the other reconstructing it. It was undoubtedly a sparring of two great minds; few people would have been able to follow along the rolling waves that the two kicked up in the sea of Torah.

Reb Dovid Potash later spoke to the Rogatchover to determine his opinion of this *rosh yeshivah*. As is known, because of the sharpness of his mind, the Rogatchover would express himself caustically, even when talking to, or about, world-famous *geonim*. Nevertheless, he replied: "This *melamed* (children's teacher) understands Torah learning very well!" Anyone familiar with the manner in which the Rogatchover spoke realized that R' Elchanan had been given lavish praise. In fact, the *gaon* maintained this opinion of R' Elchanan at a later date when he told two students, who had asked if they should study under R' Elchanan, "You want to go and study under this *melamed*? Go, go to him and you will know how to learn a *blatt* gemara!"

Accepting this evaluation, R' Dovid Potash donated a large amount of money to the yeshivah and continued to contribute time and time again, throughout the duration of the war. There were times when the channels of overseas support became blocked, and Reb Dovid's contributions literally kept the yeshivah alive. From the sums received from Reb Dovid Potash, R' Elchanan provided for his students and he even organized a soup kitchen with an enormous urn to provide food for the poor refugees in Smilovitz with one hot meal per day. He never took one penny for the support of his own household.

An Officer's Burden and Redemption

As the Second World War drew to a close, thousands of Polish citizens who had fled to Russia in the last days of the war were now trying to return home. The special Russian-Polish commission in charge of issuing exit visas was centered in Lvov (Lemberg), and the city soon became terribly overcrowded.

Eliezer, a young Jew who had made his way to Lvov from Bukhara, met a group of Jewish youths who had banded together in the city for support, living in an overcrowded apartment while awaiting their visas. Unfortunately, before they even arrived in the city, it was discovered that the special Russian-Polish commission was no longer accepting applications. To the thousands of refugees with nowhere else to turn, it was a terrible blow. But Eliezer and his friends would not give up hope.

After discussing the matter at great length they concluded that there was only one solution, even though it seemed to be a long shot.

For some time, a rumor had been circulating among the refugees that the N.K.V.D. (Russian secret police) officer in charge of visa applications, Boris Sapokvini, was Jewish. As an officer of the U.S.S.R, he maintained an outward appearance of unapproachable coldness. Deep down, though, it was said that he was a warmhearted individual, who would help his Jewish brethren. Everyone was well aware that the rumor was only speculation, nobody really knew for sure. But without any viable alternative, Eliezer and his friends decided to forge ahead with their plan.

The next night, Eliezer and another young man went to N.K.V.D. headquarters. In exchange for a bribe, the watchman gave them several applications and the home address of Boris Sapokvini. They hurried back to their apartment and filled out the forms.

The following morning they were waiting on the sidewalk when Sapokvini left for work. As always, the officer's uniform was impeccable, his hair carefully coifed. Despite the cold, the two young men were drenched in sweat, terrified by the risk they were about to take.

As the officer walked past them, they took a deep breath and blurted out, "We represent ten young Jews who wish to leave Russia. Please help us, for otherwise we will be forced to take drastic action."

Boris Sapokvini gave no sign that he had heard them and continued walking. But a few yards later he stopped and spun around. "No! It's already too late. And who told you about me, anyway? How did you get my address?"

The N.K.V.D. officer was clearly furious.

A full minute passed as Sapokvini scrutinized the two young men. Then, in a whisper he asked them, "Do you have the exit forms?" With a trembling hand Eliezer held them out. The officer stuffed them into his pocket and said quietly, "Eleven o'clock tonight. In my office," and walked on.

That evening, which happened to be the first night of Chanukah, Eliezer went to Sapokvini's office by himself. The officer quickly locked the door after Eliezer was inside.

The two men sat on opposite sides of the desk and looked at each other. Suddenly, two tears rolled down the Russian's cheeks. As if wishing to unburden himself, Sapokvini began to tell Eliezer the story of his life, which quickly verified the rumor that he was Jewish. He also revealed that he had successfully enabled thousands of Jews to leave the Soviet Union.

In the slight pause that followed, Eliezer reminded the officer that it was the first night of Chanukah. Startled by the news, Sapokvini checked the windows to make sure the blinds were drawn and walked over to the glass jar in the corner that contained an emergency candle, in case of electrical failure. Striking a match, he lit the wick and began to chant the Chanukah blessings.

Two days later, Eliezer and his friends crossed over the border and arrived safely in Poland. Eventually Eliezer made his way to Israel, where he lives today. According to reliable information, Sapokvini's activities were eventually uncovered and he was put to death before a firing squad, but not before he had saved the lives of thousands of his brethren.

| RAV YECHEZKEL ABRAMSKY |

"All is Heavenly-Directed Except Cold and Heat."

After he was released from a Siberian prison where he was sentenced to five years of hard labor, Rav Yechezkel Abramsky *zt"l* would often relate the following: "For twenty years, our patriarch Yaakov shepherded the flocks of sheep belonging to his father-in-law Lavan, even under extreme outdoor conditions, as he said: 'By day heat consumed me and frost by night.' (Bereishis 31-40)"

R' Yechezkel would compare his situation to that of Yaakov Avinu. "When I was imprisoned in Siberia, there were mornings when the temperature would plummet to forty degrees below zero. The bitter cold and the biting winds were absolutely unbearable. Nevertheless, our Russian captors would force us to take off our shoes and run barefoot in the snow. Can you imagine the torture? Believe me, from this torture alone, even the strongest of men fell like flies.

"I knew that there was no way I could survive this situation. I looked toward Heaven and cried, 'Master of the Universe, You have taught us: 'All is Heavenly-directed (except illness) through cold or heat.' (Kesubos 30) Cold and heat are in man's own hands since man can guard himself from the elements by donning a coat or removing a sweater. This reason, however, no longer applies to me, for my captors not only fail to provide me with clothes, but force me to remove whatever I am wearing. My obligation to guard my health, therefore, is no longer my responsibility. It now returns to You. Please protect me, Hashem, for I trust in You!'"

R' Yechezkel concluded: "As a child, my mother always bundled me up warmly due to my frailty and yet, while in the midst of that Siberian cold, I never once took sick or even caught a cold!"

| RAV ELIYAHU ESSAS |

The "Bubba" of Moscow

T he Creator works in mysterious ways. Behind the folds of Russia's Iron Curtain and the constant persecution of religion that was a staple of the Communist doctrine, Rav Eliyahu Essas *shlit''a* discovered the Torah while still a student at the Vilnius Academy. All it took was a tiny spark to ignite his passion for his religion and, through perseverance and diligence, he soon became the inspiration for all Russian *refuseniks* and *baalei teshuvah*. R' Eliyahu became a vocal leader of Russian Jewry when there wasn't much Jewry to speak of and, incredibly, he became an accomplished Torah scholar and teacher.

But if Rabbi Essas can be called the father of the Soviet *baal teshuvah* movement, a short, stocky, elderly woman - possessor of a pair of shrewd eyes and an indomitable spirit - by the name of Frieda Koronova, deserves to be known as its grandmother, its "Bubba."

The men and women who were returning to Jewish observance in Moscow, Riga, and Leningrad knew little about the elderly widow who served as the caretaker for the Moscow *mikvah*. She wore a kerchief, living alone in a small Moscow apartment - and she was there when anyone needed her.

As the network of observant Jewish families grew, so did the number of women determined to fulfill the mitzvah of family purity. By the mid-1980s, the once moribund Moscow *mikvah* was serving more than one hundred and twenty women, all under the shadow of the KGB who was unaware that this "bathhouse" was in fact being used for religious purposes! The network spread the word: To use the *mikvah*, contact Frieda Koronova. And so they did, in ever-increasing numbers.

At first, Frieda was suspicious. Was this a KGB ploy, or some kind of practical joke? Why were all these women calling her out of the blue? But once convinced of the seriousness of these women's commitment, Frieda Koronova joyously embraced the group.

Aside from the *mikvah,* many families were in desperate need of inspiration, of Torah. Finding a place to hold *shiurim* was always a continual challenge. Most people lived in small apartments, and there was simply no room for the increasing number of participants. Many of the students still lived with their parents, who refused to tolerate these strange, dangerous goings on.

When Frieda heard about the problem, she decided to solve it by offering her own small home as a meeting place. From then on, she would sit in her miniscule kitchen, a saintly smile on her face, listening in on the learning that she couldn't understand a word of, beaming proudly at her "grandchildren." The *shiur klali* (general lecture) delivered by R' Essas and others was held there for the most advanced students. Her small apartment near the Voykovskaya Station of Moscow's subway ultimately saw more scholars, and heard more words of Torah spoken than any other in the city. "*Dos iz mein gantz leiben* - This is my entire life," she once told a visitor from Israel who delivered a *shiur* in her home.

The young people got a taste of her indomitable spirit one evening, when their *shiur* was interrupted by a knock on the door. The secret police had found them!

Panic ensued in the little apartment. The terrified participants scurried about but there was no place to hide. The little woman - the "Bubba" - however, never panicked. Her small frame took position in front of the doorway, a bulwark protecting her loved ones. She was a fierce lioness protecting her young. She opened the door and announced to the men standing on the other side, "I went through Hitler's camps. Fascists killed my entire family. These people are my only grandchildren. Hitler couldn't kill me and you won't kill me either."

In the face of such determined opposition, and perhaps with the memory of their own *babushkas* in their minds, the police shamefacedly turned away to wait for their quarry downstairs, where it was "safer."

That was all the Jewish men and women huddling in the apartment needed. Used to police ways, the participants simply climbed up to the roof, found a small crawl space, and made their careful way to the next entrance. Hardly glancing at the ominous black Volga sedan parked in front of Frieda's apartment house, they nonchalantly walked home, unspoken mixed feelings of triumph, anxiety, and gratitude in their hearts.

Such was the movement's "Bubba."

A Stamp of Approval

Many stories are told of the great effort and *mesiras nefesh* of the Lubavitcher Rebbe, Rav Yosef Yitzchak Schneerson *zt"l*, on behalf of the Jews of Russia during the time when the Czarist regime still ruled the Russian Empire.

One incident, though, stands out. A new decree against the Jewish community was in the works, aimed at forcing changes in the structure of the rabbinate and Jewish education. R' Yosef Yitzchak, then a young man, was dispatched by his father, the previous Rebbe, Rav Shalom Dov *zt"l*, to the Russian capital of St. Petersburg to see what he could do to prevent the decree from being passed.

Upon his arrival in St. Petersburg, R' Yosef Yitzchak learned that the decree had already reached the desk of a man by the name of Stolipin, the feared and hated interior minister of Russia and arguably one of the most powerful men in the entire Russian Empire. The ruling czar's lack of decisiveness made him a virtual rubber stamp for whichever minister the prevailing political climate favored. At that particular time, the czar was influenced by Interior Minister Stolipin, a heartless tyrant and rabid anti-Semite who was personally responsible for many of the devastating pogroms which were "arranged" for the Jews of Russia.

This was indeed a problem, but for the Lubavitcher Rebbe, it was not insurmountable. He made a few inquiries and learned that living in the capital city of St. Petersburg was an elderly non-Jewish scholar, a former teacher and mentor of Stolipin. This man, reasoned R' Yosef Yitzchak, may prove to be a valuable asset. R' Yosef Yitzchak succeeded in befriending this man, who was greatly impressed by the scope and depth of the young scholar's knowledge. For many an evening, the two would sit and talk in the old man's study.

One day, R' Yosef Yitzchak told his new friend the purpose of his stay in St. Petersburg and pleaded with him to assist him in reaching the interior minister.

The old scholar eyed him carefully. Then, he replied, "This is not an easy matter. I know Stolipin. To speak with him would be useless. The man has a cruel and malicious heart, and I have already severed all contact with this vile creature many years ago. But there is one thing I can do for you. Because of my status as Stolipin's mentor and my stature in the intellectual community, I have been granted a permanent entry pass into the Interior Ministry building. These days, I do not have much use for this pass. I can 'lend' you my pass for a short time which will allow you access into the building and perhaps an audience with the man you seek. But I need not explain to you the consequences, for both of us, if you are found out. It is only because I have come to respect you and what you stand for, that I have decided to help you."

R' Yosef Yitzchak thanked him dearly and promised that he would be careful. The old man handed over his precious pass and the younger man prepared his strategy.

The next morning, when R' Yosef Yitzchak presented the pass at the gates of the Interior Ministry building, the guard on duty was stupefied; few cabinet-level ministers were granted such a privilege, and here stands a young Jew, complete with beard, sidelocks, Chassidic garb and Yiddish accent, at a time when to even reside in St. Petersburg was forbidden to Jews. But the pass was in order, so he waved him through.

R' Yosef Yitzchak entered the building and proceeded to look for Stolipin's office. He thought if he could get just a few words with the man, he may just succeed. Those who he passed in the hallways could only stare at the strange apparition confidently striding the corridors of the Interior Ministry. But Russians are trained not to ask questions or even delve into anything which was not directly related to them. They walked on by and let him go. After much effort, R' Yosef Yitzchak managed to locate the minister's office at the far end of a commanding hallway, on the fourth floor of the building.

As R' Yosef Yitzchak walked toward the office, the door opened and Stolipin himself walked out and closed the door behind him. The future Rebbe and the hated Interior Minister passed within a few feet of each other, but the feared Russian never even turned in his direction. Thinking quickly, R' Yosef Yitzchak went straight to the office, opened the door, and walked right in.

The office was empty. R' Yosef Yitzchak searched the entire room quickly looking for papers or documents pertaining to the decree against the Jews. It took a few short minutes, but eventually, after rummaging through the desk, he found what he was looking for, sitting right inside Stolipin's desk.

R' Yosef Yitzchak held his breath as he read through the documents as quickly as he could - and then he made a decision. On the desktop sat two rubber ink stamps, bearing the Russian words 'APPROVED' or 'REJECTED' above the minister's signature and seal. Quickly, R' Yosef Yitzchak grabbed the stamp 'REJECTED' and stamped the proposed decree with a forceful bang. He scrutinized his handiwork until he was satisfied. Then, he inserted the newly stamped papers into a pile of vetoed documents which sat in a tray on the desk.

With a quick backward glance, he walked out of the room and closed the door quietly behind him. He got out of the building as fast as he could reasonably walk without arousing suspicion, and left St. Petersburg that very day. Mission accomplished!

Biographies of Great Men Mentioned Within the Pages of this Book

Rav Yoel Teitelbaum zt"l

(1887 - 1979)

known as "Reb Yoelish," was the saintly Rebbe of Satmar. He was already a highly regarded Rebbe in Hungary and when the Nazis invaded Hungary in 1944, he was rescued from death in Nazi-controlled Transylvania as a result of a deal between a Hungarian official, Rudolph Kastner, and a deputy of Adolf Eichmann. Although Kastner intended to rescue only Hungarian Zionists on a special train bound for Switzerland, R' Yoel and a few other religious Jews were also given seats. (It has been said that this was the result of a dream in which Kastner's father-in-law was informed by his late mother that if the Grand Rabbi of Satmar was not included on the train, none of the passengers would survive.) En route, the train was re-routed by the Germans to Bergen-Belsen, where the 1600 passengers languished for four months while awaiting further negotiations between rescue activists and the Nazi leadership. In the end, the train was released and continued on to Switzerland. R' Yoel briefly lived in Jerusalem after World War II, but, at the request of some of his chassidim who had emigrated to the United States, he settled there instead and established a large community in the densely Orthodox neighborhood of Williamsburg located in northern Brooklyn in New York City.

(1886-1959)

known throughout the world as the "Brisker Rav" ("rabbi of Brisk") was the oldest son of the great Rav Chaim Soloveitchik zt"l of Brisk.

He was the rabbi of the Jewish community in Brisk and was the *rosh yeshivah* of its yeshivah. While vacationing away from his home, World War II broke out and he was unable to return to Brisk. He lived in Warsaw and later moved to Vilna, where he was looked upon for guidance by so many suffering Jews. He was fortunate and was able to flee the Holocaust together with three of his sons. His wife, mother and three small children perished.

When the Brisker Rav was in Europe and all was burning, he had a choice where to escape: America or Palestine. Despite the danger posed by the German army, which at that point had already reached Egypt, he chose to go to Jerusalem, because in Jerusalem, he said, "there is a small group of Jews who truly fight for the honor of Hashem *Yisbarach*." In a place where the Jews never gave up the fight - that would be the guarantee that he would raise good children and future generations. He moved to the Holy Land, where he re-established the Brisk Yeshivah in Israel. In Jerusalem he continued educating students as his father did, with what would come to be known as the Brisker *derech* (the "Brisk method" or "Brisk approach") of analyzing Talmud.

Rav Aharon Rokeach zt"l

(1877 - 1957)

was the fourth Belzer Rebbe in the illustrious line of the Belzer Chassidic dynasty. He was Rebbe from 1926 until his passing in 1957. Known for his piety and righteousness, R' Aharon was called the "wonder rebbe" by Jews and gentiles - even the Nazis - alike for the miracles he performed. R' Aharon's rule as rebbe saw the devastation of the Belz community, along with that of many other chassidic dynasties in Galicia and elsewhere in Poland during the Holocaust. During the Holocaust, R' Aharon was high on the list of Gestapo targets as a high-profile Rebbe. He and his brother, Rav Mordechai of Bilgoray, spent most of the war hiding from the Nazis and moving from place to place, with the support and financial assistance of their chassidim both inside and outside Europe. Eventually, they were taken out of Europe via a series of escapes, many miraculous in nature. R' Aharon and R' Mordechai immigrated to the British Mandate of Palestine in 1944. The two lost their entire extended families, including their wives, children, and grandchildren.

Rav Yekusiel Yehudah Halberstam zt"l

(1905 - 1994)

was the first Klausenberger Rebbe, founding the Sanz-Klausenberg chassidic dynasty. He was known for his personal righteousness, kindness toward others, and Torah wisdom that positively influenced whole communities before, during and after the Holocaust. He was a natural leader, mentor, and father figure for thousands of Jews of all ages. The Klausenberger Rebbe became one of the youngest rebbes in Europe, leading thousands of followers in the town of Klausenberg, Romania, before World War II. When the Nazis invaded Romania, he was taken away from his family and incarcerated under terrible conditions, in a number of concentration camps. The Nazis murdered his wife, eleven children and most of his followers. He managed to survive through his great faith and encouraged others to believe all throughout the war. After the war, he rebuilt Jewish communal life in the displaced persons camps of Western Europe, re-established the Klausenberg dynasty in the United States and Israel, and rebuilt his own family with a second marriage and the birth of seven more children.

Rav Aharon Kotler zt"l

(1891 - 1962)

was a prominent *rosh yeshivah* in Lithuania before the war, and later became the leader of the yeshivah movement and litvishe Jewry in the United States of America, where he built up one of the first and largest *yeshivos* in the U.S. After learning in the famed Slabodka Yeshivah in Lithuania, he joined his father-in-law, R' Isser Zalman Meltzer, to run the yeshiva of Slutsk. When the Soviets took over, the yeshivah moved from Slutsk to Kletsk in Poland. With the outbreak of World War II, R' Aharon and the yeshivah relocated to Vilna, then the major refuge of most *yeshivos* from the occupied areas. Through the intervention of American Jewry, R' Aharon was able to escape Europe for the United States via Siberia, but many of his students did not survive the war. He was brought to America in 1941 by the Va'ad Hatzalah rescue organization and soon assumed its leadership, guiding it during the Holocaust and using any means at his disposal to try to rescue the remnants of European Jewry. In 1943, R' Aharon assumed leadership of Bais Medrash Govoha in Lakewood, New Jersey and continued to lead American Jewry until his untimely passing in 1962. Today, Bais Medrash Govoha has grown into the largest institution of its kind in America with thousands of students and married *kollel* members, as well as a number of satellite yeshivos.

(1895 - 1986)

 was a world-renowned *posek* (halachic arbitrator) and was regarded as the supreme rabbinic authority for Orthodox Jewry of North America. R' Moshe grew up Uzda, near Minsk, Belorus, where his father was rabbi. In 1921, at the age of 26, he became rabbi of Luban, near Minsk, where he served for sixteen years. Under increasing pressure and torment from the Soviet regime, who enacted decrees to limit his authority and control over the community, he moved with his family to New York City in 1937 where he lived for the rest of his life. Settling on the Lower East Side, he became the *rosh yeshiva* of Mesivta Tifereth Jerusalem. He later established a branch of the yeshiva in Staten Island, New York, now headed by his son Rabbi Reuven Feinstein. In the Orthodox world, it is universal to refer to him simply as "Rav Moshe" or "Reb Moshe." R' Moshe became the leading halachic authority of his time and his rulings were accepted worldwide. He was a dedicated, selfless and beloved leader for the Jewish people to whom anyone could approach at any time with any problem.

(1882 - 1968)

was the president of the Agudas HaRabbonim of America and among American Jewry's foremost religious leaders. He helped save many thousands of Jews in the Second World War and held several rabbinical positions in New York, Pennsylvania, Massachusetts and Ohio. R' Silver convened an emergency meeting in November 1939 in New York City, where the Va'ad Hatzalah (Rescue Committee), was formed, with R' Silver as president. He spearheaded its efforts in rescuing as many European Torah scholars as possible from Nazi Europe. He launched a fund-raising drive that raised more than $5 million, and also capitalized on an exemption to U.S. immigration quotas allowing entry to ministers or religious students. At his direction, synagogues in Cincinnati and across the country sent contracts to rabbis, thereby securing 2,000 emergency visas that were telegraphed to Eastern Europe. R' Silver used all channels, whether legal or not, to save as many lives as possible by bringing Jews to the U.S., Canada and the Holy Land. Sympathetic foreign diplomats provided fake visas for immigration; counterfeiters were paid to produce phony passports. In October 1943, as the scale of Nazi atrocities was becoming clearer, R' Silver helped organize and lead a mass rally of more than 400 rabbis in Washington to press for more decisive action by the US government to save European Jews. After the war, he distributed relief funds and helped expedite visas to Jews in eight European nations - wearing, with government permission, a U.S. Army uniform for extra protection in areas where anti-Semitism was still rife. When donations were insufficient, R' Silver often spent his own money to meet refugees' needs.

(1888-1967)

the Kapyschnitzer Rebbe, was renowned for his supreme kindness and great *ahavas yisrael* (love of ones fellow Jew). On his weak and frail shoulders, he carried the pain and suffering of countless individuals, and often when he heard of the problems of others, he would break down weeping uncontrollably. With the outbreak of the First World War in 1914, R' Avraham Yehoshua fled with his family to Vienna. When Jewish life was shattered by the German occupation of Vienna, the Rebbe was seized and forced to clean the streets to the amusement of the jeering Germans. On one occasion in an attempt to humiliate the Rebbe, the Germans sent one of their officers to cut off his beard. The Rebbe promptly stuck out two fingers and told the officer, "Rather cut off my fingers, but don't touch my beard." The German, startled by the Rebbe's courage, left without carrying out his evil orders. Despite the pleas of his chassidim that he flee Vienna, the Rebbe stayed put, refusing to leave his followers behind. Tortures and threats did not bother him. Only when it became increasingly difficult to keep the Torah and mitzvos did he finally give in and reluctantly agree to leave Vienna. On his arrival in America, the Rebbe settled in the Lower East Side of New York where he opened his *beis hamedrash* (study hall) and immediately threw himself into the task of saving the lives of the *Yidden* he had left behind in Europe. His dedication to refugees of the war was especially extraordinary. He opened an orphanage in Petach Tikvah, Israel called Beit Avraham, which exists until this day.

(1891 - 1986)

studied in Minsk and then for 21 years in the Slabodka yeshiva. It was there that he met his lifelong friend Rabbi Aharon Kotler, who would go on to lead the Lakewood Yeshivah. R' Yaakov was appointed rabbi of Tzitavyan in 1926 and moved to North America in 1937, where he initially took a rabbinical position in Seattle and then Toronto. From 1948 to 1968 he headed Mesivta Torah Vodaath in Brooklyn, New York. Along with R' Moshe Feinstein, he led American Jewry in issues of halachic and spiritual guidance until 1986, when both men passed away. Aside from his extensive Torah scholarship, R' Yaakov was known for his ever-present warm smile and his expertise in Hebrew grammar. Today, his son Rabbi Shmuel Kamenetsky is one of the leading Orthodox rabbis in America. Dozens of his descendants serve in key leadership positions across North America and in Israel.

Rav Yisrael Meir Hakohen Kagan zt"l

(1838 - 1933)

is commonly known as the "Chafetz Chaim," the name of his famous work on guarding one's tongue from speaking evil. The Chafetz Chaim was the undisputed *Gadol Hador* (leader of his generation) and his counsel, blessings and insight, was much sought after. As a young man, he refused the rabbinate of a number of towns and eventually settled in Radin (Poland) where he subsisted on a small grocery store which his wife managed and he did the "bookkeeping"- watching every penny to make sure that no one was cheated. He spent his days learning Torah and disseminating his knowledge to the common people. As his reputation grew, students from all over Europe flocked to him and by 1869 his house became known as the Radin Yeshivah. When the Bolsheviks seized power in Russia in 1917, the upheaval forced the Chafetz Chaim who had split up the yeshivah when he left Radin temporarily during World War I, to settle in the small city of Snovsk where it remained until 1921. In addition to his yeshivah, the Chafetz Chaim was very active in Jewish causes. He traveled extensively (even in his 90's) to encourage the observance of *mitzvos* amongst Jews. One of the founders of Agudas Yisrael, the religious Jewish organization of Europe and later the world, the Chafetz Chaim was very involved in Jewish affairs and helped many *yeshivos* survive the financial problems of the interwar period. The Chafetz Chaim passed away in 1933 at the ripe age of 95.

Rav Yechezkel Abramsky zt"l

(1886 - 1976)

studied at the *yeshivos* of Telshe, Mir, Slabodka and particularly Brisk under Rabbi Chaim Soloveitchik. At the age of 17 he became a rabbi, serving, in turn, the communities of Smolyan, Smolevich and Slutsk. Following the Russian Revolution, he was at the forefront of opposition to Communist attempts to repress the Jewish religion and culture. As a result the Russian government twice refused him permission to emigrate to the land of Israel and take up the rabbinate of Petach Tikvah, in both 1926 and 1928. In 1928, he started a Hebrew magazine, *Yagdil Torah* (lit. "Make [the] Torah Great"), but the Soviet authorities closed it down after two issues appeared. In 1929, he was arrested and sentenced to five years hard labor in Siberia. However, in 1931 the German government under Chancellor Brüning, who exchanged him for six Communists they held, rescued him. He immigrated to London in 1932, where he was appointed rabbi of the Machzike Hadas community in London's East End. In 1934, he became the senior *dayan* of the London Beth Din, holding the post until he retired to Jerusalem in 1951. While living in Israel, he also served as a *rosh yeshiva* of the Slabodka yeshiva in Bnei Brak. R' Yechezkel passed away in Jerusalem on September 19, 1976.

(1863-1940)

was a world renowned pre-war *Dayan*, *Posek* and Talmudic scholar in Vilna. R' Chaim Ozer was a founding member and administrator of the *Va'ad HaYeshivos* in Lithuania. He also established a network of Jewish schools that provided traditional Jewish education and the Agudas HaRabbanim of Poland. The Chafetz Chaim would not initiate any public action, or sign any public document, until he consulted with Rabbi Grodzenski, considering him to be a living embodiment of Torah. R' Chaim Ozer passed away in 1940, in the Lithuanian capital of Vilna, where he had served as Chief Rabbi for many decades, after a protracted illness, thought to be cancer. He did all he was able at that difficult period of time when thousands of yeshivah students poured into Vilna, fleeing from the Nazis in the west and the Soviets in the east. The overcrowding conditions in Vilna were merciless and the hardships facing the many refugees became unbearable. Through it all, R' Chaim Ozer, worked tirelessly to provide assistance for all. His door remained open for much of the day and night, to all the questions, advice and solace that he could provide for the needy masses. R' Chaim Ozer was no youngster and his illness was progessive, yet he resolutely carried on on behalf of his people. His passing prompted massive grief and a huge funeral was held, attended by most of Lithuanian Jewry and many war refugees from Poland, led by the most eminent rabbis of the time.

Chacham Rabbeinu Yisrael Abuchatzeira zt"l

(1890-1984)

the Baba Sali, was a Moroccan-born *Chacham* and Kabbalist teacher. Baba Sali has become legendary to Moroccan Jews and is known as the "Praying Father" of the Moroccan Jewish community, who made *aliyah* to Israel in the middle of the twentieth century. The Baba Sali was part of a lineage of great Talmudic scholars. When the Germans invaded North Africa, during World War II, its Jews feared that their end was near. Yet even then, the Baba Sali continued to pray, promising his community that if they did teshuvah, the enemy would not overtake them. A short while before the German troops reached Arpud, the capital city of the Risani district in southern Morocco, where the Baba Sali served as chief Rabbi, the Americans arrived on the scene, saving the entire district. After that, Morocco's Jews continued to pray for the welfare of their brothers in Eretz Yisrael, to where the Germans were rapidly advancing. While the Germans reached El Alamein in Egypt, they were turned back before ever entering the Holy Land. The Baba Sali is known for miracles performed and for being instrumental in helping Moroccan Jews make *aliyah* to the young State of Israel. An estimated 100,000 people attended his funeral in 1984, and his tomb has become a pilgrimage site to Moroccan Jews.

(1891-1965)

was a born leader; his strong personality and authoritative voice commanded respect of Jew and gentile alike. At the beginning of World War II, the *rav* and his family reached the United States, while his beloved Mirrer Yeshivah escaped from Mir to Vilna, to avoid Soviet persecution. At that time, Vilna - like the entire Lithuanian Republic - was only a temporary haven, for Russia would soon swallow the entire little country. The yeshivah moved again - this time from Vilna to Keidan, until emigration procedures could be arranged. The *rav* began to work frantically from the U.S., knowing that he was fighting for time. A fortune had to be raised immediately. The Rav did not rest until his beloved yeshivah was safely on its way across Siberia. The yeshivah finally arrived in Vladivostok, and from there by boat to the Japanese port of Kobe, Japan. A short time later, the yeshiva relocated again, to (Japanese-controlled) Shanghai, China, where they remained until the end of World War II, when the majority of Jewish refugees from the Shanghai ghetto left for Palestine and the United States. R' Kalmanowitz worked tirelessly, as only a father would - to rescue his children, the remnants of the European *yeshivos*. But he also made sure that they would not be the last of a species - by founding the Mirrer Yeshivah in Brooklyn, NY. He also imported new *talmidim* from the Maghreb region, the term generally applied to all of Morocco, Algeria, and Tunisia. To his *talmidim*, admirers, and to all who owe him their very lives, he was indeed the last of a unique species, a man who served Hashem with inexhaustible zeal.

(1907 - 2000)

the third Bobover Rebbe re-established the Bobover dynasty in the United States after World War II. He was the son of Rabbi Ben Zion Halberstam *zt"l hy"d* (1874-1941) of Bobov, who died in the Holocaust. During World War II the beautiful *Chassidus* of Bobov was destroyed, the second rebbe himself perishing in the Holocaust together with thousands of his followers. His son, R' Shlomo, through *bitachon*, and no short supply of cunning, managed to stay one step ahead of the Nazis, miraculously escaping from Poland, where he organized an underground escape route enabling many to get away to Hungary and Czechoslovakia. He, his mother and his young son Naftali Tzvi (later to succeed his father as Bobover Rebbe) were from the few members of his family to survive the Holocaust. After the war, he made his way to Italy, with the intention of emigrating to Palestine, which refused him entry. Instead, he came to London, urging British Jews to rescue the remnants of European Jewry. Barely 300 Bobover chassidim survived, and R' Shlomo took it upon himself to rebuild Bobov. He eventually settled in Boro Park, New York, and married his second cousin Freidel Rubin, with whom he went on to have five daughters and one son. R' Shlomo was known as a very wise man, a giant in good *middos* and a true gentleman. He was noted for his steadfastness in not taking sides in disputes. This brought him great popularity and respect.

(1880–1950)

known as the "Rebbe Rayatz" was the first Lubavitcher Rebbe in the United States. Following the tradition of his predecessors, he took charge of the Chabad movement upon the death of his father and led it until his death in 1950. He fought against the Bolsheviks by attempting to preserve Jewish life in Russia. In 1927, he was arrested and imprisoned in the Spalerno prison in Leningrad, and sentenced to death for spreading Judaism. After international protests, his life was spared and he went on a world tour in the early 1930s. He returned to Warsaw in 1934, disillusioned with the secularism of the United States. He stayed in Warsaw with his chasidim through 1940 and the capture of the city by the Nazis. A desperate struggle to save his life ensued. Ultimately, he was granted diplomatic immunity, and arrived in New York in March 1940, reputedly with the help of Admiral Wilhelm Canaris. Bolshevik governments and the Nazi invasion in 1941 destroyed most of the Chabad Yeshivah system, and many of its students were killed.

Rav Eliezer Zusia Portugal zt"l

(1898-1982)

the Skulener Rebbe, succeeded his father as rabbi of Skulen at the age of 17 upon the latter's death in 1915. Before the outbreak of World War II, upon the urging of the Sadigorer Rebbe, the Skulener Rebbe moved to the city of Chernowitz. Chernowitz changed hands several times during World War II, eventually ending up in the Soviet Union. On a number of occasions, both the Germans and Russians persecuted the Rebbe. More than once, his life was in danger. One day he was even taken out to be executed, but he was saved from the Germans by a miracle. The Russians also imprisoned him several times. But despite everything, he never stopped his appointed task. After the war he moved to Bucharest, the capital of Romania, where he opened an orphanage for the orphans left after the Holocaust. When the Communists took over Romania it became dangerous for him to continue to educate the children in the ways of Judaism, yet the Rebbe continued unafraid. In 1959 the Communists arrested the Rebbe and his son, the present Rebbe, for teaching religion and for supporting and educating orphans. An international effort to free the Skulener Rebbe and his son was mounted, and eventually, through the intervention of United Nations Secretary-General Dag Hammarskjld, they were freed and immediately immigrated to the United States in 1960. Upon moving to America, the rebbe continued his works helping the underprivileged and began an international charity organization known as Chesed L'Avraham. The Rebbe authored Noam Eliezer and Kedushas Eliezer, and composed many popular Chassidic tunes. He passed away in 1982 and is buried in the Viznitzer Cemetery in Monsey, NY.

(1886-1969)

was the founder and *rosh yeshiva* of the Ponevezh yeshiva. At the age of 33, R' Kahaneman was appointed the new rabbi of Ponevezh, one of the largest centers of Jewish life in Lithuania. There, he built three *yeshivos* as well as a school and an orphanage. He was even elected to the Lithuanian Parliament. However, all of his institutions were destroyed and many of his students and family were killed during World War II. R' Kahaneman immigrated to the British Mandate of Palestine in 1940 and built Kiryat HaYeshivah ("Town of the Yeshivah") in Bnei Brak and Batei Avos orphanages. He traveled widely in the Diaspora to secure financial support for his yeshivah, which he constantly improved and extended. In the face of skepticism and opposition, he succeeded in turning the re-established Ponovezh Yeshivah into one of the largest in the world. He sought to take care of many orphans and tried to rescue them from the clutches of secular Zionist organizations, especially the Yaldei Tehran ("Children of Tehran") - children who escaped from Nazi Europe by walking across Europe to Tehran (including the famous Biala Rebbe - Rabbi Ben Zion Rabinowitz). R' Kahaneman was a distinguished member of the Council of Torah Sages of Agudas Yisrael, a man of deep piety and wit.

(1901 - 1980)

was a businessman, philanthropist and a major lay leader of Orthodox Jewry in the United States from the 1930s until his passing in 1980. As the trusted assistant to R' Aharon Kotler, he was deeply involved in all aspects of Torah dissemination, philanthropy and Holocaust rescue. Together with other American Orthodox leaders, Mr. Bunim established the *Va'ad Hatzalah,* an organization created to save yeshivah students and teachers from captivity and probable death in Eastern Europe. Later, the Va'ad's scope expanded to include all suffering Jews in Europe and helped them by sending food and other relief supplies, or by giving them refuge in non-European countries of safety. The hardest aspect of his rescue work was negotiating with the Nazis themselves. A series of negotiations called the Musy Negotiations, named after Jean-Marie Musy, the pro-Nazi former president of Switzerland, was initiated. In these negotiations the Va'ad agreed to pay the Nazis ransom to free Jews from concentration camps. After some dealings the Vaad agreed to pay $5 million for 300,000 Jews or $250,000 each month for 20 months to free 15,000 Jews. These negotiations failed, though some one thousand Jews, out of the 300,000 Jews promised to be freed, were saved from a certain death. After the war the Va'ad kept working to supply the survivors with food and other relief supplies. Irving Bunim was a philanthropist who gave loans and did the best he could to help people in need. His main goal was spreading the word of the Torah to all Jews who had forgotten it, or never been exposed to it, in America, Israel and the rest of the world. He was devoted to fund-raising work. Irving Bunim passed away in 1980 at his home in New York City.

(1889 - 1989)

the Bluzhever Rebbe, was the scion of the illustrious Bluzhever dynasty, of which he remained the sole survivor after the war. He had been the *rov* in the small town of Pruchnik until 1932 and only assumed the title of Bluzhever Rebbe after his arrival in the United States in 1946. His *rebbetzin* and their daughter, with her husband and children, were among the six million who perished. At the outbreak of World War II, he moved from Istrik to Lvov. Lvov was then under Soviet rule due to the Soviet-German non-aggression pact that was signed on August 23, 1939, which effectively divided the soon-to-be conquered country of Poland into two. The Eastern half was to fall under the sphere of Soviet influence, while the invading Germans would control the western sector. Of course, the Germans could not be trusted and in the summer of 1941, the Germans broke the treaty and occupied the Soviet areas. R' Yisroel found himself in the Lvov Ghetto under horrid conditions until its liquidation in June of 1943, where he and the remaining Jews were deported to Bergen Belsen and later to the infamous Janowska road camp, from where almost no one survived. R' Yisroel suffered for nearly five years in a succession of labor, concentration, and death camps but was a constant bastion of faith and inspiration in the camps where he helped as many Jews as he was able. After liberation, he emigrated to the U.S., rebuilt the Bluzhever Chassidus, and became one of the leading lights of Chassidic Jewry until his death in 1989.

Rav Michoel Ber Weissmandel zt"l

(1904-1957)

a son-in-law of the Nitra Rav and a Jewish resistance leader working to rescue Jews during the Holocaust - had tried to warn the Hungarian Jews of their impending doom. The Nazis captured him shortly after he sent a letter to the outside world demanding that the Allied forces bomb the Auschwitz Death Camp in order to disable it. He escaped this capture by jumping off a moving transport train as did many of the war survivors, as it headed for Auschwitz. During the height of the war, Rabbi Weissmandel managed to stop the deportation of 25,000 Romanian Jews by bribing Adolf Eichmann's second-in command. Encouraged by this success, Rabbi Weissmandel conceived an incredibly bold plan to try and buy the life of every Jew in Europe. The Europa Plan, as it was called, was an attempt to rescue every remaining Jew by giving the Nazis a massive bribe. After protracted negotiations, the Nazis agreed to stop all deportations everywhere except from Poland, for two million dollars. With the receipt of the first $200,000 the Nazis would halt the transports for two months. After that, the next payment would be due. In spite of almost superhuman efforts, Rabbi Weissmandel was unable to raise the first $200,000 dollars, and negotiations broke down in September 1943. He later settled in the U.S. but remained broken and bitter at American Jewry's inability to rescue their brethren. He reestablished the Nitra Yeshiva in Mt. Kisco, NY, and remarried. He was blessed with five exceptional children who carry on his legacy till this day.

the revered Viznitzer Rebbe, was a spiritually energizing force in the entire region, but the war brought all this to an abrupt halt. Miraculously the Rebbe escaped war-torn Romania and survived. When the Romanian Jews were deported in 1941 to Transnistria (a death camp in the Ukraine, administered jointly by the Germans and the Romanians from July 1941 to March 1944), R' Chaim Meir threw himself, heart and soul, into the rescue operation helping to alleviate the suffering in Transnistria and established a rescue apparatus that saved thousands of Jewish souls from certain death. Within a short time, the Viznitzer Rebbe gathered around him a group of survivors, thirsty for spirituality. He changed their lives, taking broken despondent refugees on the road to nowhere and turning them into optimistic chassidim. It did not take long to realize that Europe would no longer yield the harvest of holiness that it had in the past. Consequently, he set his sights on the Holy Land, where he had a huge following, including the thousands of settlers of Shikun Vizhnitz, and the hundreds of students of the Viznitzer Yeshivah, both in Bnei Brak. He was a member of the Moetzes Gedolei Hatorah (Council of Torah Sages) of the Agudas Yisrael of Eretz Yisrael; he was the scion of a noble Chassidic dynasty; but, perhaps equal to all of these elements, his personal warmth, and the triumph of joy over adversity that he personified, won him vast admiration beyond the confines of any one group.

(1882 - 1980)

was the grandson of Rav Shamshon Raphael Hirsch *zt"l*, who fought the battle for religious principle, known as *"Austritt"*, in the Frankfurt *kehillah* a struggle that he inherited from his illustrious father and grandfather. From his rise to prominence and leadership in Frankfurt to the tumultuous Nazi years to the rebirth of his Khal Adas Yeshurun in Washington Heights, Rav Breuer hewed to the vision of Rabbi Hirsch. From the time Hitler came to power in February 1933, it became clear that German Jewry was in danger, especially institutions so obviously "Jewish" as his yeshivah. In a attempt to anticipate the worst, Rav Breuer accepted the invitation of the Jewish community of Fume, Italy, to become its rabbi and bring his yeshivah with him. However, the experiment was unsuccessful and they moved back to Frankfurt. There the oppression of Jews became progressively worse and following Kristallnacht in November 1938, the yeshivah was disbanded. Rav Breuer and his family immigrated to Antwerp, Belgium in December 1938, where a former student, the late Jacob A. Samuel of New York - who was to become a major supporter of Torah institutions - persuaded him that he was needed on the American Jewish scene. He eventually settled in the Washington Heights section of Manhattan, where he became the spiritual leader of the Khal Adas Jeshurun (KAJ) German-Jewish kehillah for the next 42 years.

(1909 - 1967)

was the leader of Agudath Israel of America for many years during the 1900s. He changed it from a small group to a major organization almost singlehandedly. He even sold his business to help pay for the needs of the organization. He fought tirelessly for Jewish education, and was at the forefront of the effort to save Jews from the Holocaust. The war years were one long fundraising campaign by the Youth Council of Agudath Israel on behalf of the Jews of Europe. It would be impossible to detail the seemingly endless series of fundraising campaigns, dinners, and "nights". Between 1939–41, Zeirei Agudath Israel was under Mike's leadership and was the most active group in America procuring visas for Jews trapped in Europe. In addition, Zeirei sent food packages to Jews in Polish ghettos and conducted massive fundraising campaigns to ransom Jews from the Nazis. Books could be filled with all that Mike organized or guided during those early years of frantic rescue work. He grew far beyond all the amateur efforts, as he answered the challenge to ever larger and wider tasks thrust upon him by Divine Providence. He was called upon to work with world rescue and relief organizations on a global level. He began to travel the continents, and even received permission to tour the D.P. camps after the war in order to encourage and assist the unfortunate refugees. The name Mike Tress and the name of Agudath Israel became respected and beloved far beyond the confines even of his own keen vision.

Rav Avraham Mordechai Alter zt"l

(1866 – 1948)

also known as the Imrei Emes, was the third Rebbe of the chassidic dynasty of Ger, a position he held from 1905 until his passing in 1948. He was one of the founders of the Agudas Yisrael in Poland and was influential in establishing a network of Jewish schools there. It is claimed that at one stage he led over 200,000 chassidim. During World War II, R' Avraham Mordechai was a prime target of the Nazi authorities in Poland. Through a miraculous chain of events, he managed to escape Warsaw at the outset of the war and reached Italy. From there, he boarded a ship bound for Palestine in 1940 with several of his sons and began to slowly rebuild his chassidic dynasty. With the outbreak of the 1948 Arab-Israeli War he was trapped in Jerusalem. He passed away during the siege of the city by the Jordanian Arab Legion. As bodies could not be removed to the Mount of Olives during wartime, he was buried in the courtyard of the Sfas Emes Yeshivah, located near the Machane Yehuda Market in Jerusalem.

Chronology of Events

Important Dates, 1933–1945

1933

> **JANUARY 30**

Adolf Hitler is appointed Chancellor of Germany.

> **FEBRUARY 27–28**

Fire destroys the *Reichstag.* All one hundred Communist party members of the *Reichstag* are arrested.

> **MARCH 23**

The first concentration camp opens in Dachau, a German town near Munich.

> **MARCH 27**

In response to a planned boycott of Jewish-owned stores and businesses in Germany, 55,000 people protest at a rally in New York City's Madison Square Garden, and those present threaten to boycott all German goods. Nazis change their plans and limit their boycott to one day.

> **APRIL 1**

Boycott in Germany of Jewish-owned stores and businesses.

> **APRIL 7**

Jewish government workers are ordered to retire.

> APRIL 26
The Gestapo, the German secret police, is established.

> MAY 10
Books written by Jews and opponents of Nazism are burned.

> JUNE 27
Mass Jewish rally in London to protest Nazi anti-Semitism.

> JULY 14
Nazi party declared the only legal party in Germany.

> OCTOBER 14
Germany withdraws from the League of Nations.

> OCTOBER 27
Arabs in Palestine riot to protest Jewish immigration there.

1934

> APRIL 7
Several thousand attend a pro-Nazi rally in Queens, New York.

> MAY 17
More than 20,000 people attend a pro-Nazi rally at Madison Square Garden in New York.

> JUNE 30-JULY 2
Night of the Long Knives. Leaders of the SA (Brown Shirts), once among Hitler's closest friends and allies, are killed by the SS (Black Shirts) on Hitler's orders.

> AUGUST 2
Paul von Hindenburg, president of Germany, dies. Hitler becomes President and Commander-in-Chief of the Armed Forces.

1935

> **MARCH 16**

Hitler rejects the Treaty of Versailles and begins to draft Germans into military service.

> **MAY 31**

Jews may no longer serve in the German Army.

> **JUNE**

Anti-Jewish riots in Poland.

> **SEPTEMBER 15**

The Nuremberg Laws are passed. Among them are laws denying Jews citizenship in Germany. The Nazi symbol, a black swastika within a round white sphere was instituted as the German national flag.

> **NOVEMBER 15**

German law defines a Jew as anyone who considers himself a Jew and has two Jewish grandparents, or anyone with three or more Jewish grandparents whether he considers himself a Jew or not.

1936

> **FEBRUARY 4**

Swiss Nazi leader Wilhelm Gustloff is assassinated as a reprisal for Nazi anti-Semitism.

> **MARCH 3**

Jewish doctors are no longer allowed to work in German government hospitals.

> **MARCH 7**

German troops march into the Rhineland in violation of the Treaty of Versailles.

> APRIL 21

Arabs riot in Tel Aviv-Jaffa to protest Jewish immigration to Palestine.

> JUNE 30

Polish Jews strike to protest anti-Semitism.

> OCTOBER 25

Hitler and Mussolini sign treaty, forming Rome-Berlin Axis.

1937

> MARCH 15

Large anti-Nazi rally in New York City.

> JULY 16

Buchenwald concentration camp opens.

> SEPTEMBER 5

Hitler views parade of 600,000 German soldiers in Nuremberg.

> NOVEMBER 25

Germany and Japan sign military agreement.

1938

> JANUARY 21

Jews in Romania lose their rights as citizens.

> MARCH 13

The *Anschluss*. The German Army marches into Austria. German anti-Semitic decrees now apply to the Jews in Austria.

> APRIL 26

All Jewish property must be registered with the Nazis.

> MAY 29

Anti-Jewish laws passed in Hungary.

➤ JULY 5
Evian Conference on German refugees opens.

➤ AUGUST 17
German Jewish women must add "Sara" to their names. Men must add "Israel."

➤ SEPTEMBER 29-30
At the Munich Conference the leaders of Britain and France agree that Germany may annex the Sudetenland.

➤ OCTOBER 5
All German Jews must have their passports marked with a large red *J*.

➤ OCTOBER 28
Polish Jews living in Germany are expelled.

➤ NOVEMBER 7
In Paris, Herschel Grynszpan shoots Ernst vom Rath, a German embassy employee.

➤ NOVEMBER 9
Kristallnacht, the Night of Broken Glass. Many thousands of Jewish-owned stores and businesses are broken into and robbed. Synagogues are burned. Jews are arrested and degraded. Some are killed.

1939

➤ NOVEMBER 15
Jewish children may no longer attend German schools.

➤ JANUARY 30
In a speech before the German Parliament, Hitler declares that if there is war, the Jews of Europe will be destroyed.

➤ FEBRUARY 9
Anti-Jewish laws are passed in Italy.

➤ MARCH 15
Germans occupy Bohemia and Moravia (regions of Czechoslovakia).

➤ MARCH 25
In New York, 20,000 people march in a huge public "Stop Hitler" protest while an estimated 500,000 line the streets and watch.

➤ AUGUST 23
Germany and the Soviet Union sign the Molotov-Ribbentrop Pact, agreeing not to attack each other.

➤ SEPTEMBER 1
The German Army invades Poland. World War II begins.

➤ SEPTEMBER 3
France and Britain declare war on Germany.

➤ SEPTEMBER 27
German orders are issued to establish ghettos in Poland.

➤ OCTOBER 24
Jews in Wloclawek, Poland, are required to wear a large yellow triangle.

➤ OCTOBER 30
The British government publishes a report of Nazi brutality in concentration camps.

➤ NOVEMBER 23
Polish Jews are ordered to wear in public at all times armbands with yellow Stars of David.

➤ NOVEMBER 28
A ghetto is set up in Piotrkow, the first in Poland.

1940

> **FEBRUARY 8**

Orders are issued to set up a ghetto in Lodz, Poland.

> **APRIL 9**

The German Army invades Denmark and Norway.

> **APRIL 27**

Orders are issued to set up a concentration camp in Auschwitz, Poland.

> **MAY 1**

The Lodz ghetto is established.

> **MAY 10**

The German Army invades Holland, Belgium, and France.

> **JUNE 4**

French and British troops are evacuated from Dunkirk.

> **JUNE 22**

France surrenders to Germany.

> **SEPTEMBER 27**

Japan signs a treaty with Germany and Italy, forming the Rome-Berlin-Tokyo Axis.

> **NOVEMBER 15**

Walls surrounding the Warsaw ghetto are completed and closed.

1941

> **JUNE 22**

The German Army invades the Soviet Union. *Einsatzgruppen* (Nazi murder squads) begin mass killings of Soviet Jews.

> ## JUNE 28
Red Friday. Nazis burn the Jewish section in Bialystok, Poland. More than 1,000 Jews, forced into the synagogue, are killed.

> ## JULY 31
Reinhard Heydrich is appointed to carry out German anti-Semitic strategy.

> ## SEPTEMBER 1
Jews in Germany are required to wear a yellow star on their clothing.

> ## SEPTEMBER 28
Murder of Jews at Babi Yar (near Kiev, in the Ukraine) begins. More than 30,000 were killed in two days.

> ## OCTOBER 15
Orders are issued that any Jew in Poland found outside a ghetto will be shot.

> ## DECEMBER 7
The Japanese attack Pearl Harbor, Hawaii. The United States declares war on Japan.

> ## DECEMBER 8
Mass killings begin at Chelmno death camp.

> ## DECEMBER 11
Germany and Italy declare war on the United States.

1942

> ## JANUARY 20
At the Wannsee Conference, plans are developed by the Nazis for the total destruction of the Jews in Europe, the "Final Solution."

> ### FEBRUARY 24
The S.S. *Strumia,* a small boat with 769 Romanian Jewish refugees on board, sinks in the Black Sea.

> ### MARCH 1
Gas chambers begin operations in Sobibor. Trains begin to arrive at Auschwitz.

> ### MARCH 17
Killings begin in the Belzec, Poland, death camp.

> ### JUNE 1
Treblinka death camp opens.

> ### JUNE 30
Jewish schools in Germany are closed.

> ### JULY 22
Deportations from the Warsaw ghetto to Treblinka begin.

> ### JULY 28
The Jewish Fighting Organization (ZOB) is established in the Warsaw Ghetto.

> ### DECEMBER 22
Jewish resistance fighters in Krakow, Poland, attack German troops.

1943

> ### JANUARY 18
Jewish resistance begins in the Warsaw Ghetto.

> ### FEBRUARY 5
Jewish resistance begins in the Bialystok Ghetto.

> ### APRIL 19
The Warsaw Ghetto revolt begins. At the Bermuda Conference, U.S. and British representatives discuss the resettlement of refugees from Nazi persecution. No action is taken,

> ### JUNE 11
Heinrich Himmler orders all Jews in Polish ghettos to be sent to camps.

> ### JUNE 21
Himmler orders all Jews in Russian ghettos to be sent to camps.

> ### AUGUST 2
Rebellion of the inmates in Treblinka.

> ### AUGUST 16
Revolt begins in the Bialystok Ghetto.

> ### OCTOBER 2
The Danish underground helps 7,000 Jews escape to Sweden.

> ### OCTOBER 14
Prisoners revolt at the Sobibor death camp.

1944

> ### MAY-JUNE
An estimated 400,000 Hungarian Jews are killed at Auschwitz.

> ### JUNE 6
D-day, the Allied invasion of Nazi-held Europe.

> ### JULY 20
German Army officers attempt to assassinate Hitler, but fail.

> ### JULY 24
Soviet forces discover abandoned Majdanek death camp.

> OCTOBER 7

Revolt in Auschwitz.

> NOVEMBER 8

Death march of the Jews from Budapest to Austria begins.

1945

> JANUARY 17

Death march from Auschwitz begins. Raoul Wallenburg is arrested by the Soviet police in Budapest. His fate remains unknown.

> APRIL 15

Bergen-Belsen is liberated by the British.

> APRIL 25

Invading American forces from the west and Soviet forces from the east meet in Torgau, Germany.

> APRIL 29

Dachau is liberated by American troops.

> APRIL 30

Hitler commits suicide.

> MAY 8

Germany surrenders to the Allies.

> NOVEMBER 22

The Nuremberg Trials of Nazis begin.

GLOSSARY

Aktion: German for "round-up."

Al Kiddush Hashem: Lit. "To sanctify the Name." Jews who died with Hashem's Name on their lips.

Allies: The nations, including the United States, Britain, France, and the Soviet Union, that joined in the fight in World War II against Germany and the other Axis nations.

Anschluss: The 1938 German invasion and annexation of Austria.

Anti-Semitism: Prejudice against Jews.

Appeasement: The policy adopted by European leaders in the late 1930s of giving in to Hitler's demands in order to avoid war.

Appell: German for "roll call."

Aryan: An ancient people of Central Asia. Used by the Nazis to mean a superior, white gentile.

Auschwitz-Birkenau: Nazi labor and death camp located in Poland.

Axis: The nations, including Italy and Japan, that fought in World War II alongside Germany against the Allies.

Beis Medrash: Study hall, where Jews go to study Torah.

Baruch Hashem: Lit. "Blessed is the Name."

Bergen-Belsen: Nazi concentration camp located in Germany.

Blitzkrieg: German for "lightning war."

Bubby: Grandmother.

Buchenwald: Nazi concentration camp located near Weimar, Germany.

Cantor/Chazzan: Leader of synagogue prayer.

Challos: Loaves of bread used for the Shabbos meals.

Chazal: The Sages of blessed memory.

Chanukah: The eight-day holiday celebrating the Jewish victory over the Greek oppressors.

Chol Hamo'ed Sukkos: Intermediate Days of the holiday of Sukkos when work is permitted.

Churchill, Sir Winston: Prime Minister of Britain during most of World War II (May 1940-July 1945) and again after the war (1951-55).

Concentration Camp: A prison in which "enemies of the German nation" were concentrated. Before the end of World War II, more than one hundred such camps had been set up.

Crematorium: Oven in which death-camp victims' bodies were burned.

Dachau: The first Nazi concentration camp, near Munich, Germany.

Death Camps: Camps built to kill Jews and other "enemies of the German nation." There were six death camps: Auschwitz, Belzec, Chelmno, Majdanek, Sobibor, and Treblinka.

Death Marches: Near the end of the war, Nazi S.S. forced prisoners in concentration and death camps located in Poland to march to other camps located in Germany.

Deportation: The Jews' forced relocation from their homes to other places, usually ghettos or Nazi camps.

Eichmann, Adolf: S.S. officer who directed the roundup of Jews and their transport to concentration and death camps. Was captured and executed by the Israeli's.

Einsatzgruppen: Killing squads. Mobile killing units of the S.S. that followed the German Army into Poland and the Soviet Union.

Elul: The Jewish month before the New Year, which signifies repentance and circumspection.

Emunah: Faith and trust in the Almighty.

Erev Pesach: The day before the holiday of Pesach.

Erev Rosh Hashanah: The day before Rosh Hashanah, the Jewish New Year.

Esrog: Citron, the special fruit used on the holiday of Sukkos to fulfill a mitzvah.

Final Solution: The Nazi term for their plan to murder every Jew in Europe.

Fuhrer: German for "leader." Used in reference to Adolf Hitler.

Gabbai: Hebrew term to define one who assists a Rebbe or runs the services in the synagogue.

Gas Chambers: Sealed rooms in the death camps. Jewish prisoners were crowded into these rooms and poison gas was released, killing the prisoners.

Gemara: Individual part of the Talmud which Jews study all over the world.

Genocide: The systematic killing of a nation or race of people.

Gentile: Non-Jew.

Gestapo: The Nazi secret police.

Ghetto: A closed off section of a city in which thr Jews were forced to live.

Hakadosh Baruch Hu: Lit. "Holy Blessed One blessed be He." A glorifying expression of Hashem.

Halachah: Code of Jewish law.

Hitler, Adolf: Nazi party leader, 1919-45. German chancellor, 1933-45. Committed suicide in a Berlin bunker. May his name be blotted out.

Hitler Youth: Nazi youth organization. From 1936 the only legal youth organization in Nazi Germany.

Holocaust: "Destruction by fire." This word came to be used to refer to the Nazi killing of six million Jews, in the years 1933-45.

Hoshanah Rabbah: Last day of the holiday of Sukkos, when Jews walk around the shul seven times, chanting special prayers.

Juden: German word for "Jews."

Judenrat: "Jewish council." Jews appointed by the Germans to govern the ghettos.

Judenrein: German for "free of Jews."

Kaddish: A prayer praising the Almighty. Recited by Jewish mourners.

Kapos: Prisoners within concentration camps who were selected by the Nazis to oversee other prisoners.

Kristallnacht: "Night of Broken Glass." November 9-11, 1938, when there were wholesale arrests of Jews and destruction of Jewish property in Germany and Austria.

Labor Camp: A Nazi concentration camp in which the prisoners were used as slave laborers.

Kol Nidrei: The awesome prayers said at the opening of Yom Kippur.

Lager: German for "camp."

Lagerfuhrer: German for "camp commandant." One of the most feared men in any given concentration camp.

Luftwaffe: German Air Force.

Majdanek: Nazi labor and death camp located in Poland.

Matzah: Flat, cracker-like bread not given time to rise. Eaten on Pesach in remembrance of what the Jews ate as they fled slavery in Egypt.

Mauthausen: Nazi concentration camp located in Austria.

Mengele, Josef: The medical doctor and S.S. captain who in Auschwitz made "selections" and conducted sadistic medical experiments on prisoners. Escaped to Paraguay after the war, where he was presumed to have died of natural causes.

Menorah: Candelabra used on the eight days of Chanukah to light candles or oil wicks.

Mikvah: A ritual bath, separate for men and women, where Jews go to purify their bodies before prayer and/or performing a mitzvah.

Muller, Heinrich: Gestapo chief, 1939-45. Directly responsible for carrying out the "Final Solution."

Mussolini, Benito: Absolute ruler of Italy, 1922-43, and an ally of Adolf Hitler. Killed by his enemies in 1945.

Orthodox Jews: Traditional Jews who follow the many precepts of the Torah, including the eating of only kosher foods and observing the laws of Shabbos.

Pesach: The Jewish holiday celebrating the Jews' exodus from Egypt, where they had been slaves, in ancient times.

Purim: Jewish holiday celebrating the rescue from Haman, Prime Minister of ancient Persia, who had intended to kill every Jew in the empire.

Rabbiner: German for "Rabbi."

Rav: Rabbi, teacher.

Rebbe: One who teaches Torah.

Ribbono Shel Olam: Lit. "Master of the Universe." A glorifying expression of Hashem.

Reichstag: The German Parliament, and the building in which it met.

Ribbentrop, Joachim von: German foreign minister. Negotiated an agreement between the Soviet Union and Germany in 1939 that neither country would attack the other.

Righteous of the Nations: Righteous gentiles. The term used for gentiles who risked their lives to save Jews from Nazi persecution.

Roosevelt, Franklin Delano: U.S. President from March 1933 until his death in April 1945, almost the entire period of Nazi rule in Germany.

Rosh Hashanah: The Jewish New Year, celebrated on the first day of the Hebrew month of Tishrei.

S.A.: Storm troopers, or Brown Shirts. Organized to protect Nazi rallies and to terrorize those not sympathetic to the Nazis.

Scapegoat: An innocent person or people blamed for other people's troubles.

Sedarim: The special feasts that Jews hold on the first two nights of Pesach, where tales of redemption are recounted and the children are an integral part of the evening.

Sefer: Jewish book.

Sefer Torah: The Torah scroll which is read each Shabbos and Yom Tov.

Selektion: The process of deciding which prisoners in Nazi camps would be sent to their deaths immediately and which would be spared.

Shalom Aleichem: Traditional Jewish greeting. It means, "Peace unto you."

Shabbos: The weekly day of rest beginning before sunset on Friday and ending after sunset on Saturday.

Shemini Atzeres: The small but unique holiday which follows the festival of Sukkos.

Shivah: The traditional Jewish mourning period.

Shochet: Traditional ritual slaughterer.

Shofar: A ram's horn which is used on Rosh Hashanah to blow one hundred sounds.

Shoftim: Book of Judges.

Shtiebel: Classic Chassidic synagogue.

Shtreimel: Classic Chassidic headress.

Shul: Yiddish for "synagogue."

Siddur: Prayer book.

Simchas Torah: The Festival of the Torah. It follows the holiday of Shemini Atzeres and is characterized by dancing, singing and unbridled joy of the Torah. The Torah is read on this day until its completion and then rewound to the beginning where it is started all over again.

Sobibor: Nazi death camp located in Poland.

Sonderkommando: Prisoners in the death camps assigned to take the bodies from the gas chambers to the crematoriums.

S.S.: Protection squad, or Black Shirts. Established in 1925 as Nazi protection squads. Included the Gestapo, squads that ran the Nazi concentration and death camps, and squads that fought with the German Army.

Stalin, Joseph: Dictator of the Soviet Union 1929-53.

Sudetenland: The western section of Czechoslovakia, which borders on Germany.

Sukkos: The holiday when Jews erect small booths outside their homes and eat, sleep and live there for the duration of the seven day festival.

Swastika: An ornament, adopted by the Nazis as their party symbol.

Tallis: Rectangular cloth with specially prepared fringes (tzitzis). Worn by Jews during prayer.

Tefillin: Phylacteries which Jewish men don each morning during prayers.

Tehillim: Book of Psalms

Terezin: Also known as Theresienstadt. Nazi concentration camp located in Czechoslovakia. Set up to show the outside world, including Red Cross investigators, how well the Jews were being treated. Most Jews held here were later killed in Auschwitz.

Tishah B'Av: The saddest day on the Jewish calendar. It is the day when Jews commemorate the destruction of the Temples in Jerusalem and is characterized by fasting, mourning and refraining from wearing leather shoes.

Third Reich: Hitler's name for Germany during his years as dictator, 1933-45.

Torah: Written and Oral Law. The great gift the Almighty gave His Jewish Nation.

Treblinka: Nazi death camp located in Poland.

Tzedakah: Charity.

Vidui: The Jewish confession, usually recited preceding death.

Wehrmacht: The German Army.

Wiesenthal, Simon: Holocaust survivor who helped capture and prosecute more than one thousand Nazi war criminals.

Yad Vashem: Memorial in Jerusalem to Holocaust victims, and center for Holocaust study.

Yahrtzeit: A day when Jews remember and commemorate the life of a dead loved one. The Kaddish prayer is recited and some eat and drink and bless the memory of their loved one.

Yamim Noraim: Days of Awe. The days beginning Rosh Hashanah and ending with Yom Kippur when Jews repent their sins from the previous year.

Yarmulke: Small cap worn on the head of Orthodox Jews, as a sign of respect for the Almighty.

Yeshivah: Jewish Academy for Torah study

Yiddish: Also know as Jewish. The language spoken by the majority of East European Jews before World War II.

Yiras Shamayim: Lit. "Fear of Heaven." A G-d-fearing Jew who follows the dictates of the Torah.

Yom Kippur: The Jewish Day of Atonement, a fast day spent mostly in prayer. Falls on the tenth of the Jewish month of Tishrei.

Yom Tov: Jewish holiday.

Zaidy: Grandfather.

Zemiros: Jewish songs which are often sung on Shabbos and holidays during the festive meals.

Zhid: Polish for "Jew."

ZOB: The Warsaw Ghetto Jewish fighting organization.

Zt"l: Acronym for "of blessed memory."

WHEN WAS THE LAST TIME YOU READ A GOOD...

STORY

DVAR TORAH

MASHAL

HALACHAH

DRUSH

HASHKAFAH

MIDDOS/ DERECH ERETZ

(over please)

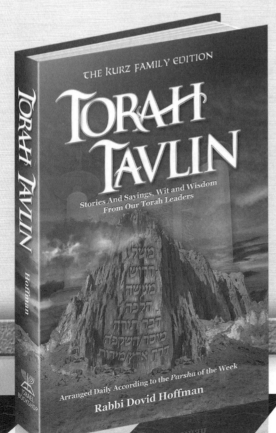

...Sephardic, Ashkenazic, Litvish, Chassidish, man, woman, young or old – you'll find enjoyment here, among the satisfying pages of Torah Tavlin.

ותקם רבקה ונערותיה ותרכבנה על הגמלים
ותלכנה אחרי האיש (כד-מא)

Rivka and her maidens set off. They rode on the camels and followed the man.

When Eliezer traveled with Rivka to bring her to _____ Eliezer was to keep a watchful eye on the females tra_____ did not ride behind them. Instead, he rode ahead of th_____ proximity to them.

R' Pesach Eliyahu Falk shlit"a quotes the *medrash*_____ maidens traveled behind Eliezer, rather than ahead of _____ in conduct dictates that females are not to be observe_____ a position to be easily observed. Furthermore, the _____ states that it is wrong for a man to walk behind even _____ is considered a lack of *tznius*. We find that Manoach _____ *ha'aretz* – ignorant person, because, as it states, *"Vay_____ ishto* - and Manoach walked behind his wife" (Shoftim _____ ignoramus, as he did not know such an elementary hal_____

Every step taken by the servants of the *Avos* reflecte_____ conduct that pr_____ is more to learn _____ the Torah of fu_____

Many of ou_____ related matters_____ writes that a ma_____ his wife. Sadly,_____ so ingrained in _____ one an *am ha a_____

R' Yosef Leib_____

"If you ne_____ than someone _____ resorts to beg_____ mercy on him _____ automatically _____

ת (כה-כ)

*Sa_____
Av_____*

A number of yea_____ when a well-known,_____ **R' Chaim Kanievsk_____** comfort the mourne_____ was a teacher on her_____ and we know that th_____ *nizokin* - [one who is]_____ How could such a ter_____

R' Chaim answere_____ *Parshas Chayei Sarah*_____ Yitzchak, because aft_____ soul left her and _____ direct result of the *Ak_____* the thought that the g_____

The answer, expla_____ mitzvos that causes _____ decides that a person_____ is now ready to mov_____ or she is a *tzaddik* wi_____ Matriarch Sarah, the_____ of a mitzvah. This a_____ died with an extra m_____ regarding a person w_____ if he has fulfilled the _____

Thus, never look at death as "untimely." It is always "timely." Hashem evaluates a person's actions and adjusts his "time" on this world accordingly.

R' Tzvi Hirsch of Riminov zt"l would say:

"Hashem, give the Jewish People wealth and sustenance and You will see we won't sin. As the *pasuk* states, 'ותמח הצעיף ותתכס' - the word 'עצמך' spells out 'עמך ישראל צריכים פרנסה' - *Your nation, Yisrael, needs sustenance.'* If we are able to take this – 'ותתכס' - our sins will be covered over!"

PARSHAS CHAYEI SARAH • פרשת חיי שרה

וישקל אברהם לעפרן את הכסף אשר דבר באזני בני חת (כג-טז)

And Avraham weighed-out for Efron the silver that he spoke of in the hearing of the sons of Cheis.

Mashal:

A woman in Poland had a daughter who was getting older and finding it hard to find a mate. A matchmaker suggested that she claim to be younger than her true age. He knew a Polish passport official, who, for the right price, could make her any age she would like.

The official met the woman and then looked at the girl.

"Oh, this is not a major problem," he said. "Of course, we can rectify this. In fact, for a fee of five hundred zloty, I can have her listed as twenty-one years old!"

Despite the steep charge, the mother agreed and took the money from her purse. Seeing how quickly the woman gave in to his first offer, the official held up his hand. "You know what," he offered, smiling, "for seven hundred zloty, I can make her twenty years old!" The lady reluctantly agreed and gave him the full amount.

At that, the officer began to get greedy. "But for an additional three hundred zloty," he pressed slyly, "I could make her eighteen!"

"No, thank you," the mother said. "Twenty years old is fine! Quick!" she shouted, grabbing her daughter. "Let's get out of here, or we'll be left with no zloty and no years!"

Nimshal:

The **Ponovezher Rav, R' Yosef Kahaneman zt"l**, once told this to a rich man who was stalling in an effort to get out of giving *tzedakah*:

"Avraham Avinu knew with whom he was dealing. He understood that the longer he waited, the more expensive the deal would become, and he was not interested in prolonging negotiations that would only leave him without money and perhaps without land. The minute Efron quoted a price, exorbitant as it was, Avraham paid it without further question. All he wanted to do was close the deal and leave. Often, it is worthwhile to take a hit and leave, because the pain of the moment is far less than the agony of insincerity." The Rav's message struck its mark, and the man handed over a sizable donation.

הגדה של פסח

TORAH TAVLIN
HAGGADAH

Stories and Sayings, Wit and Wisdom
from our Torah Leaders
on the Haggadah shel Pesach

By:
Rabbi Dovid
Hoffman